Sex Life of an Emperor:
The Many Loves of Napoleon Bonaparte

Sex Life of an Emperor:
The Many Loves of Napoleon Bonaparte

by

Frederic Masson

Fireship Press
www.FireshipPress.com

ISBN-13: 978-1-934757-63-5
ISBN-10: 1-934757-63-2

BISAC Subject Headings:
BIO006000   BIOGRAPHY & AUTOBIOGRAPHY / Historical
BIO008000   BIOGRAPHY & AUTOBIOGRAPHY / Military
BIO022000   BIOGRAPHY & AUTOBIOGRAPHY / Women

This work is based on the 1894 edition of *Napoleon and the Fair Sex* by Frederic Masson, Philadelphia: J.B. Lippincott and Co.

Address all correspondence to:
Fireship Press, LLC
P.O. Box 68412
Tucson, AZ 85737

Or visit our website at:
www.FireshipPress.com

1.0

Contents

Introduction

A LARGE proportion of the Chapters in this book appeared in the literary supplement of the *Figaro* from April to September, 1893. The idea of writing them was suggested to me in the following manner.

In the *Chronicle,* published periodically in connection with the journal, an anonymous correspondent asked the questions: *"With what women is Napoleon known to have had temporary relations as a young man, as Consul, and finally, as Emperor? Had he an absorbing passion for any one woman? And if so, for whom?"*

Answers to these queries appeared at intervals, but were far from convincing. It came to the knowledge of M. Perivier, the editor of the literary supplement, that I had for some time past collected documents bearing on the private life of Napoleon. He applied to me for the desired information, and I gave it. But it was impossible to do justice to the subject within the prescribed limits, and my summary was but a brief outline of the facts I had gathered. It was then suggested that I should fill in this outline, and the result was a series of articles, in the form and production of which I was allowed absolute liberty, but to which the *Figaro* offered a hospitality I now most gratefully acknowledge.

The articles found favor with the public, and were quoted in many journals, both at home and abroad. But on the other hand, they drew down upon me no small share of anonymous abuse and covert reproach.

Many of those with whom I had stood shoulder to shoulder in the Bonapartist ranks between 1870 and 1879, from the fall of the Empire to the death of the Prince Imperial, took exception to these articles as ill-timed and disrespectful. Though they acquitted me alike of dissimulation of present sympathies, or treachery to past traditions, they held — and some among them openly told me — that my passion for writing, my desire to figure prominently in a well-known review, and to cater for a public greedy of unpublished gossip, had seduced me into revelation and discussion of matters I ought to have suppressed. They pronounced my Bonapartism not at all to their liking, and declared that a devotee of Napoleon who dealt thus with his memory was hardly to be distinguished from his enemies.

Such were the accusations brought against me. I seek neither to exaggerate nor to minimize them. It would be easy to pass them over in silence. But for twenty years I shared the passions, the hopes, the joys and sorrows of my accusers. The friendship of many among them is very dear to me; nor would I willingly forfeit the esteem of any. I therefore gladly take this opportunity of justifying myself. I ask the indulgence of a public to whom these disputes are of little interest, to whom my very existence is almost unknown, who are ignorant of my past, and who may look upon these pages as a superfluous affix to the book for which they have paid their money. But hitherto my loyalty has never been called in question. I have held my course with all singleness of heart and purpose, and it would ill become me to shrink from an explanation that has long seemed to me necessary, and has now become imperative. The present book is the first of a series of studies I propose to publish successively. In these it is my intention to give the result of my researches with absolute independence. I therefore owe it to my old political friends to explain what led me formerly to join their ranks, and why I now feel at liberty to follow my own bent, and write after my own fashion, recognizing in them no rights either as dictators or censors.

The Bonapartist staff after 1870 was largely recruited from the ranks of the Orleanist and Legitimist parties; even those sometime supporters of the Revolution of 1848 who had rallied to Prince Louis Napoleon were largely influenced by reactionary sympathies. They were all pledged to the cause of the fallen Empire by virtue of places they had held, favours conferred on themselves or their families, anxiety to play a new part, and a very natural ambition to recover a lost position, or achieve one yet more brilliant.

They prided themselves on their knowledge of the sole system of administration proper to their country. This system they had applied with unquestionable ability, with a rectitude to which the world is now beginning to do tardy justice, and with a professional equity no longer to be found among politicians. Each one among them may fairly claim to have largely contributed to the material prosperity enjoyed by France for forty years. They had all the virtues of their caste, together with one not common in that caste — the virtue of self-sacrifice.

They were agreed that in 1852, as in the year XII., the Empire was clearly in principle a delegation of the national sovereignty. Great therefore as was the repugnance of some among them to universal suffrage, they were bound to refrain from overtly attacking it. But they held the rights of discussion already acquired to be amply sufficient, resigned themselves much against the grain to a new *plébiscite*, and looked with abhorrence on all schemes of democratic government that ignored hereditary rights. The Empire found favor among them, not only because it was an authoritative system agreeable to men who frankly detested Parliamentarianism — at least so long as they themselves had no part in it — but because they saw in its dynastic and hereditary formulae a practical compromise between the monarchy they regretted, and those elements of democracy they recognized as inevitable. They beheld in the Emperor, not the predestined organizer of a new society, but the guardian of the interests of the old. On these issues, the majority of them were so closely allied to *Conservatism*, that they were finally merged among the *Conservatives*, or partisans of the two Bourbon dynasties. With these they were agreed on all points, save that of the origin of authority, and some few secondary details of its application, and doubtless had a Napoleon set himself to impugn their doctrines, they would have sacrificed the leader to the creed.

The legislative, religious, and political program formulated in the first Napoleon's acts, edicts, and plans of government were accepted by them with certain explicit reservations; on some points they altogether withheld their adhesion. But Napoleon III was too present a reality to be thus set aside upon occasion. His advanced tendencies were, however, freely canvassed; some of the measures proposed by him were denounced as strangely revolutionary; and though his followers were by no means loath to accept the credit of certain improvements in the condition of the people initiated by him, they considered that the maximum had been attained in this direction, and that further progress on lines formerly marked out would imperil the whole social fabric. To give but two instances in illustration, it is undeniable that the right of workmen to strike, and the necessity of primary education, had few, if any, supporters. In foreign policy, the anomaly was even greater: not one among them would have upheld the principle of nationality; nor would any voice have been raised in defense of the war undertaken in the cause of Italian independence; the Crimean and Chinese campaigns found few apologists. In fact, any who had attempted to sum up the opinions held by Napoleon III., which the chiefs of the Bonapartist faction had assimilated, would have been surprised to find how few were the doctrines in common between the chief and his followers. The latter, indeed, professed theories adapted from Legitimists, Orleanists, and even Parliamentary Republicans. And thus there grew up a Bonapartism lacking Bonapartist spirit, as conspicuously as it now lacks a Bonaparte.

This annihilation of the Napoleonic doctrine by those who in all sincerity declared themselves its champions was a gradual process. The work of disintegration was first clearly manifested when certain members of the party in the National Assembly formed a faction, and combined with other factions for the overthrow of Thiers, and the nomination of MacMahon. Thenceforward they formed a mere item in the conservative union, and as the great majority of that union was Royalists, the Bonapartist interest was gradually merged in theirs. Daily contact, parliamentary alliances, and social intimacy caused a fusion of opinions which differed rather in degree than in principle, until, after a lapse of twenty-three years, it is difficult to distinguish between the politics of deputies who were elected as Bonapartists, and those who had declared for monarchy.

It may be readily supposed that this group of politicians considered themselves invested by popular mandate with special authority. They naturally held that their presence in the field of politics, their participation in the actual government of the country, and their facilities for keeping watch on the course of public events, marked them out as guardians of their party's interests. They therefore only accepted their Prince's mandates *ad referendum*, and subject to discussion, on many occasions rejecting them altogether. When the execution of his orders seemed likely to imperil their re-election they openly rebelled, for it was a cardinal doctrine with them that their presence in the senate was essential to the welfare of the party. And thus, unconscious apparently that they were degrading the one political principle that remained to them, they substituted for the doctrine of authority a Parliamentarianism all the more rigid, that the atoms of their own parliamentary microcosm had lost the habit of obedience, each considering himself peculiarly fitted to command.

Thus by degrees the stronger elements of Bonapartism were watered down. During the minority of the Prince Imperial, Parliamentarianism gained ground among the leaders of the party. When, on the attainment of his majority, the Prince sought to assume his rightful authority, he met with such strong opposition that he probably planned his expedition to Zululand in the hope of winning a prestige that would enable him to hold his own on his return. No sooner did Prince Napoleon attempt to assume the leadership than the party broke into open revolt, which was even more violent in its manifestations when he ventured to dissociate himself from the Royalists. Matters are less complex at the present time; both faction and party are no more. The one has effaced the other. The party is merged in the nation. But should the nation discover a man in whose person her aspirations towards glory, authority, and social reform take tangible shape, the popular current will revert to its former channel, the party will take a new lease of life, and if the man be equal to his destiny, the machinations of the middle-class Parliament man will prove futile indeed when opposed to the triumphant progress of him whom Carlyle so aptly calls " The Hero."

Such a vision will find realization sooner or later, or France will be no more. This is my earnest conviction, a conviction that has survived even the strange episode of some few years ago. The man whose wonderful fortune seemed to be bearing him on towards supreme power failed to grasp the prize, and fell almost at the moment of attainment. But this was because of his inherent weaknesses; he was unequal to the great part he was called upon to play. A Caesar is neither to be improvised nor developed; he must be born.

I owed nothing to the Empire; no family ties, no past favors bound me to the Bonapartes. Up to the age of sixteen I received a national pension of six hundred francs, the price of my father's life. He was killed June 23, 1848. The Republic, adopting me and other orphans in the same cause, made the award. It will hardly be contended that it was excessive, or that I became a Republican on the strength of it.

An ardent Republican I was, however, under the Empire, a result brought about by my classic education, my lonely youth, my passion for literature, and a certain austerity of temperament. I dreamed of a Republic founded on virtue, such as Montesquieu desired, and seen through the mists of legend, the men of the Revolution seemed to me the most virtuous beings who had ever existed. I had no misgivings as to the rectitude of their successors, and believed the Mountain to be the chosen asylum of high-minded patriots, pure of soul and spotless of hand. One alone of all constitutions seemed to me to rest on a legal basis, to emanate from the sovereignty of the people, and to contain the fundamental articles of the Republican faith; this was the Constitution of '93. It is true that it had never been carried out to its logical conclusions; but its theories might have been the creation of Rousseau himself.

Such dreams are healthy. Napoleon himself has said "There have been good men among the Jacobins. At one period all exalted natures were attracted to Jacobinism. I myself was so attracted, like thousands of other well-meaning persons. "I need not blush to confess myself of the company. Those who feel no draught towards such notions in their youth, who are never in extremes, who confine their ambitions to the practical and the moderate, will no doubt prove the better architects of their own fortunes, the surer guardians of their own interests. But these will never have felt upon their brows the refreshing shadow of those vast wings on which the spirit soars above the mud of earth to the eternal home of true and generous souls, the land of the sage and of the seer. They will not have retained, from this rapid flight through ideal heights, a perpetual aspiration towards progress, the one religion that stands the test of criticism and analysis. They will know nothing of the joys of disinterested search after truth. They will be men, not of principles, but of expedients. They will adapt themselves to circumstances, and will support the form of government that offers them the highest wages. These are the successful men, who are praised for their dexterity. But for oneself, it would seem the better part to accept the blame of the herd, and to dwell among honest men."

Belief in the Constitution of 1793 is apt to be a passing phase with one who has a taste for research and a passion for knowledge. My enthusiasm for the men of the past gradually died out under the weight of evidence gleaned from books, pamphlets, and newspapers, and a little experience of humanity showed me the men of the present very much as they actually were.

Among the constitutions which had been submitted to the nation, and so were of legal origin according to the democratic code, that of the year VIII seemed to me to have been vitiated by Brumaire the 18th,[1] that of 1852 by December the 2nd; yet I found it difficult to understand why such a solemn consultation, four times repeated, should have had identical results. Whatever the pressure brought to bear upon the people, was it possible to suppose that they could not have found some means of expressing their hatred and contempt, if the men who solicited their votes were indeed as odious to them as they were represented to be, and if the program submitted to them were indeed so repugnant to their feelings? This was a mystery on which I pondered deeply. Further, if the *plébiscite* of 1851 were void, the popular election of 1848 held good, and in that connection there could be no question of pressure or intimidation. If undue influence had been used, it had been on the other side. The popular mind, throwing off the trammels of the middle classes, had declared itself with one accord on that eventful day, and with marvellous unanimity had pronounced for Napoleon. And this in the face of the most unblushing official candidature, the most frantic Parliamentarian efforts, the dread of deportation, the shadow of civil war, the spectacle of blood-stained bayonets — in the face, too, of ridicule and lampoons, of an unscrupulous press, of the whole body of the police in full cry, of a ministry of worthy gentlemen stopping coaches. It was a manifestation no less magnificent than extraordinary, and almost unique in history. Here was the true birth-certificate of the Second Empire, a document of unimpeachable authenticity. I recognized its authority, and this recognition was of no slight moment, seeing that it involved condonation of a violated oath, of projected massacres, of the dissolution of the Assembly, and a negation of all the doctrines of the *Chatiments*, the text-book of my generation. This was not to be achieved without a struggle, especially by one who had contributed to the literature of the political controversy.

I had reached this stage of my mental evolution, when in May, 1870, the Emperor proposed a renewal of the compact between himself and the people. No open-minded witness can contend that the subsequent deliberations were not absolutely free, nor deny that the enemies of the Empire had recourse to the most unworthy weapons, while the defence of their opponents was unparalleled in

---

[1] *Editor's Note*: Throughout this book Masson makes references to dates using the Revolutionary Calendar which was in vogue during Napoleon's day. Wherever possible, we have translated those into Gregorian dates. For a more complete explanation of this calendar, see Appendix B.

its moderation. I was present at the *plébiscite*, and took part in it. The result made it evident that the treaty between sovereign and people, if proposed by the former, had been solemnly ratified by the latter. It was idle to hark back upon December 2, and to maintain that its events vitiated the vote of some nineteen years later.

Yet this was but a part — no inconsiderable part assuredly, but still only a proportion — of the satisfactions demanded by the theoretic mind. For one who was haunted by the desire "to ameliorate the condition of the poorest and most populous class of the community," there was another set of ideas which a government was bound to apply, before it could be admitted as a desirable government, suitable both to present and future requirements.

Left without a leader, a nation perishes. With a leader, even when that leader has not been freely chosen, even when he has seized, rather than accepted, supremacy, a nation lives. But when the chief is chosen by the voice of the whole people, how great is his power for good, how vast the field opened out to him for the accomplishment of his work! The *plébiscite* is the only instrument by which it is possible to restrict and direct the powers of that Third Estate, which has hitherto furnished orators and wire-pullers to every party, even to the most avowedly democratic, from the ranks of which all governments have recruited their administrators, and in which consequently all power is vested, even in the days of universal suffrage. This has been the case for a century, the only interludes in this dictatorship of the Third Estate being the periods of Imperial sway. The Constituent Assembly proclaimed the apotheosis of the middle classes, and suppressed the three powers that held them in check — the King, the nobility, and the clergy. The *bourgeoisie* became supreme in the Legislature and the Convention. The Directory existed by and for it. Important as were its functions under the Restoration, the latter was not sufficiently submissive for its taste, and it accordingly substituted the Monarchy of July, under which its supremacy was assured. In the Constituent Assembly of '48, as in the Legislature, it attacked the anointed of the people, firstly because of the popular origin of his power, secondly because it dreaded to find in him an adversary such as it had encountered half a century before. The *coup d'etat* of December the 2nd was an attack, not upon the sovereignty of the people, — for its author was the chosen leader of the people, — but upon the sovereignty of the middle classes in the persons of their parliamentary representatives, whose resentment was the keener that they foresaw further encroachment on their usurpations, and feared that the popular Dictator would take the utmost advantage of the national vote, which had invested him with supreme powers.

Simultaneously with this assumption of political authority by the middle classes from 1830 onwards, an economic transformation had been taking place. The toil of the individual workman, and the output of small workshops directed by petty traders, who worked side by side with their employees, had been gradually superseded by vast collective enterprises, by huge factories, depending on anonymous and external funds, under the control of impersonal and irresponsible managers.

These funds were furnished by the Third Estate, whose first thought was the highest return possible for their capital, to secure which they placed the laws, the government, and the army at the disposal of their agents. They invented Protection, to increase the value of their goods, and inaugurated a long series of petty tyrannies, by which they forced the proletarian manufacturer to remain wretched and poverty-stricken, and prevented the coalition by which he might have improved his status. They thus created antinomy as between capital and labour, and justified the reprisals of that class which we are beginning to call the Fourth Estate. Two dates will be sufficient to mark the genesis and growth of this new power: June, 1832, when a popular outbreak lasted barely two days; and June, 1848, memorable for an insurrection which took an army to quell it, and cost the lives of more generals than a great battle. It was easy to foresee the Commune from the very first days of 1870.

One course only could have prevented this revolution, which was merely postponed by the victory of the Third Estate in 1871, from becoming in due time, not only in France, but throughout the world, the most bloody and terrible ever dreamed of, a catastrophe which will replunge humanity into barbarism. This course was the establishment of a moderate Dictatorship, with a Dictator sufficiently alive to the interests of the Third, and the needs of the Fourth Estate to act as mediator between the two, to enforce the sacrifices necessary on both sides, and to bring about a sort of concordat between the conflicting classes. But the authority of a dictator who should successfully bring about such an evolution in the industrial order as was accomplished by Napoleon I. in the agrarian order, could only be sustained by national suffrage, and this, by virtue of its democratic character, would restore the balance of power as between the moneyed minority and the indigent majority, and ensure the election of a chief by that majority. If a sovereign, basing his claims on divine right, be radically disqualified for such leadership by his origin, his surroundings, his supporters, the very principle of his power, how much more is this the case of an assembly made up of the very persons it is proposed to dispossess? The nobility indeed may cite that 4th of August, when it renounced its hereditary privileges. The sacrifice was immense, but it was a sacrifice of pride only, and not of purse. The nobles did not renounce their pecuniary privileges, but agreed to their redemption by the nation. There will be no 4th of August in the history of the Third Estate. Its privileges are based on money, and money it will never be induced to relinquish.

Personally, Napoleon III. perceived the greatness of his mission. Personally, not as a man of strong will, for he had little force of character, nor as a man of genius, for he had no genius, but as a man of intelligence, honesty, and deep convictions, he had prepared himself to play his part. Unhappily, throughout his reign he was the hostage of the Third Estate, in spite of which, and as the opponent of which, he had been elected. Forced by the Constiturion from the very beginning to choose his ministers from a middle-class assembly avowedly hostile to him, he was obliged to govern through an executive not one member of which had voted for him. In later times, when he had shaken off the yoke of the Assembly, he was driven by force of circumstances to choose all his instruments of government from among the Third Estate. Whether they came from the Right or the Left, they were all alike, and it was only by dint of that gentle obstinacy peculiar to him that the Emperor succeeded in forcing upon them those principles of social reform he himself had at heart. Had he not found supporters among a certain class of men, whose middle class extraction had been neutralized by a phase of adhesion to the Saint-Simonian sect, and who still professed the cult of Humanity, the dreams of the exiled author of *L' Extinction du Pauperisme* [*The End of Poverty*] would have remained but dreams. It is possible that a greater part might have been played by some other leader. But none other, fettered as he was, could have shown a more entire comprehension of, and devotion to, the cause of the people.

At the time, however, I saw nothing but the result. It was already great; but realities will always fall far short of a youthful ideal, with its impatience of gradual development. It was no inconsiderable victory over my acquired prejudices, to admit that the imperial power rested on a legitimate basis. The further concession, that the man who wielded this power had to a great extent understood and fulfilled his mission, was a logical result of wider experience, and honesty itself compelled it. But to establish in my mind the sovereign conviction that absorbs all other sentiments, and produces the fanaticism born of faith, some electric spark, falling upon the scattered elements, and fusing them into sudden illumination, was still necessary. This too was forthcoming. I lived through September the 4th and all its horrors — the disgrace of that shameful revolt in the enemy's presence, of cries for "Peace!" raised among soldiers laying down their arms. Rage against the invader, disgust at imbecile bravado, hatred of the Orleanist lawyers who flung open the gate of that Palace in which they had sworn fidelity to the Emperor to a horde of ruffians and prostitutes — I suffered the tortures of all these. In the brilliant autumn sunshine, I saw and heard a reeling, dancing mob pour into the Rue de la Paix, insulting the column as they passed, plunge into the Rue de Rivoli, and blacken as with a darkly swelling tide the Place de la Concorde. I saw and heard, and would have gladly laid down my life to save France from the shame of these things on the morrow of Sedan.

And the justification of this betrayal of their country by certain Parisians was offered in the very phrase which our good friends the allies were fond of using in 1814: "Prussia is not at war with France, but with the Emperor!" Then I felt and understood that, consciously or not, those who argued thus were the accomplices of the invaders; that the overthrow of the Empire meant the surrender of France; that now as then, the Napoleons and the nation were inseparable, not only as for us, but as against monarchical Europe, and that they alone had made the nation formidable.

Meanwhile a tumult of half-forgotten youthful sensations rose once more in my breast. The religion that had breathed round me in my cradle, the teaching of a time distant and dimly remembered as if it had formed part of some previous life, awoke, and claimed its disciple. I recalled gentle old men, who loved children and flowers, and whose tender patience overcame my childish timidity. I remembered how they would take me on their knees, and with failing voices, the tones of which linger in my hearing after forty years, would tell me things like some strange fairy tale, but even more marvellous! For they had seen and taken part in the wonders of their story, and if I seemed to doubt, they would take my little fingers in their maimed hands, and make me touch the scars left by ball, or lance, or sword. And my curiosity, inexhaustible as their patience — the infinite patience of the strong — plied them with never-ending questions about him whose marble face, pale and superb, rose above us in the hall, like that of a god above his altars.

They told what he had done and suffered, how he had lived; they spoke of battles, victories, apotheoses; of conquered capitals and liberated peoples; of armies swimming across icy rivers; of Cossacks carried off and cast at his feet; of levies raised spontaneously by the magic of his name; of duels, combats about his memory. And we wept together — they, his old soldiers, and I, a little child. Sacred are those tears, which I have seen flowing on proud faces seamed with scars, when, after some such burst of speech, the iron veterans would sit silent awhile, with lips compressed, so pale that their wives, rising, would rebuke them tenderly— "You should not talk of these things. It is bad for you!" To which they would answer — "It is right that the child should hear!" Those tears, falling on my brow, were my baptism, a baptism to which I am still faithful.

That infant faith of mine may have slumbered for many years. On that memorable day it awoke, and mastered my whole being. I too witnessed things strange and terrible, such as my old friends had told me: a treacherous faction striking down the Elect of the People, and giving up their fatherland to the invader. I saw joy which made me think of the joy of noble ladies, kissing the lips of the Cossacks; I saw the human brute let loose against the vanquished, while urging it on, goading its frenzy, and directing its attack, I saw the same men as of old, with like passions and appetites; and with them others, like unto them, the children of our own century — our governors of yesterday, our governors of to-day.

From that day forward I neither reasoned nor doubted. I acted. An unknown volunteer, I served the Emperor Napoleon III.; a nameless soldier, I served the Prince Imperial. Later, I held the post assigned to me in my brigade, and obeyed orders, for which I may claim some credit, seeing that at the time the Napoleonic Party was, to my mind, diverging lamentably from its true precedents and its rightful goal. But I had faith in the future. The young leader had the virtues proper to a Napoleon — faith, courage, sincerity; he would have understood and accomplished his mission. He disappeared, and chance brought me into contact with Prince Napoleon. He honoured me with a confidence unsolicited on my part, and deigned to call me his friend. In his will, my name occurs immediately after those of his own family. He called upon me to vindicate his memory, and if I have not yet accomplished the task, it is through no fault of mine.

I feel that an impassable gulf now separates me from those in whose ranks I once fought. We have not a thought, not a hope left in common. My place is among the dead; I have finished with conflict, and the opinions I cherish are purely historical. All that remains to me of activity, of energy, of faculty for work, I desire to dedicate to the study of him whom I look upon as our saviour in the past, and whose tradition — now distorted and forsaken — might have been our salvation in the present. For the last twenty years I have been endeavouring to form an idea of him, and everything I have read has proved to me more and more conclusively that the history of Napoleon has yet to be written. Going back to the root of the matter, I have tried to consider him apart from the deeds he accomplished, and the events he brought to pass. As legislator, as diplomatist, as financier, as administrator, his figure is a great and attractive one; but it is not that of the *man* himself. Before we can form any just idea of the man, must we not see how his brain worked; how each minute of his time was spent; what proportion of it he bestowed on pleasure; how far he was influenced by the senses, the passions, the affections; what part he played as son, as lover, as husband, as father? At the present distance of time it is necessary, in order to reconstruct the man, to inquire carefully into his daily life, and to invoke all available testimony. This it has been my endeavour to do. I have collected round me all I could find that shows him as he was, that speaks of, or that emanated from him: manuscripts, books, pamphlets, newspapers, drawings, engravings, busts, statues. In this task I have found many powerful allies, and have received many flattering marks of confidence. I had no intention of publishing my notes. I felt my own limitations too deeply to aspire to be the biographer of Napoleon. But the endless scribblers who have furnished more or less apocryphal accounts have at last forced me to break silence, were it only in the cause of truth. So it has come to pass that I have distilled the essence of documents that have been accumulating for years, consisting of notes gleaned from State or private archives, from books, newspapers, and pamphlets — all I had seen, read, or heard that seemed to me of some value as evidence. The result is a narrative of the facts as they appear to me from these various evidences.

Neither in this volume, nor in those that may follow it, shall I reveal my sources of information. Many to whom I owe valuable documents exacted a secrecy which debars me from any public expression of my gratitude. As I cannot name them, it seems to me better to name no one. Neither do I care to draw attention to certain items taken from private papers in my possession. Such references often serve no other purpose but to gratify the vanity of the writer. Besides which, such displays of erudition, calculated to dazzle a certain section of the public, are by no means proof of good faith. Several authors, whose attacks upon Napoleon have been recently printed, bristle with references to authorities. In each case where I have verified these references, I have found them to be false. For my own part, I have given my best work to my task. I am convinced of the authenticity of the documents I have used, as I am ready to prove by offering my portfolios for inspection. But I neither care nor intend to convince any who doubt my good faith. As is the historian, so is the history. Hitherto I have been accounted an honourable man, and such I claim to be. The circulation of these articles has been very considerable, yet I have only received two corrections as to matters of fact. One referred to a date, the other to the name of a place. I therefore venture to think that had more serious errors crept in, they would hiave been pointed out to me. I am far, however, from supposing that my work is absolutely free from mistakes or omissions. And in laying these collected essays before the public, I cordially invite communications from any who may have information to give, or documents to make public.

As to the spirit in which these studies have been produced, I have heard it said that I have lowered the reputation of my hero, and belittled the man I sought to magnify. This may be the result of the minute analysis and precise detail of my narrative. To show the Emperor as he was, it was necessary, not to chant his glory in the sonorous periods of the poet, but to examine the more intimate habits and functions of his personality. To this end, no circumvolution of his brain was without interest, no motive of his actions insignificant, no fact in his life without its bearing, nor any individual of his circle altogether unimportant. My long preparation was for other purposes than the drawing up of a declamatory *apologia*, or unsupported generalization. My inquiry is rigorous as that of a judge, bound to neglect no element of his case. In the following pages this inquiry turns upon the feelings and affections; later, it will be occupied with the Emperor's domestic life, and with certain periods of Napoleon's career, in dealing with which I feel qualified to bring out his character, his modes of thought and action. Will the final result justify my endeavours? I have every confidence that it will. But if I falsified evidence to give a favourable turn to the inquiry, if I failed to allow due weight to every fact that presents itself, I should fail in my duty, and forfeit my claims to belief.

Are there any who wish to see Napoleon painted other than as a man? who conceive of him as having lived without the daily development of his nature; who think of him as the same in 1769 as in 1821; who admit of no modifications between his apparition in France as the young scholar of Autun, and his death at St. Helena, after having dominated nations, and swayed the destinies of Europe? Would they have had him pass from the cradle to the grave guiltless of an indiscretion, superior to impulse, untouched by experience? Would they have had him so far above the rest of humanity as never to have shared its passions, felt its emotions, nor yielded to its governing instincts? Were these things true of him, he would have been no man, but a god; one of those supernatural beings created by the imagination of a people, whose first lispings proclaim truths divine as those of his maturest utterances; who have neither childhood, youth, nor maturity, seeing that throughout their earthly passage they are but the instruments of a divine mission. But if we take it that Napoleon was a man like other men, though of exceptional intellectual gifts, it is evident that his ideas, and the actions these ideas suggested, were not classified and regulated for him by a special providence from his birth; they were his own, and not the promptings of a god; the product of his brain, and not the effect of external influences. He himself was not the predestined instrument, the germ of which, passing spotless and incorruptible through a long line of elect beings, is transmitted from generation to generation, from sex to sex, bearing in that atom which is to become its brain the fate of nations. He was a being who retained, no doubt, some confused impressions of previous atavisms, but whose mind was formed by education, instructed by history, who gleaned some new idea from every fresh experience, whose gradual evolution may be followed, his passing sensations observed, a being in whom his fellow-man can recognize a brother, for he shared the emotions common to mankind at large.

And therefore it is essential to note Napoleon's relations with women. Nature has associated with the special function of the male animal, the propagation of species, a host of sensations which govern and subjugate him, which determine his course, and to which the majority of his actions are subordinated. In the case of man, these sensations are active and even violent; they inspire a large proportion of his sentiments and ideas, and occasion or determine the liveliest manifestations of his character. Even when the man in question is Napoleon, and woman plays a comparatively mediocre part in his life, it is essential to see what sort of woman attracted him, what were his relations with her, and what the feelings, physical or moral, she inspired in him; to inquire which of his actions were attributable to woman's influence, and how far his thoughts and ideas were modified by the beauty and conversation of women in daily intercourse.

He who embarks on an inquiry of this nature, of course lays himself open to the charge of mere scandal-mongering. The lists I have drawn up, the evidences I have collected, the details I have accumulated will no doubt shock the modesty of Tartuffes, who, fresh from an attempt on Elmire's virtue, exhort Dorine to cover her breast. There are beings so ethereal and spotless that they can brook no allusion to the process without which all animated nature would perish, a process which, if in itself unvarying, and consequently uninteresting, is capable of infinite variety in its preliminaries and its consequences; which exhibits man in the most diverse aspects; which explains and annotates his life, revealing its secrets, and strengthening its foundations. Of this process we must needs take cognizance, for without it, preliminaries and consequences would be alike unmeaning; yet, strange to say, it is held to be indecent to allude to it in connection with historical personages, although it is avowedly the text of all conversation, the chief interest of all social gatherings, the attraction of every ball, the nucleus of every play, the theme of every novel, the basis of family life, the tie that binds society together. History, nevertheless, must be expurgated, as if its public were recruited solely in young ladies' schools. The writer of history alone is forbidden to show that one of the strongest motives of human action is the desire to find favour with woman. He alone is expected to ignore that love — or what passes for such — has been the root of most of those events which have shaped the destinies of the human race. This form of hypocrisy I willingly leave to others. A candid account of some *liaison* of Napoleon's throws more light on his character, to my mind, than the history of a campaign or a treaty. What we desire to know is the man himself, his soul, his heart, his mind. And it will hardly be contended that such knowledge is complete, if we ignore his attitude towards women, and the part they played in his life.

The contemporary novelist is permitted, in deference to the exigencies of a thesis which invariably deals with sexual passion, to analyze every amorous sensation, moral or physical, of his imaginary hero; the public applauds his inventions, women wax hysterical in admiration, drawing-rooms and academies combine in ecstatic eulogy. The psychology of such books is certainly interesting, but it is purely fictitious, built up on hearsay, or based on confidences and episodic observation. Nevertheless, it is accepted as a science; it receives official recognition, and soon, no doubt, it will be taught from professorial chairs in the Sorbonne, just as it is already expounded and demonstrated in society. But dare to inquire how a man, who holds perhaps the supreme place in history, understood, judged, and loved women, basing your inquiry on the letters, admissions, and conversations of the man himself, on a wide variety of evidences, and on every sort of information that affords material for the reconstruction of his career; approach your subject never so frankly, liberally, and chastely, eschewing all coarseness of expression, all superfluous details — and you will be branded as one of those pornographic scribblers whom all serious students despise! So be it!

I honour the incomparable man to whom I would fain see altars raised by his countrymen, after my own fashion. I am convinced that the more deeply one studies his history, the greater is one's admiration for him; that one cannot do his memory a greater service than by making known the facts of his life; that my present contribution to such knowledge, indispensable to the appreciation of his moral being, will have its value to the sincere and unbiassed section of the public; and looking for no reward, aspiring to no place, seeking no suffrages, I go my way.

Frederic Masson

Clos des Fees.
    August 15, 1893

Chapter 1
Youth

Thursday, November 22, 1787.
Paris, Hotel de Cherbourg, Rue du Four St. Honore.

"I HAD come out from the *Italiens*, and was walking rapidly along the alleys of the Palais Royal. That tumult of strong emotions peculiar to my temperament made me indifferent to the cold for a time; but as my imagination cooled, I became conscious of its severity, and sought the shelter of the arcades. I was at the threshold of the iron gates when my eyes fell upon a woman. The time and place, no less than her general appearance and her extreme youth, left no doubt in my mind as to her calling. She stopped, and I noticed that her bearing was not in the least brazen, but had a certain propriety that harmonized with her personality. This *(the next word is illegible)* impressed me. Encouraged by her timidity, I spoke to her — I, whose repugnance to her class is such, that I feel myself contaminated by a glance from one of its members! But her pale complexion, her frail physique, and her soft voice decided me at once. 'Either,' said I to myself, 'this is a person who will be useful to me for the observations I wish to make, or a mere simpleton.'

" 'You are very cold' I began; 'how can you venture into these alleys?'

" 'Ah, sir, the cold refreshes me. I must finish my evening.'

"The indifference of her manner, the business-like nature of her reply interested me, and I turned to walk by her side.

" 'You look delicate. I am surprised at your taking to such a calling.'

" 'Ah, well, sir, one must do something!'

" 'Certainly. But are there not other pursuits of a healthier kind?'

" 'No, sir; one must live.'

"I was delighted. I saw that she was willing at least to answer my questions, a measure of success which had not always crowned similar attempts on my part.

" 'You must be a native of some northern district, as you bear the cold so well.'

" 'I come from Nantes, in Brittany.'

" 'I know it well.... Mademoiselle, you must tell me your story. How came you to lose your virtue?'

" 'I was seduced, sir, by an officer.'

"' 'And do you regret your fall?'

" 'Oh, yes, indeed.'(Her voice took on a sweetness, an unction I had not before remarked.) 'My sister is comfortably married, and I might have been as she is.'

" 'How did you get to Paris?'

" 'The officer who ruined me, and whom I hate, deserted me. I fled from my mother's anger. A second presented himself, and brought me to Paris. He left me in his turn, and was succeeded by a third, with whom I lived three years. Though a Frenchman, he was called to London on business, and is there now. Let me come home with you.' "

" 'What shall we do there?'

"' 'Oh, we can warm ourselves, and then —'

"I had no scruples in the matter. I had led her on in order that she might not be able to escape when pressed by the train of reasoning I had prepared while counterfeiting a severity I determined to show her was not natural to me."

When he wrote the above, Bonaparte was eighteen years and three months old. He was born on August 15, 1769.

There is every reason to suppose that this was the first woman to whom he had addressed himself; a hasty glance through the records of his childhood will suffice to show the grounds of this conviction. The more important dates he noted himself, and where it has been possible to verify these, they have proved scrupulously exact.

He left Ajaccio for France on December 15, 1778, at the age of nine years and a half. His feminine reminiscences of his native isle centred round his foster-mother, Camilla Carbone, afterwards the widow Ilari; his elderly nurses; and a little school-fellow, La Giacominetta, of whom he often spoke at St. Helena. In his later life he showered benefits upon his foster-mother, upon her daughter, Madame Tavera, and her grand-daughter, Madame Poli, to whom he had himself given the name of Faustina at her baptism. If he did nothing for his foster-brother, Ignatio Ilari, it was because the latter espoused the English cause at an early age, and entered the British navy.

One of his nurses, Minana Saveria, remained in Madame Bonaparte's service till her death; the other, Mammuccia Caterina, died long before the Empire, as did also the little Giacominetta, whose childish tears Napoleon had so often dried.

During his sojourn at the College of Autun, from January 1 to May 12, 1779; at Brienne, from May, 1779 to October 14, 1784; at the military college in Paris, where he spent a year, from October 22, 1784 to October 30, 1785, we find no mention of any woman. If, as Madame d'Abrantès states, he spent a week at M. Permon's house, No. 5, Place Conti, contrary to the regulations of the military school, to recover from a sprain, it was when he had just completed his sixteenth year.

Any adventure prior to that of November 22, 1787, could therefore only have taken place between the dates of his quitting the military school and of his return to Paris. But if Bonaparte started for Valence on October 30, 1785, he left Valence for Corsica during the term, on September 16, 1786, after a sojourn of less than a year. He did not return from Corsica till September 12, 1787, on which occasion he made the journey to Paris.

His emancipation did not take place in Corsica, nor at Valence, during the ten months of his first sojourn. He was known there as a shy, somewhat melancholy youth, much engrossed in study, but anxious nevertheless to make a good impression, and find a favourable reception in society. Monseigneur de Tardivon, Abbé of Saint-Ruff, to whom he had been recommended by the Marbeufs, and who, as a mitred dignitary, and general of his order, took the lead in social life at Valence, introduced him to some of the best houses, among others to those of Madame Grégoire du Colombier, Madame Lauberie de Saint-Germain, and Madame de Laurencin.

These ladies, especially the two latter, were among the best bred people in the province. Members of the lesser nobility, or of the more aristocratic section of the middle class, they were very particular about the conduct of the officers they admitted into their circle, and would not allow any intercourse between their daughters and young men whose morals could be called in question.

Bonaparte, though he was but seventeen and the lady was older, seems to have had some vague ideas of a marriage with Caroline du Colombier, whose mother allowed her rather more liberty than was usual. But the mutual fancy they may have felt for one another resulted only in a chaste and reserved courtship, of a somewhat infantile character, quite in the spirit of Rousseau — the Rousseau of Mademoiselle Galley. Bonaparte may have said to himself, when gathering cherries with Mademoiselle du Colombier — "Would that my lips were cherries! How gladly would I offer them to her thus!" She soon became the wife of Monsieur Garempel de Bressieux, a retired officer, who took her to live at his country-house near Lyons. Nearly twenty years later, towards the end of the year XII., Napoleon, who had never met his cherry-gatherer again, received a letter from her at the camp of Boulogne, recommending her brother to his notice. He replied by return of post, promising to take the first opportunity of serving Monsieur du Colombier, and assuring Madame *Caroline* de Bressieux that "his recollections of her and of her mother had always been among his most interesting memories." "I see by your letter," he continues, "that you live near Lyons, and I take it somewhat ill that you did not come to the city during my stay there, for it would have been a great pleasure to me to meet you."

The hint was not lost on Madame de Bressieux. When the Emperor passed through Lyons on his way to be crowned at Milan (Germinal 22, year XIII.; April 12, 1806), she was one of the first to greet him. She was much changed and aged — a mere shadow of the fair Caroline of his youth. In spite of which the Emperor granted every request she made: erasures from the lists of *émigrés*, a post for her husband, a lieutenancy for her brother. In January, 1806, she wrote to the Emperor for the new year, inquiring after his health. He replied himself at once. In 1808 he appointed her Lady-in-Waiting to his mother, and appointed Monsieur de Bressieux President of the Electoral College of Is ère; in 1810 he made him a Baron of the Empire.

Such was the grateful remembrance in which he held all who had shown him kindness in his youth, that there was not one among them whose fortune he did not make, and whose name was not often on his lips during his captivity. To women he showed, if possible, a double portion of this gratitude, and even when he had good reason to bear them malice, it was enough that they had once felt kindly towards him to make him forget the rest. Thus, Mademoiselle de Lauberie de Saint-Germain, whom he once thought of marrying, preferred her cousin, M. Bachasson de Montalivet, a native, like herself, of Valence, and a comrade of Napoleon's. Bonaparte showed no resentment, and it is notorious how richly M. de Montalivet benefited by his friendship, receiving successively the posts of Préfet of the Manche and of Seine-et-Oise, Director-General of Roads and Bridges, Minister of the Interior, and Count of the Empire, with a settlement of 80,000 francs. Madame de Montalivet, "whose virtues he had once loved as much as he had admired her beauty," as he himself puts it, he appointed Lady-in-aiting to the Empress in 1806. She accepted the post on certain conditions. " Your Majesty," she said, " knows my convictions as to woman's mission here below. The much-coveted honour you graciously bestow on me would become a misfortune, to my mind, if it prevented me from nursing my husband when he has the gout, or my children, if Providence should grant me any." The Emperor frowned at first, but presently bowed graciously — "Ah, Madame de Montalivet, you make conditions, and I am not used to that. However, I submit. You must be a lady-in-waiting, and matters shall be so arranged that your duties as wife and mother shall not be neglected." Madame de Montalivet was exempted from regular attendance, and Napoleon never failed to treat her with special distinction. He had a great affection for the whole family. "They are scrupulously honest," he used to say, "and sincerely affectionate. I have every confidence in their attachment."

Such were the cherished memories Napoleon carried away from Valence. They are such as any young girl might be proud to inspire. No other intimacies are recorded, even in his most private notes, which show him as an Hippolytus, in love with glory rather than with woman. We may quote the following in proof — "If I had to draw a comparison between our own times and those of Rome and Sparta, I should say that love was the ruling power in the one, and love of country in the other. The effects of these two passions are so diverse, that we may well pronounce them incompatible. It is not to be denied that a people given up to gallantry soon loses even the strength of mind necessary to conceive of the existence of patriotism. To such a condition we seem to have come in our own age." We may conclude that his adventure with the young woman of the Palais Royal was his first experience of the sort. Common-place as it is, the episode is strongly characteristic. We recognize his misogynistic tendencies, his critical spirit, his brusque affirmations, his habit of cross-examining his interloc- utor, and also his extraordinary memory, for he reproduces the girl's words, phrases, and exclamations, even the familiar expletives that proclaim her Breton origin.

Did he ever see her again? Probably not. Among the papers written by him during this sojourn in Paris is one on patriotism, addressed to a young lady. But this was hardly a subject of much interest to a frequenter of the Palais Royal arcades.

After this sojourn in Paris from October to December, 1787, we find that Bonaparte returned once more to Corsica, where he arrived on January 1, 1788. He spent his furlough there, rejoining his regiment at Auxonne on June 1. We find no trace of any love-affair at this period. At Seurre, however, where he was sent on detachment duty at the beginning of 1789, he is supposed to have made conquests of a certain Madame L—z, née N—s, wife of the collector of the salt dues; of Madame G—t, a farmer's wife, whose dairy he visited to drink new milk; and of "the daughter of the house in which he lodged." It is a good record for a term of some twenty-five days, during which his note-books further prove him to have been working strenuously! But it is nevertheless true that fourteen years later, on Germinal 16, year XIII. (April 6, 1805), when Napoleon passed through Seurre on his way to Milan, M. de Thiard, his chamberlain, presented the " young woman " to him, and that he gave her a scholarship at one of the government schools for her son, a child of *twelve years old*. The age of the boy precludes the idea that Napoleon may have thought it his own. If he had felt any doubts on- this score, his bounty would have been not only greater, but unsolicited.

We hear of nothing during his sojourn at Auxonne throughout the year 1790; nothing either during his stay at Valence, in Corsica, or in Paris, in the middle of the year 1792, nor during the first southern campaign against the Federals, nor at Toulon.

We must pass over a space of some four years. The lieutenant has become a general; Bonaparte commands the artillery in the army of Italy.

Attached to this army, as emissary from the Convention, was the citizen Louis Turreau, called Turreau de Lignières, one of its most influential members. Accompanied by the young wife he had lately married, the daughter of a surgeon of Versailles, he arrived at Cairo in Piedmont, where Napoleon was quartered, at the close of the year II., probably on the fifth Sans-culottide, September 21,

1794. Bonaparte found great favour with the deputy, and still more with the deputy's wife. Their connection can hardly be termed a *liaison*, for Madame Turreau was the most fickle of her sex, but it was more than a mere passing caprice. So much were both husband and wife impressed by the young general's talents, that Turreau, conjointly with Barras, moved that the command of the troops should be given to Bonaparte, on the 13th of Vendémiaire, that day of peril for the Convention, and associated himself with the Corsican deputies as surety for his nominee.

Bonaparte remembered this service. On his appointment as Commander-in-Chief of the army of Italy, he took Turreau, who had not been re-elected, as store-keeper. Turreau was again accompanied by his wife, who, failing generals on this occasion, was content with smaller game. Hence many storms in the Turreau household, and the husband is even said to have died of grief at his wife's conduct. Madame Turreau returned to Versailles, and lived there for a time in great poverty during the Empire, after various fruitless attempts to find a protector. One day at a hunting party, Napoleon mentioned her to Berthier, who had known her from her childhood, being like herself a native of Versailles. He had hitherto put her off when she appealed to him, but now took the opportunity of presenting her to the Emperor. "Napoleon at once granted all her requests, and even went far beyond her expectations."

The love-passages of Napoleon's youth seem so far to have consisted of unimportant flirtations, or commonplace intrigues. [1]

With the exception of Madame Turreau, who threw herself at his head, and may be accounted a conquest, women seem to have taken little notice of the young officer, thin, pale, badly dressed, and careless of appearances. He, on his part, seems to have been too much occupied with dreams of glory to bestow much thought on them. Another excellent reason for his chastity existed. He was poor, and like other poor men, he began to think of securing a woman for himself by marriage.

---

[1] It is impossible to give the slightest credence to the fables in a pamphlet called *Forty Unpublished Letters of Napoleon*, col- lected by L— F—. Paris, 1825. 8vo.

Chapter 2
Matrimonial Projects

WHEN visiting his sister-in-law, Madame Joseph Bonaparte, at Marseilles, Bonaparte amused himself by playing the lover to Madame's sister, Désirée-Eugénie Clary, a pretty girl of sixteen, whom he was fond of calling his "little wife." Désirée took the matter seriously; her childish ways were soon laid aside, and as by magic, a passionate, attachment was developed. "Oh! my beloved!" she writes to Napoleon, "take care of yourself, if only to preserve your Eugénie, who could not live without you. Be faithful to the vows you made me, as I will be to mine."

There is a genuine and spontaneous tenderness in these letters of Eugénie's. After the fashion of the day, the young girl, who was known by the name of Désirée, re-christened herself for her lover's benefit, desirous that the name by which he called her should be sacred to him alone. Rough copies of the letters were discovered sixty-five years later among the papers of her who had written them, and preserved them as relics. They are conceived in the very spirit of that age, an age of reaction towards love and life, after a period when death had long been the only spectacle, the only preoccupation. Women, more especially, were turning to love as to a new religion — the only creed that had survived the wreck of civilization.

The acquaintance dated from January of the year 1795. The betrothal, if any formal engagement were entered into, must have taken place on April 21 , the day that Napoleon passed through Marseilles on his way to Paris.

Joseph and his wife, Julie Clary, favoured the match. They, in fact, had planned it together, and no opposition was to be feared from the Clary family. The father, to whom has been attributed the remark that "one Bonaparte was enough in a family," died on January 20, 1794 (Pluviose i, year II.). Désirée — who was not thirteen or fourteen at the time, as she afterwards wrote, declared, and caused to be officially printed — but sixteen or seventeen, the date of her birth being November 9, 1777, had only her mother and sister to consult; or rather, seeing the strength of character she exhibited, it would perhaps be nearer the mark to say that she had only herself to please.

No objection could be made on the score of age. In those days it was usual for girls to marry before eighteen, and the author of the first Civil Code had just fixed the legal age at thirteen for the woman. As to fortune, if Julie had been content with the elder brother, who had no sort of position, Désirée might well take the younger, who was at least general of his brigade.

Bonaparte, who arrived in Paris in May, in a very poverty-stricken plight, placed all his hopes on this marriage. If it should fall through, there seemed to be nothing left for him but to go and take service in Turkey, or to become, like so many others, a speculator in the national property. Even when his fortunes mended somewhat, and he was employed by the Commission of Public Safety in drawing up plans of campaign, he felt that the occupation chance had procured for him was extremely precarious. From these difficulties Désirée alone could deliver him, and he pressed his brother to get him an answer. In every letter he wrote to Joseph there were messages for her. She, for her part, was also corresponding with him. She asked for his portrait. He had it taken, and sent it to her. When she travelled to Genoa with her sister and brother-in-law, and ceased to write, he reproached her for her silence, and remarked that "the river Lethe had apparently to be crossed by those who entered Genoa." At last he abruptly demanded a definite answer. Joseph was commissioned to speak to Eugénie s brother. "Let me know the result, and end the matter."

The next day, before Joseph could receive his letter, he wrote again — "The affair must be settled one way or the other," he declares: "I await your reply impatiently." A month passed, bringing nothing but occasional messages of remembrance. Between him and the little fourteen-year-old maiden of Marseilles, not strictly beautiful perhaps, but full of charm, with her pencilled eyebrows, her soft eyes, her tip-tilted nose, her delicately curling lips, her chaste, reserved, yet tender air, Paris had interposed — that great unknown city which Bonaparte had entered with patched boots, a shabby uniform, and two famished aides-de-camp. And Paris had shown him her women, creatures matchless in grace, in elegance, in trickery, whose painted cheeks lend a strange brilliance to their eyes, whose cunning toilettes accentuate all the charms of their persons, and disguise, or rather beautify, all their doubtful points; beings of gaiety and pleasure, modified and refined by society, like hot-house fruits in their opulent maturity, decked by the merchant for the market with false colours and a suspicious bloom, that have never felt the touch of sun or wind — fruits very different to the somewhat green produce of the ungrafted tree, which, ripening under the flame of the one and the keen blast of the other, is apt, in spite of its fresh and tonic properties, to leave a slightly crude and pungent flavour on the palate.

"Here alone," wrote Bonaparte, "among all the places upon earth, woman might justly aspire to dominion. A woman needs six months of Paris to learn what is due to her, and what her empire may really be." And a few days later he writes — "Women, more beautiful here than anywhere in the world, are the all-absorbing business of life in Paris."

Yes, they were indeed the fairest of their century, those women of thirty, of thirty-five, and even of forty years old, adepts in the art, if not of loving, of making themselves beloved. Bonaparte, having nothing but his hand to offer, promptly offered that to Madame de Permon, and to Madame de la Bouchhardie, afterwards Madame de Lesparda, before that eventful Vendémi-aire [first month of autumn] came round, when Madame de Beauharnais was finally induced to take him at his word.

Hence silence, complete and unbroken on his side, towards Désirée, and on hers a lament, soft and tender as the vibration of broken heart-strings — "You have made my life a misery, and I am yet weak enough to forgive you. So you are married! Your poor Eugénie must no longer love you, or think of you. . . . My sole consolation now is to know that you believe me faithful to your memory. Beyond this I have nothing to desire but death!

"Life has become a torture to me, now that I may no longer hope to dedicate it to you. *You* married! I cannot face the thought! I cannot survive it! You shall see that I will be truer to our vows, and though you have broken the bonds that united us, never will I plight my troth to another, never will I marry. ... I wish you all happiness and prosperity in your marriage. I pray that the wife you have chosen may make you as happy as I had hoped to make you, and as you deserve to be. But, in the midst of your happiness, pity the fate of Eugénie, and do not quite forget her."

Bonaparte, whose nature was incapable of forgetfulness, looked back with a regret not untinged with remorse upon the episode. The youthful love, of which he had no doubt inspired a larger share than he had felt, had been at first a childish pastime, on which he had gradually built up a scheme of ambition. But it had broken the heart of the young girl. He seems all his life to have sought to atone for and repair the disaster. When at Milan in 1797, he devised a marriage for Désirée, who at the time was at Rome with her sister, and her brother-in-law, Joseph, who held the appointment of ambassador at the Papal Court. He despatched General Duphot, with a warm letter of recommendation — "a distinguished officer, a man of the highest character. A marriage with him would be most advantageous." Duphot arrived, and was well received; the betrothal was about to take place. Then came the terrible scene of December 28, Désirée's bridal robe was stained with her lover's blood.

At last, after rejecting various proposed suitors, Désirée agreed to marry General Bernadotte. This was during Bonaparte's Egyptian campaign. The suitor was undeniably a good match, though one of the most insufferable of Jacobinical prigs, a Béarnais without the quick wit and lively manners of the Gascon, but with a calculating astuteness that stood its owner in good stead in the double game he was constantly playing. Madame de Stael's congenial pedantry was his ideal of feminine perfection, and he spent his honeymoon in giving dictation lessons to his young wife. The news of the marriage reached Bonaparte at Cairo. It was not altogether to his taste, for Bernadotte was his enemy, but he cordially wished Désirée happiness — "the happiness she deserves."

One of his first supplicants after his return from Egypt was Désirée. She begged him to be godfather to her infant son. A son! The gift so coveted by Bonaparte already, so doubly to be coveted in the future! Désirée, not averse to this form of revenge upon her hated rival, the "old woman" as she called Josephine, paraded her maternity to the utmost; and Napoleon, hiding his chagrin under a gracious bearing, accepted the sponsorship, and chose the name of

Oscar, from the lays of his favourite Ossian. A trifling gift this! But he held richer ones in reserve for his godson.

"Bernadotte may thank his marriage for his marshal's bâton, his principality of Pontecorvo, and his crown," said Napoleon. "His treacheries under the Empire were overlooked on the same grounds."

The record of these treacheries is no trifling one! Bernadotte proclaimed his opposition at the outset, on Brumaire 18. Notwithstanding which, he was summoned to take part in the Council of State of the following day, and appointed to the command of the Army of the West. Holding this post, he not only opposed, but conspired against the First Consul, and even attempted to raise an insurrection against him. The details have become history. For this offence he received no punishment whatever. Bonaparte contented himself with endeavouring to get rid of him by appointing him ambassador to the United States. Bernadotte characteristically agreed to go, but by a series of adroit manoeuvres contrived to postpone indefinitely the equipment of the frigates that were to convey him.

A year later he was implicated in Moreau's conspiracy, and escaped because Bonaparte spared him once more, for Eugénie's sake. He did a good deal more than spare him, in fact. For having bought all Moreau's possessions, his estate at Grosbois, and his house in the Rue d'Anjou, he presented the latter, for which he had paid 400,000 francs, to Bernadotte.

Then came the days of the Empire, when Eugénie's husband was made a Marshal of the Empire, Commander of the eighth cohort of the Legion of Honour, President of the Electoral College of Vaucluse, and Knight of the Black Eagle. On Eugénie herself he bestowed a revenue of 300,000 francs, a sum of 200,000 francs in ready money, and the sovereignty of the principality of Pontecorvo. For her sake he forgave Auerstadt, Wagram, and Walcheren, and overlooked two military blunders, undoubtedly deserving of a harsher name, following on an intrigue with the royalists, in which Bernadotte, Fouché, and Talleyrand essayed the methods that resulted finally in the return of Louis the Desired in 1814.

Meantime he was unwearying in attentions and kindnesses to Désirée, which might seem excessive, but for his evident anxiety to make reparation. When Bernadotte was wounded at Spanden, Napoleon wrote to him two days afterwards, rejoicing that "Madame Bernadotte was able to be with him," and adding —

"Give Madame la Maréchale a thousand kind messages from me, together with one little reproach. She might have written me a few lines, telling me the Paris news, but I will defer my quarrel with her on this score until we meet."

There was no end to the marks of favour by which he distinguished her. One of the three magnificent fur pelisses presented to him by the Emperor of Russia after Erfurth was put aside for Désirée. Costly gifts — Sévres vases, Gobelin tapestries — were sent to her on all occasions, though she seldom appeared at Court, and made no secret of her hatred for Josephine and the Beauharnais. Was it not of Désirée Napoleon was thinking, when-— after Walcheren! — he proposed the appointment of Bernadotte as Governor-General of Rome — and consequently as grand dignitary of the Empire — to hold a vice-regal court at the Quirinal, with a civil list of three millions, a position equal in splendour to that of Borghese at Turin, and Elisa at Florence, and little inferior to that of Eugène at Milan?

When Bernadotte was elected hereditary Prince of Sweden, after the rejection of the title by Eugène, who declined to apostatize, the result was largely due to the benevolent neutrality of Napoleon. The Emperor's policy on this occasion has seemed to some obscure and unintelligible. They failed to read his heart. "He was dazzled by the prospect of seeing a woman in whom he took an interest a queen, and his godson a royal prince." He himself arranged all the details of Désirée's presentation at Court, when she came to take leave as Princess of Sweden. He invited her to the family dinner on Sunday, an unprecedented honour. To Bernadotte he made a grant of a million francs from the public service fund; he further compounded handsomely with him for the various benefactions he had himself made him, notably the principality of Pontecorvo, and crowned his bounty with a pension and a title to Bernadotte's brother.

He had indeed proved his right to say in a subsequent letter to Eugénie, "I am sure you have long been convinced of my strong attachment to your family."

Four months later, Bernadotte leagued himself with Russia against Napoleon, and in less than a year a rupture between France and Sweden was imminent. Désirée had only consented under strong pressure to a short sojourn at Stockholm. "I thought," she said, "that Sweden, like Pontecorvo, was merely a place from which we were to take our title." At the first signs of the approaching storm, she hastened back to her house in the Rue d'Anjou.

Napoleon very cautiously approached the Minister for Foreign Affairs at this juncture, desiring him to hint to the Swedish Minister his great regret that the Princess of Sweden should have returned to Paris without permission, and the desirability of showing her that her conduct was contrary to etiquette, and her absence from her husband at such a crisis most unseemly. Désirée chose to ignore the message, and made all preparations for remaining. In November, on the eve of the declaration of war, the Emperor wrote again. He sent word by Cambacérès to the Queen of Spain (Désirée's sister), that he wished the Princess to leave at once and return to Sweden; that her presence in Paris at such a time was scandalous.

Désirée, however, had made up her mind to stay. She went on ordering dresses from Leroy, receiving her friends, and giving entertainments. She went to drink the waters with her sister, came back to Auteuil, and finally returned to Paris as if nothing had happened. She even thought it very extraordinary that her French friends should blame the former Marshal of the Empire, who had now become Generalissimo of the combined forces of Northern Germany. If we are to accept the testimony of several well-informed persons, we must believe that while conveying Napoleon's final adjurations to Bernadotte, she also acted on various occasions as intermediary between her husband, Fouché, and Talleyrand.

If it could be clearly proved that Désirée took advantage of the Emperor's weakness for her to be the willing tool of conspirators who knew each other of old, what should we be forced to think of her? Let us give her the benefit of the doubt, and believe that her motives in remaining were her passion for Paris, and her reluctance to give up her sister, her nieces, her favorite society and habits.

She was still in Paris in 1814, and took part in the reception of the Russian Emperor. She was there, too, in 1815, during the Hundred Days, and on June 17, the eve of Waterloo, she ordered from Leroy a nankeen riding-habit, and a cambric dressing-gown trimmed with Valenciennes.

It was Eugénie now who was forgetful! [1]

---

[1] A communication from M. Félix Verany, author of the interesting pamphlet, *The Clary Family and Oscar II.*, Marseilles, 1893, enabled me to rectify the date of Désirée's birth, and gave me various other items of information.

Chapter 3
Josephine De Beauharnais

TOWARDS the close of Vendémiaire, year IV. (October, 1795), chance brought about a meeting between the Vicomtesse de Beauharnais and General Bonaparte. The latter had suddenly become famous; the name, which was almost unknown but a day before, the name with which Barras was so unfamiliar that he wrote it *Buona-Parte*, had echoed through France with the thunder-peals of the cannon that scattered the rebel sections of the Convention.

Appointed second in command of the Army of the Interior, and afterwards General-in-Chief, one of Bonaparte's first measures was the disarmament of the Parisians. A youth presented himself at head-quarters, and begged for permission to keep his father's sword. Bonaparte saw the lad himself, took a fancy to him, and granted his request. Whereupon he received a visit of thanks from the boy's mother, a lady, a great lady, a *ci-devant* vicomtesse, the widow of a President of the Constituent Assembly, a courtier, a general in command of the army of the Rhine. All of which, the title and rank, the refinement, the easy and aristocratic grace of his visitor, made a great impression upon Bonaparte. For the first time, the twenty-six year old provincial, hitherto unnoticed by any Woman of this class, found himself face to face with one of those elegant, seductive, delicate beings whom he had hitherto admired from afar. And the part of protector he was called upon to play for the first time flattered his pride, and was eminently to his taste.

Josephine, who was in extremities, at once saw with what manner of man she had to deal. A Creole from Martinique, married at the age of sixteen to the Vicomte de Beauharnais by an adroit aunt, who lived openly with the Vicomte's father, the Marquis de Beauharnais, Josephine Tascher de la Pagerie had led a stormy life since her arrival in Paris in 1779. Her husband, after deceiving and deserting her, had separated from her through no fault of hers. She had no social amusements to console her, for her aunt's equivocal position had barred the entrance both to the Court and to society. After her separation from her husband she had more liberty and took advantage of it, said scandal. She travelled, and spent a considerable time in Martinique. After the Revolution, she was reconciled to her husband, who became successively deputy in the States-General, President of the Constituent Assembly, and Commander-in-Chief of the army of the Rhine. For a brief space she lived happily, and had a salon, finding herself for the first time in "the world," and profiting by the experience. Then came the Terror. Beauharnais was imprison-ed, guillotined; she herself, also a prisoner, escaping death by a miracle.

When she was released from the Prison des Carmes on Thermidor 9, she was past thirty; she had two children, and was completely ruined. By the help of certain feminine friends she had made – chiefly in prison, for few others were left her – she again entered society. Borrowing right and left, running into debt, and eking out these resources by occasional supplies from the West Indies, she managed to keep up appearances. She left her lodging in the Rue de l'Université, and took a small house, No. 6 in the Rue Chantereine, which she rented from Louise-Julie Carreau, Madame Talma, for 4000 livres, or 10,000 livres in *assignats*. There she installed herself on Vendémiaire 10, year III (October 17, 1794).

A year passed. Debts accumulated, but nothing came in to meet them. No doubt her sunshiny Creole disposition enabled her to drift along, shutting her eyes to the critical facts of her position, or hoping to be presently delivered from them by a miracle – some such miracle, perhaps, as her aunt had encountered in the person of M. de Beauharnais! At the places of amusement she frequented, and in the so-called "society" of the day – a society that came together in public gardens, where good company was to be had for a few pence! – Josephine had made a few acquaintances, who exerted themselves on her behalf, and effected the restitution of some few acres that had belonged to her husband. But she had realized, and was gradually consuming these. Other resources she had none; the nominal dowry of 100,000 francs she had received at her marriage was to have produced an income at five per cent. interest on the capital. But her father had died, her mother was left in poverty, and the West Indian colonies were blockaded by the English. She had further been portioned by her aunt, Madame Renaudin, with the reversion of certain properties, which had since been sold, and with claims on certain creditors, which had lapsed. This, however, was of little moment, for the lady could not live on a reversion. Madame Renaudin gave her some little help, which she supplemented by loans from complaisant bankers, who accepted drafts on Martinique, and who even advised her to go to Hamburg, where she would be able to receive remittances more easily. Hut her credit was waning, her years increasing. What card had she yet to play?

At this critical juncture General Bonaparte rang at the outer gate to return the Vicomtesse de Beauharnais' call. He did not know that the house belonged to the Citoyenne Talma, and was, in fact, a present from a rich protector of the days when she was known as Mademoiselle Julie. Nor did he note that the house and its surrounding 1200 metres of land, in this outlying quarter of the city, close to the Rue St. Lazare, was worth barely 50,000 francs, the sum it fetched in 1781, and was again to fetch in 1796.

The gate having been opened by the concierge–for a concierge there was – the General traversed a long passage, on one side of which he saw the stables, with two black horses of about seven years old, and a red cow. The coach-house on the other side discreetly concealed its shabby carriage.

The passage gave admittance to a garden, in the center of which stood the dwelling-house. On the ground-floor were four lofty windows, surmounted by a low attic storey. The kitchens were underground. Bonaparte passed up four stone steps to a terraced platform enclosed by plain balusters, and entered an ante-room, the scanty furniture of which consisted of a copper urn, an oaken chest, and a deal cupboard.

The man-servant Gonthier conducted him into a small dining-room, and left him to seat himself on one of the four horsehair chairs near the round mahogany table, or to examine the half-dozen prints in black and gold frames on the walls. There was little of luxury in his surroundings; but remnants of former elegance were scattered here and there, in the shape of tables and dumb-waiters of mahogany, and the yellow wood of Guadeloupe, with marble tops, and gilded copper mouldings, while in two large cupboards with glass doors, a tea-urn, some vases, and a series of table accessories in Britannia metal did their best to supply the place of silver. Of this latter commodity the house could boast no more than fourteen spoons, fifteen forks, a soup-ladle, six soup-spoons, and eleven coffee-spoons.

But of all this Bonaparte knew nothing.

Josephine, fresh from the hands of her maid, the citoyenne Louise Compoint, emerges from her dressing-room, and hastens into the dining-room to receive this visitor, the harbinger of better fortunes. She cannot well receive him elsewhere; for on the ground-floor she has only, besides the dining-room, a little semi-circular chamber, of which she has made a dressing-room, and her bedroom. The latter is pleasant, but simple enough. The furniture is upholstered in blue nankeen, with a pine pattern of blue and red; the little bed is of plain wood; a few more elegant pieces of furniture, made of mahogany, or of the yellow wood of Guadeloupe, complete the plenishing, together with a harp by Renaud, and a little bust of Socrates in white marble, the only ornament of the room. In the dressing-room, the most important feature, after a piano by Bernard, were the mirrors. One stood on a large dressing table, another on a mahogany chest of drawers, a third on a side-table, while a fourth, an ornamental glass with two panels, crowned the mantel-shelf.

Such were the household goods of this lady of fashion! Her table was served with earthenware, except on great occasions, for which she reserved a dozen blue and white china plates. The table linen consisted of eight table-cloths, so much the worse for wear that they, together with the table napkins, were valued at four livres in Josephine's inventory. But Bonaparte knows nothing of this. How should he know that the charming woman before him, whose infinite grace dazzles him, whose tasteful costume is a positive feast to the eye, possesses in all but four dozen chemises, a good deal worn, two dozen handkerchiefs, six petticoats, six night-jackets, six pockets, eighteen lawn neckerchiefs, and a dozen pairs of silk stockings of different colors? As a set-off, however, to this meagre linen-chest, she owns six muslin scarves, two taffetas gowns of brown and violet respectively, three muslin dresses embroidered in colors, three plain muslin dresses, two of Indian muslin, three of cambric, one summer taffetas gown, three of woollen material, and one of white embroidered lawn. The scanty under-linen and the comparative wealth of outer garments is characteristic of Josephine! Her six petticoats as against her sixteen frocks reveal the woman!

But all this matters little! Bonaparte sees only the dress, or rather he sees only the wearer. Her chestnut hair, fine and silky rather than abundant, was less remarkable for quantity than quality in those days of blonde wigs and powder. Her skin, somewhat brown in color, and no longer youthfully smooth on the face, owed not a little of its bloom to rouge and white paint. Her teeth were bad, and she never displayed them, the dainty mouth wearing invariably a faint, sweet smile, in charming harmony with the infinite sweetness of the deeply-fringed eyes, the tender expression of the features, and the exquisite modulations of a voice which in later years, it is said, would cause the very servants passing along the corridors to pause and listen. A delicate nose, small, mobile, slightly *retroussé*, the nostrils quivering at the least emotion, was not the least provocative feature of the attractive face.

The face, however, was insignificant as compared with the beautifully moulded figure, and long, lithe limbs, terminating in a pair of dainty feet, arched and slender, the feet of a queen, made for homage and kisses! We can divine their form and texture, see them, feel them almost, as we look at the shoes that once encased them. Of stays, or any artificial support, her figure was innocent; the slender and even meagre development of the bust enabling her to dispense with such contrivances. Hers was an individual charm that triumphed over minor defects, an elegance of which she alone possessed the secret; it was said of her that "she even went to bed gracefully." Her grace was due to the perfect proportion of the supple limbs to the lissom figure, a proportion which resulted in an easy elegance of movement that made her seem tall, though she was really of mediocre height. Add to all this, a profound knowledge of effect in pose and gesture, a coquetry that displayed itself in infinite refinement, neglecting no opportunity, and leaving nothing to chance, and that indefinable languor that makes the Creole the most essentially feminine of women, that sensuous element, vague yet intoxicating, that seems to pervade the facile *abandon* of her personality. Was not the vision one that might have charmed the most experienced? How much more then such a novice as Bonaparte? Captivated by the *woman*, he was dazzled by the *lady*, awed by her air of dignity and breeding: "the calm and noble bearing of the old French aristocracy," as he himself expresses it.

She, for her part, saw that he was won. He returned the next day, and the next. Soon no day passed without a visit from him, and when he found Madame de Beauharnais surrounded by personages of the late court, men whose birth seemed to him of the highest compared with his own "petty gentility," as he called it, when he saw her treated as a friend, an equal, in fact somewhat as a comrade, by a Ségur, a Montesquiou, a Caulaincourt, he did not detect the shade of familiarity in their bearing, nor does he seem to have been struck by the fact that these men, whose prestige was so great in his eyes, paid their visits alone, and that their wives were never seen in Madame de Beauharnais' salon. Fresh from the Jacobinical society in which he had lived at Vaucluse, at Toulon, at Nice, and in Paris, and to which he owed his promotion, he felt an infinite satisfaction at finding himself in such company. He took appearances for realities, and, dazzled by his senses, continued to accept them as such. For all here was equally unreal – the lady's wealth, birth, position, and apparent social standing.

A fortnight after the first meeting Bonaparte was her lover. The letters exchanged at this date seem to imply that as yet there was only friendship between them. But, says a contemporary, delicate transitions were unusual in those tumultuous times, and progress was rapid.

"They loved each other passionately." It was natural enough in his case, and it seems not unlikely that Josephine herself was sincere at this stage. Bonaparte was a new experience for her, a savage to tame, the lion of the day to lead about captive. The dawn of passion in the young man, his southern ardour, and youthful fire, his rapturous worship of her personality, were homage that could not fail to touch a woman of her age, a delicious evidence that she was still beautiful, that she would never lose her charm. But it was as a lover he commended himself to her, not as a husband. And now, he offers her his hand, he presses her to become his wife! After all, she has little to lose by such a transaction. She is desperate, and this may be a winning hazard. He is young, ambitious; he commands the Army of the Interior. The Directory remembers that he furnished the plans for the last campaign in Italy; Carnot is prepared to give him the command in the next. This way, perhaps, salvation lies. And at the worst she enters into a contract from which she can easily seek release in a divorce, if need be, for there is no question of priests, or a religious ceremony.

What is there then to fear? The bargain will hold good as long as the contracting parties are pleased to observe it, but it is one which will not be considered binding, either by the woman's conscience, or by the opinion of her former world, if that should trouble itself at all in the matter. And a great stake worth winning may be the portion of the skilful player in such a game, for the young man may rise to great heights. If he should be killed, there is always the pension.

She takes certain precautions, nevertheless. First of all, she busies herself with the falsification of her age, for she cannot own to thirty-two, either to a lover of twenty-six, or any one else. Calmelet, her business adviser, the guardian of her children, goes to a notary, in company with a certain Lesourd. "They declare themselves perfectly acquainted with Marie-Josephe Tascher, widow of the Citizen Beauharnais, and certify that she was born at Martinique, in the Windward Islands, and that it is at present impossible for her to procure a certificate of her birth, owing to the occupation of the island by the English." This was all; there was no further declaration, and no dates were given. Armed with this document, Josephine informed the registrar of the civil marriage that she was born on June 23, 1767, whereas she was as a fact born on June 23, 1 763. But she was not pressed very closely on this point.

She determined to keep up a similar fiction with regard to her means. This seemed more difficult at the first blush. But Bonaparte was in a mood to be readily cajoled. The most extraordinary marriage contract ever received by a notary was drawn up privately, in the presence only of Lemarrois, the General's aide-de-camp. No community of goods of any kind, or in any degree; each contracting party to have the sole control of his or her property; all administrative power secured to the future wife by the future husband in advance; the children of the first marriage to be under the sole guardianship of the mother; a jointure of fifteen hundred livres per annum in the event of her becoming a widow, in which event she should also be entitled to take possession of all goods she may certify as her own.

There is no mention of other settlements. All the future wife's property is said to be secured to the joint estate of herself and the late M. de Beauharnais. No inventory had as yet been made, and until this was done she could not be called upon either to accept or renounce. When two years later the inventory was drawn up, she renounced her claims, fortune having brought better things in the interim. Bonaparte's avowal of his poverty was made with less circumlocution. "On his part the future husband declares that he owns neither lands nor goods beyond his personal wardrobe and his military accoutrements, the whole valued by him at ... which he assigns." This was indeed, as the notary said to Madame de Beauharnais, the proverbial Cloak and Sword. The General, however, came to the conclusion that the declaration was superfluous, and struck the paragraph out of the contract.

The document bears the date Ventose 18, year IV. (March 8, 1796). The marriage took place the next day before the registrar, who obligingly described the bridegroom as twenty-eight years old, instead of twenty-six, and the bride as -twenty-nine instead of thirty-two. He was evidently an official with a strong sense of proportion. Barras, Lemarrois, who was still a minor, Tallien, and the inevitable Calmelet were the witnesses. No reference was made to the consent of the parents on either side. They had not been consulted.

Two days later General Bonaparte left to join the army in Italy. Madame Bonaparte remained in the Rue Chantereine. Fortunately, they had anticipated the honeymoon.

Chapter 4
Citoyenne Bonaparte

THE journey from Paris to Nice was accomplished in eleven stages; from each of these, and from almost every posting-house where the General halted for relays, a letter was despatched to the Citoyenne Bonaparte, care of the Citoyenne Beauharnais. These letters breathe nothing but passion; ambition finds no expression here, so confident is the writer in his destiny. He seems to feel no doubt, no uncertainty as to the future; his confidence is so complete that it has no need of utterance. He indulges in no speculations, gives no hint of his plans, and seems to feel no uneasiness as to his means. He might be one of those princes of some two centuries ago setting out to preside at a victory. He writes of nothing but love, of her, and of himself.

At Nice, whether issuing his laconic orders to the unruly hordes out of which he is to mould an army, or subduing with one frowning glance such mutinous subalterns as Augereau and Masséna; or rapidly devising a system whereby his exhausted soldiers may be fed, equipped, and disciplined in preparation for that rush upon the Alps with which they are to open the campaign, letter after letter flies to Josephine. "When I am inclined to curse my fate, I lay my hand on my heart and feel your portrait there; I look at it, and love fills me with joy unspeakable; life seems to have no sorrow, save that of separation from my beloved." This portrait he never laid aside. He showed it to every one, said his prayers before it, and was in an agony of despair when the glass was broken, a mishap which he looked upon as an omen of death.

It was the worship of a fanatic, the rapt adoration of a devotee. Had his soldiers known of it, they would not have laughed at him; they were of his own age and race. Like him, their brains were dizzy with supernatural visions. He was a fit general for this strange army. At its head, he, the young man of twenty-six, pale, thin, and impassible of feature, his long hair slightly powdered, his deepset eyes flashing a fire that penetrated the very souls of men, awing and subjugating the most unruly. Under him, adventurers of every type – Augereau, a deserter from every standard of Europe, an effusive swashbuckler, roysterer, and bully; Masséna, a successful smuggler, a pirate upon occasion, an ardent lover of women and of money, and as little fastidious in his taste for the one as in his pursuit of the other.

They would have rejoiced at the downfall of the little *ci-devant* who had been exalted above them. But his keen eye is fixed steadily upon them, and, growling fiercely, the wild beasts grovel at their master's feet. The inferior officers and soldiers as a whole (for there are individual rebels such as Landrieux) do not need taming; they gave in their adhesion at the first word. The majority of them are recruited from the army of the Eastern Pyrenees. They have gone through the ordeal of self-renunciation, and each man has in him something of the spirit of La Tour d'Auvergne. Their thoughts are of glory and of fatherland. In the coming war there were found officers who declined promotion as if it had been an insult, corporals who turned the tide of battles, private soldiers who approved themselves good generals in an emergency, and divined all the intricacies of strategy. An electric current of genius thrilled through the ranks, filling each young heart with a like disdain of death, a like cheerfulness in peril, a like joyful stoicism, a like romantic conception of love. Here, again, Bonaparte showed himself worthy to be their leader. Victory was a means of seeing her again, of possessing her, of having *her* near him, with him always.

With such thoughts in his mind, he had gained six victories within a fortnight in the month of April 1796, taken twenty-one standards, and compelled the capitulation of Piedmont. "Soldiers, we thank you!" Yes, from our hearts, for Josephine is coming. Junot, who has been despatched to Paris with trophies, is to bring her back. He cries out for his wife. "Come, come! If you linger, you will find me ill on your arrival. The fatigues I have undergone, and your absence, are too much." It was no excuse to hasten her. He was consumed by fever, exhausted by an incessant cough. The scurvy contracted at Toulon had weakened and emaciated him. And the one longing, the one idea possessed him day and night – "You will come? You will be here beside me, on my heart, in my arms? Oh, that you had wings! Come, come!"

The world contained but this one woman for him. At Cairo, the mistress of a Piedmontese officer was brought before him. She was young, and exquisitely beautiful. A momentary fire flashed into his eyes as he looked at her. Then, motioning his officers to remain, he received the captive with calm dignity, and gave orders for her safe-conduct through the lines, and restoration to her lover.

Such an act may be attributed to policy. But when Grassini offered him her love at Milan, and, in despair at his coldness, breathed her soul out in strains so pathetic and melodious that the whole army was converted to a passion for music, he showered money on the singer, and rejected the mistress. All womanhood for him was comprised in one woman, and all the joys of love began and ended only in her.

Why did she delay her coming? Truth to tell, the thought of following the drum by no means attracted her. She greatly preferred to rejoice over the results of the campaign in Paris, where it was delightful to find herself at the summit of her desires at last, a recognized queen and leader in the new capital! Bonaparte sent her liberal supplies, and there was unlimited credit for the wife of the commander-in-chief of the victorious army. She took part in every fete, in every assembly, in every reception at the Luxembourg, which had regained something of its princely splendour under Barras. Here a prominent place was always assigned to Josephine beside Madame Tallien, the reigning divinity.

She was conspicuous in the front row of spectators when Junot presented the twenty-one banners to the Directory, and left the hall on Junot's arm, sharing in all the glories of the triumph. Then there were "first nights" at the play, when the pit rose up to greet her as she entered her box, and she tasted the sweets of popular acclamation; then official fetes, the Festival of Gratitude and Victory, which seemed to be given specially in her honor; and above all, or rather summing up all, there was Paris, the city of which she was so enamoured that she could scarcely live outside it, the Paris which so fascinated her that her chief pre-occupation throughout the eighteen years of life that yet remained to her was how so to contrive as to remain in it.

Meanwhile Bonaparte, waiting, hoping, raging at the delay, tortured by jealousy, anxiety, and longing, wrote letter after letter, despatched courier upon courier. What was she doing? What was she thinking of? She had taken a fresh lover, no doubt – "one of about nineteen" this time. "If so, let her beware of Othello's dagger." At which outpourings she would smile, and protest with her pretty Creole lisp, that Bonaparte was really very droll!

An excuse of some sort must be found, however. Joseph Bonaparte is in Paris, urging her departure; Junot, pleasant as he finds it to play the part of dashing hussar in Paris, is about to rejoin the army. Lodi has followed on Crasco, and the troops are now at Milan. A palace and not a camp awaits her. Josephine is at her wits' end. An ordinary illness is too hackneyed an excuse. But how would it be to declare herself *enceinte*? She catches at the idea. Bonaparte is enraptured at the news. "How shall I ever atone," he writes, "for all my hard thoughts of you? You were ill, and I accused you of lingering in Paris! Forgive me, my beloved. My passion robs me of my reason, and I shall never recover it. Mine is a disease for which there are no remedies. I am oppressed by mournful forebodings. There are times when I should be content to see you once more, to press you once more to my heart, and then to die with you. . . . A child, sweet as its mother, is soon to lie in your arms! Oh, to be with you but for one day!"

He writes the same evening to Joseph – "I am in despair, my brother. My wife, the creature I love best in the world, is ill. My brain reels at the thought. The darkest forebodings oppress me. I implore you to tell me exactly how she is, what there is to fear. I beseech you, by our brotherhood, by the tender affection there has always been between us since our childhood, watch over her, tend her as I should be proud to do myself. You cannot bring my heart to the task, but you, and you alone, can in some measure take my place. You are the only man in the world for whom I have a true and lasting affection. After her, after my Josephine, you hold the first place in my heart. Comfort me. Tell me the truth. You know me. You know my passionate nature. You know too that Josephine is the only woman I have ever really loved. The thought of her illness drives me distracted. No one writes to me, all have forsaken me. Even you do not write. I am alone with my fears, my misery. If she is better, and can safely undertake the journey, I long unspeakably to have her with me. I want to see her, to hold her in my arms. I love her so madly, I cannot live without her. If she were to die, there would be nothing left me to live for. Oh, my good brother, I rely on you. See that my messenger remains no more than six hours in Paris, and send him back with new life to me. ..."

His patience is at last exhausted. He threatens to resign his command, and return to Paris, if his wife does not join him. Josephine sees that it would be dangerous to trifle further. The most plausible of her excuses, the one that appealed most strongly to Bonaparte, is no longer available, if, indeed, it ever had any foundation in fact. Joseph is not to be deceived by the plea of illness, for he sees her taking part in all the pleasures of society, and very well able to bear their fatigues.

Josephine resigns herself to her fate. After a farewell supper at the Luxembourg, she takes her seat in a travelling carriage, weeping copiously, and sobbing aloud. Her dog Fortuné, Joseph, Junot, Citizen Hippolyte Charles, aide-de-camp to Adjutant-General Leclerc, and Citoyenne Louise Compoint, accompany her. The maid is served at the same table with her mistress, and dressed in the same style. Her room in the Rue Chantereine is not that of a servant; it is better furnished than that of her mistress, with curtains and *portières* of Oriental chintz, alabaster candlesticks mounted in gilded copper, Sèvres figures of Cupids and shepherdesses, and a handsome Regency bureau, with copper fittings and marble top. It has been suggested that there was something mysterious in Louise Compoint's relations with Josephine. She seems, however, to have been merely a confidante with whom her mistress thought it well to be on good terms, and Josephine continued to pay her a pension till 1805, in spite of the rupture that took place subsequently. During the journey, which seems to have been prolonged somewhat unnecessarily, Junot made the best of his opportunities with Mademoiselle Louise; and Josephine, though – to judge by the sequel – she found Monsieur Charles by no means indifferent to her own charms, is said to have been irritated at the preference shown to her favorite.

The travellers had set out at the end of June (Messidor, IV); on July 8, (Messidor 20,) they were approaching Milan, and Napoleon, who was obliged to meet the advance of Wurmser's army, implored Josephine to join him at Verona. "I shall need you," he wrote, "for I am going to be ill." She preferred, however, to await his return to Milan. He hastened back to her, and after two days of rapture and caresses, the great crisis of Castiglione was upon them. The difficulties and perils of the situation could hardly be over-stated. The question was not so much how to avoid defeat, as how to escape destruction. Yet, while busily despatching orders for the mustering of his divisions, and working out schemes to minimize the shock of impending disaster; at this crisis, unparalleled in his career, when Fortune seemed about to forsake him, when his prestige was at stake, and he himself for the first time seemed to have lost confidence in his resources, he found time for a long love-letter each day. "Ah! it were better to show me some of your faults. Be less lovely, less graceful, less tender, less kind. But never be jealous; never weep. Your tears drive me distracted, they set my blood on fire. Come to me here, that we may at least be able to say before we die: We had so many days of happiness!"

And the next day, and the next, and every day that they are apart, he breaks out into the same frenzy of passion, showering imaginary kisses and caresses upon his idol from afar. He orders, commands, entreats her to come to him, if but for a night, an hour. Josephine, who has grown somewhat more submissive, feeling vaguely, on the soil of conquered Italy, in the presence of the enthusiastic army, that he is of the race of chieftains to whom it is well to yield at least a semblance of obedience, makes an effort to join him. And then begins a strange progress through endless lines of soldiers, one day a fugitive, the next the heroine of a triumphal entry; now received with regal honors by the magistrates of the new Italy, now under the fire of the Austrian batteries. Carriages are overturned, impeded by the debris of victorious or disbanded armies, and a love-drama is enacted to the beating of drums, the whistle of bullets, and the flaming of bombarded cities.

When she was with Bonaparte, "he was all day at her feet, as before some divinity." When absent from him, post after post was despatched with letters to her. From each of the obscure villages whose names he has immortalized he sent letters, in which declarations of tenderness, confidence, and even of gratitude are mingled with jealous imprecations and frenzied expressions of passion. Upon her worldly, expert nature he lavishes all the youthful ardour of the young man of twenty-six, whose life has been chaste hitherto; and these outpourings are the wail of unsatisfied desire, exasperated by illness, fever, and incessant mental labour.

Half unconsciously, the expression of his passion is tinged by his recollections of *La Nouvelle Heloise*, and his burning periods borrow an added glow from Rousseau's pages. Though his passion was absolutely sincere, and in no sense a pretext for fine writing, yet he too had loved in this manner, had learnt the formula, and could speak of love in no other language. In those days he was a son of Jean Jacques, and, like all those who have "plucked the periwinkle blossom," his heart retained its perfume for ever.

The periwinkle blossom was, unfortunately, not at all to Josephine's taste. She was of a different generation, a different country, a different education, a more artificial temperament. Bonaparte's perpetual rhapsodies wearied and annoyed her. It was delightful, of course, to be loved so deeply; at first it had all the charm and interest of novelty; but it became fatiguing after a time, and the want of tact, the crudities, the inexperience of youthful passion offended her maturer and more fastidious senses. There were, of course, certain compensating advantages, presents from municipalities and princes, offerings from the generals, commissions from contractors. Lavish as was her expenditure, Josephine was never mercenary. Wasteful and improvident, always open to temptation, and perpetually tempted, she often accepted out of mere civility just as she bestowed out of mere caprice. Obeying her instincts in such matters, she was only dimly conscious of wrong-doing. Nevertheless, she so contrived that Bonaparte should be kept in the dark. She knew him to have scruples that seemed strange to her, judged by the standard of her own circle and the society in which she had lived. But, such as he was, she must make the best of him. Soon after her arrival he had expressed himself very severely about a box of medals Josephine had received, and she had been forced to return them. Thenceforth, such matters were kept from him. If he had suspicions, Josephine, who secured accomplices beforehand, was always ready with some adroit lie to account for pearl necklaces, diamond parures, valuable pictures, and priceless antiques.

These were not the only secrets of which Bonaparte was ignorant. He scarcely knew of the existence of Monsieur Charles, adjutant to Leclerc, who had travelled from Paris with Josephine. Monsieur Charles had remained at Milan, in the streets of which he showed to great advantage in a smart cavalry uniform; and whenever the General was absent from the Palazzo Serbelloni, Monsieur Charles appeared. Josephine indeed declared that Monsieur Charles only came to amuse her, talk to her, and make her laugh; that the intimacy was purely Platonic. Monsieur Charles was a lively young man, robust and athletic, and remarkably lithe and active in person. He had the most imperturbable assurance, never spoke without a jest or a pun, and was an adept in all feats of strength or skill, and a master of drawing-room pastimes, mystifications, and caricature. He was the link between Josephine

– who was always in want of money – and the contractors, who imagined that Josephine's influence might be of use to them. In this capacity he showed a light-hearted liberality, a frankness, a gaiety that compared very favorably in Josephine's eyes with Bonaparte's austerity in such matters. The General, however, became suspicious of Monsieur Charles, as he had been of Murat. Monsieur Charles was arrested, it is said, probably only on the grounds of his dealings with the contractors. However this may have been, he left the army and returned to Paris, where, through Josephine's intervention, he became a member of the Compagnie Bodin, and made a great fortune as a contractor.

Monsieur Charles was a distraction after Josephine's own heart. He came from Paris, that Paris she loved – Paris the gay, the noisy, the frivolous, the licentious. She wanted the help of a Monsieur Charles to endure the *ennui* that oppressed her. "I am bored to extinction," she wrote to her aunt. Yes, everything bored her – her young husband's love, Milan, Genoa, where the Senate received her like a queen, Florence, where the Grand Duke greeted her as his cousin, Montebello, where she held her court, Passeriano, and even Venice – all, everything wearied her, except Paris! And yet, when Bonaparte at last set out for Paris, she did not accompany him. She had a fancy to see Rome, or at least said so, and it was not till a week later that she rejoined her husband in the Rue Chantereine – Rue de la Victoire – in the house for which she had ordered furniture and decorations amounting to 120,000 francs, the house Bonaparte bought some four months later (March 31, 1798) for 52,400 francs.

Thus, for a mere caprice, she renounced the glories of the triumphal journey through Italy and Switzerland, and the public entry into Paris on the arm of the man with whose name the whole country was ringing. A month after Bonaparte's departure from

Milan he was still alone. She arrived at last at the end of December. [1]

Although Napoleon no longer felt that frenzy of passion which Josephine had at first inspired, his wife was still the one woman he really loved. This he publicly avowed. "I love my wife," he told Madame de Stael. He was constantly with her, and was not concerned to hear it said that he was extremely jealous. She was no longer beautiful. "She was nearly forty, and looked her age." But what of that? To Bonaparte she could not grow old, and though the first flush of passion was over, he retained so warm and grateful a memory of his first love, that Josephine, in spite of all that was to come, remained the creature he had loved above all others, the only woman who had held absolute sway alike over his heart and his senses.

---

[1] A chronicler, whom I quote only because it is well to suppress no evidence that throws any light upon such matters, states that on the morning when Bonaparte received the oath of allegiance of the officers of the civic guards, he had in his room an actress, the former mistress of a Piedmontese officer, for whom he had sent. After the ceremony, Bonaparte, he further declares, went out on foot, and bought jewellery to the value of 128 livres from the jeweller Manini, in the Passage dei Figini. From another source we learn that before the siege of Milan he had an intrigue with the Marchesa de Bianchi, a very beautiful woman, who had come to claim twenty-five horses belonging to her husband, which had been requisitioned in Parma. Gossip further tells of his relations with a singer, named Ricardi, to whom he sent a carriage and six horses by Duroc; also with a dancer seventeen years old, Mademoiselle Therese Campini, and with the daughter of a furrier in the south, who had married a Piedmontese patriot, one Caula. This would make five altogether. None of these adventures are authenticated in any way, and the probabilities against them are very strong from the psychological point of view.

ON the 29th of Floréal, year VI., at Toulon, Bonaparte stood on the bridge of the *Océan*, the vessel to which he had entrusted his fortunes, and gazed, as long as he could see it, at the handkerchief Josephine was waving. He still loved this woman, no longer with the passion of young love, but with all the tenderness inspired by gratified desires and flattered affection. He loved her as the incarnation of grace and elegance, his ideal of femininity, the first woman who had shown him tenderness, the first who had really given herself to him.

He had arranged with her, that as soon as he had completed the conquest of Egypt – of this result he was perfectly confident – she should join him there. A frigate was to be despatched for the journey. Josephine may have made the compact in all sincerity. But very soon the thought of such a long journey to unknown regions disturbed and alarmed her. In Paris, she gradually became absorbed once more by old habits, old friends, the pleasures of society, and above all, by the lovers who had followed her from Milan. Her indiscretions at last roused Bonaparte's suspicions.

He began to show his uneasiness even during the voyage from Toulon to Malta, and hence to Alexandria. Old doubts rose again in his mind. He wished to make sure; he questioned his friends, and they answered him. On various occasions he took aside those in whom he had most confidence, and who were least likely to withhold the truth from him, and insisted on hearing from them what had been said of his wife in Italy.

To all that had happened before his marriage with Josephine he professed indifference. When, on the 23rd of Prairial, year IV., he wrote to her from Milan "Everything about you was but an added charm in my eyes, even the recollection of your errors, and of the sorrowful scene that took place a fortnight before our marriage," he gave the keynote of his own character, and of his comprehension of love. His claims upon the heart, mind, and senses of the woman he loved he conceived of as dating only from the day when she pledged herself to him, accepted his love, and seemed to return it. But from that day forth she belonged to him absolutely, and woe betide her should she deceive him!

No sooner were Bonaparte's eyes opened, no sooner was the delusion he had cherished at an end, than the idea of a divorce suggested itself to him. He considered the bond broken between his wife and himself. Had it been possible to preserve his ignorance, he would, no doubt, have been as faithful to her in Egypt as he had been in Italy. But now he may well have felt that there was no obligation to continence. Why, he may have argued, should he not take advantage of any distractions that might relieve the tedium that weighed upon the invading army? Such distractions, but a few months ago, he would have looked upon as treason to a beloved and faithful mistress. Now they seemed but the natural weaknesses of a man of nine-and-twenty.

He seems to have felt an attraction of curiosity towards the women of the East, as had many of his officers. Some half-dozen were brought before him, but their appearance, and notably their obesity, filled him with disgust, and they were hastily dismissed. He was already remarkable for the extraordinary fastidiousness of his senses, in especial for his susceptibility to smells, and the irritable delicacy of his nervous organization.

Greater attractions were to be found at the *Tivoli Egyptien*. This was a pleasure-garden, modelled on the Parisian Tivoli, the enterprise of an *émigré*, formerly a member of the Garde du Corps, and a fellow-student with Bonaparte at Brienne, who had obtained leave to follow the army. As at Paris, there was a club, all manner of games, wooden horses, swings, jugglers, *almées*; the spectators ate ices as they watched the performers, or listened to military bands. All this would have been charming, had it not lacked its chief essential, the feminine element of its French counterpart. But there were very few European women in Egypt, to the great disgust of the army of occupation. Numbers of the officers, resigning themselves to the inevitable, married native wives.

The only European women who frequented the Tivoli had followed the army. The most stringent orders had been given before the embarkation that all officers' wives were to remain at the brigade depots. Those who had reached Cairo, therefore, had all got there by means of some stratagem, the most common device being the donning of male dress. Thus disguised, they had escaped the vigilance of sentries, and had made the voyage concealed in the hold of one or other of the troop-ships.

They were naturally for the most part women of free and audacious manners, ready for adventure, bold, and even martial in an emergency, like General Verdier's wife, who handled a gun like any soldier. The flower of the flock was a little fair-haired lady, with a brilliant complexion, and exquisite teeth. She would have been attractive anywhere; in Egypt she was adorable.

Her name was Marguerite Pauline Belleisle. While apprenticed to a milliner at Carcassonne, she had succeeded in marrying her employer's nephew, a handsome young lieutenant of the 22nd Chasseurs, called Fourès. In the middle of the honeymoon came the order for the bridegroom to embark. The bride put on a chasseur's uniform, and sailed in the same ship with her husband. At Cairo she resumed her feminine habit. "She held little communication with the other officers, and the young couple were cited as models of wedded bliss." On Frimaire 20, year VII. (December 1, 1799), a féte was held at Esbekieh, the chief feature of which was the launching of a balloon, a phenomenon intended to astonish the natives of Cairo, who were, however, so little impressed that they scarcely turned their heads to look at it. Bonaparte's two young aides-de-camp, Merlin and Eugène de Beauharnais, pointed out Madame de Fourès, with such vehement praises of her beauty that Bonaparte in his turn noticed her, and began to make inquiries about her.

In the evening he met her again at the *Tivoli Egyptien*, exchanged glances with her, approached her, paid her all manner of compliments, and spent half the evening at her side. The attack thus opened, auxiliaries at once came forward to help in the siege.

Prompted either by virtue or prudence, the little woman held out for some time. Protestations, declarations, letters, costly presents were necessary. At last she surrendered. On the 17th of December, Fourès received orders to embark – alone this time –

on the *Chasseur*, Captain Laurens, to make for the coast of Italy, and thence to carry despatches to the Directory. At Paris he was to see Joseph and Lucien Bonaparte, and to return promptly to Damietta. He returned rather sooner than he was expected.

The very day of Fourès' departure, Napoleon gave a dinner-party to the little wife and several other French ladies. Madame Fourès sat beside him, and he did the honors with great gallantry. All of a sudden he threw over a decanter of iced water, as if by accident, and on the pretext of repairing the damage done to his neighbour's dress, carried her off to his own room.

"Appearances were almost saved," it was remarked. *Almost* indeed! But the prolonged absence of Madame Fourès and the General soon made evident the real nature of the episode.

The most charitable could hardly feel any further doubt on the subject, when a house was hastily furnished close to the General's palace of Elfi Bey, for Madame Fourès' reception. She was scarcely installed when Fourès suddenly returned.

The *Chasseur*, which had set sail on December 28, had been captured the very next day by an English cruiser, the *Lion*. The English, perfectly well informed of all that was going on at the French head-quarters, mischievously released Fourès, and sent him back on parole, on his pledging himself not to serve against them throughout the rest of the campaign.

Marmont vainly endeavoured to retain Fourès at Alexandria. He arrived at Cairo in a fury of wrath, and gave his wife every reason to regret her escapade. Madame Fourès demanded a divorce, "to escape his violence," and this was granted in the presence of a commissary of the army. On his return from the Syrian expedition, the husband was again ordered to return to France, and an urgent order to give him every facility on his journey was addressed to the naval commissary.

After the divorce Madame Fourès, who had resumed her maiden name of Belleisle, but who was better known throughout the army, as formerly at Carcassonne, by the pretty sobriquet Bellilote, appeared openly as the General's mistress. Richly dressed, and living in great luxury, she did the honors of the palace to the few French ladies with the army, and entertained the generals at dinner-parties. She was constantly to be seen on the public promenades, either driving by Bonaparte's side in an open carriage, the aide-de-camp on duty riding beside – Eugène de Beauharnais among others – or riding an Arab horse that had been trained for her, in a general's uniform, a three-cornered hat on her head. "There's our Generaless," the soldiers would cry. The more cultured called her *Clioupatre.*

Round her neck she always wore a long chain, to which was attached her lover's miniature. The *liaison* thus flaunted in the eye of day caused very little scandal. From '92 onwards, it was usual to find among the staff of a Republican general, young women in male attire, who sometimes performed the duties of aides-de-camp, like the Demoiselles de Fering, sometimes other functions, like Illegrine de Morency, Ida St. Elme, and others.

A suit of man's clothes was an essential item in the wardrobe of all the emancipated women of those days, and the custom of carrying a mistress, or even a wife, to the seat of war became so usual among the generals, that from the time of the Peninsular campaign to the end of the Empire, scarcely one among them was unaccompanied. We may instance Masséna in 1810 - 1811. Eugène at last took exception to the public drives. He retained his post as aide-de-camp to his step-father, however, and was exempted from duty on these occasions.

Bonaparte became so infatuated with Bellilote that he discussed with her the possibility of repudiating Josephine, and even proposed to marry her, the ex-milliner of Carcassonne, in the event of her bearing him a child. "But the little idiot doesn't know how to have one," he pettishly remarked. To which Bellilote retorted, when the speech was repeated to her, that it "certainly was not *her* fault!"

She remained at Cairo during the Syrian expedition, and Bonaparte wrote her the most affectionate letters. When, after the battle of Aboukir, the General embarked for France on the *Muiron*, he left orders that the *ci-devant* Madame Fourès should rejoin him as soon as possible, in the first vessel that could be equipped.

Kleber, however, had his own views on the subject. Succeeding Bonaparte in the command of the army, he no doubt considered Bellilote one of the perquisites of the Commander-in-Chief, and put one obstacle after another in the way of her departure. At last, thanks to Desgenettes, Madame Fourès was allowed to embark with Junot, and a few scientific men who had accompanied the expedition – Rigel, Lallemand, and Corancez the younger – on a neutral vessel, the *America.* The *America*, however, fell into the hands of the English.

Bellilote remained a captive for a time. She was finally released, and sent under safe-conduct to France. When she arrived, however, it was too late. A complete reconciliation had taken place between Josephine and Bonaparte, and the events of Brumaire the 18th had made her lover the first magistrate of the Republic, the man to whom all looked for an example of dignity of life and austerity of morals.

It has been said that he forbade Bellilote to enter Paris. Be this as it may, she appeared openly at the Francais, and other theatres. The Consul, however, always refused to see her.

On the other hand, he granted every request she made for money. On March 11, 1811, he made her a grant of 60,000 francs from the theatrical fund, in addition to large sums already received. He bought a country house for her near Paris, and married her to a returned *émigré*, M. Henri de Ranchoup, a sometime artillery officer.

The marriage took place in 1800 at Belleville. The husband, who was of a good Auvergnat family, received as a wedding gift the Vice-Consulship of Santander, whence he was promoted in 1810 to Gothenburg.

In spite of her new husband's appointments, Madame de Ranchoup seems to have spent most of her time in Paris. She was there in 1811, and again in 1813. In 1814 she had become a *persona grata* in fashionable circles, and was a frequent visitor at the houses of the Baronne Girard, the Comtesse de Sucy, and the Baronne Brayer. She also made an excursion into literature, and Delaunay published a novel in two volumes by her, called *Lord Wentworth*. This, however, concerns us less than the novel she herself had lived. She painted too, and not without a certain charm, to judge from a pretty portrait, in which she has represented herself plucking the petals from a daisy. A strange fancy, for, if she had known something of "passionately," she had undoubtedly concluded with "not at all!" [The french version of "He loves me – He loves me not."] Her saucy, vivacious head is charming, though it smacks somewhat of the milliner; the hair is cut short, and curls all over, like a child's; the figure is delicate and seductive, the arms remarkably beautiful. The whole has a something fresh, gay, and attractive, a blooming grace that atones for the lack of distinction.

About 1816, Madame de Ranchoup, having finally separated from her husband, sold her furniture, which was of considerable value, and sailed for Brazil with a certain Sieur Jean Auguste Bellard, a retired officer of the Guard. There were rumours in Paris that she had realized her entire fortune, and that she proposed to open up communications with St. Helena, and effect the escape of the Emperor. Nothing was further from her thoughts, as a fact. She had taken a strong aversion to her former lover, and professed the most rigid Legitimist principles. When Madame d'Abrantès repeated the rumour in her Memoirs, with many admiring comments, Madame de Ranchoup protested. It might have got her into bad odour with the police, who kept her under surveillance as "a former mistress of Bonaparte's," and who had her every movement carefully watched when she returned with Bellard in 1825.

Her sole object, indeed, seems to have been the re-construction of her fortunes. She took over a cargo of goods, which she bartered in Brazil for rosewood and mahogany. Returning with the woods, she sold them, bought another stock of furniture, which she again took out to Brazil, and continued these journeys to and fro until 1837, when she settled again in Paris. She then turned once more to literature, and published a second novel, *A Chatelaine of the Twelfth Century*. In her modest dwelling in the Rue de la Ville-l'Evèque, surrounded by her pet birds and monkeys, she led a life which many would envy up to the advanced age of ninety, for her death did not take place until March 18, 1869. Her faculties remained unimpaired to the end; she wrote, painted, played the harp, bought pictures, renewed her friendships of earlier days, and even formed new ones, among others, an intimacy with Mademoiselle Rosa Bonheur.

Her artistic sympathies may be divined from the pictures she bequeathed to the Museum of Blois. (She had been attracted to Blois by her friend the Baronne de Wimpffen.) They comprised a good many copies, a good many so-called pictures of the schools of Raphael, Titian, Leonardo, and Boucher; a few canvases attributed to Prud'hon, others ascribed to Reynolds, Terburg, Jan Miel, Carlo Maratti, and Jeaurat; two modern pictures, one by Rosa Bonheur, the other by Compte-Calix; *Infant Christs, Gipsies, Venuses, Cupids, Psyches, Hermits, Flute-players* – not a hint of her Egyptian, days, of the palace of Elfi Bey, of the man who had played so important a part in her life. Before her death, Madame de Ranchoup – the Comtesse de Ranchoup, as she liked to be called – burnt all the letters written to her by Bonaparte.

It seems as if she had wished to destroy even the memory of that love which still invests her name with an interest for the student of history, a youthful, sensual, unsophisticated passion, chiefly important as giving the first indications of the desire that was to become so imperious an ambition – Bonaparte's longing for a child, a son to whom he might bequeath the heritage of his name and his glory. [1]

---

[1] After the publication of this Chapter in the *Figaro*, an interesting communication was made to a local newspaper in the Haute-Loire by Monsieur Boutin, of Craponne – "Madame de Ranchoup lived at Craponne from August, 1812 to March, 1814. The Ranchoup family, originally of Craponne, quitted the neighbourhood at the beginning of the eighteenth century. Their estates, Ranchoup and Polagnat, were acquired by the Torillons and the Sasselanges.

"The name was almost forgotten in the district, when, in July, 1812, M. Barrès, Secretary-General to the Prefecture, and afterwards Vicar-General at Bordeaux, wrote to M. Charles Gallet, then a lawyer at Craponne, desiring him to receive Madame de Ranchoup, banished by Imperial decree from Paris. A few days afterwards, a young lady, very fashionably dressed, arrived with a servant. She announced herself as one of the Empress's Ladies-in-Waiting, who had come into the country for her health. She received a number of newspapers, which she read, seated in front of M. Gallet's house, or smoking at the open window, to the great amazement of the ladies of Craponne, with whom she was not chary of her sarcasms. She often went out walking accompanied by a dog with long silky hair, for which she had a great affection, generally taking him to church with her, to the great scandal of the devout. She left Craponne at the approach of the first invading army."

It is not impossible that Madame de Ranchoup may have been requested to try the air of Craponne. I think, however, that she was in Paris in 1813.

For a communication of still greater importance, which I received at the last moment, I must refer the reader to Note A. at the end of this volume.

Chapter 6
The Reconciliation

JOSEPHINE was dining at the Luxembourg with Gohier, President of the Directory, when she received the startling news that Bonaparte had landed at Fréjus. She seems to have almost forgotten his existence, and to have given up all thoughts of his return, so little place had he in her plans for the future, and so kindly had she taken to the part of a widow in search of consolation.

While the husband was considering the possibilities of a divorce in Egypt, the wife was making repudiation a duty in France.

Forsaking Barras, who could scarcely be regarded as a lover, whose influence also was on the wane, and whose term of power was almost at an end, she made desperate overtures to the Gohiers, husband and wife, as soon as the husband became a member of the Government after *the coup d'état* of Prairial, year VII.

Gohier, a citizen of Rennes, who affected a Spartan integrity and purity of manners, was Minister of Justice under the Terror, and the author of the legal formulae insisted on by Fouquier-Tinville. He was the casuist of the guillotine. Nothing gives such a semblance of austerity as the constant search after judicial expedients; it is the form of hypocrisy which best cloaks prevarication. Gohier was reputed austere. This reputation, together with Josephine's influence, had won him his office. She had made him the confidant of her love-affairs, and Gohier, in his character of protector, had urged her to divorce Bonaparte, and marry M. Charles. Divorce is a legal and republican institution, enabling a woman who has been a man's mistress to become his concubine.

Josephine hesitated, almost persuaded. Meanwhile she came to open rupture with her brothers-in-law, Joseph and Lucien, who were Gohier's strongest opponents in the Council. The Bonapartes headed the faction favorable to Napoleon, those who expected, hoped for, and staked their future on his return, and had dreams of re-constructing France with his help. Gohier was the leader of the opposition, comprising Napoleon's bitterest enemies – Bernadotte, Championnet, Jourdan, Moulin, all the *political* generals. The Jacobins had invented Gohier, the virtuous Republican civilian, only to checkmate the conqueror. But the more Gohier showed himself hostile to Bonaparte, the more acceptable he seemed to Josephine. To secure the continued protection and help of the Gohiers, she even proposed a marriage between their son and her daughter Hortense, the girl whose happiness she invariably subordinated to her own interests and convenience, and whom she was now prepared to sacrifice without the least remorse, as indeed she effectually did later on.

The negotiations were at their height, and the families were dining quietly together, when the news burst upon them. Bonaparte had landed, and was on his way to Paris. Swift as the posts had been, he was doubtless following close on their heels. He would not have broken quarantine in order to make triumphal entries into the towns on his route. There was no time to deliberate or ask counsel. Only one course was open – to face the situation boldly, and carry matters with a high hand. This Josephine at once proceeded to do with Gohier, whose adhesion she was determined to secure at any price. "President," she said, "have no fears as to Bonaparte's intentions. They are not hostile to liberty. *But we must combine to prevent him from falling under the influence of traitors!*"

Gohier will serve his turn, no doubt, upon occasion, but at the moment Bonaparte is the all-important person. Josephine orders post-horses without a moment's delay. She proposes to meet the traveller half-way, thus avoiding all explanations, to fall into his arms, to revive his dying passion, and, her lover recaptured, to enter Paris in his carriage, to return to the Rue Chantereine on his arm, and thus to receive the mortified Bonapartes, who would never dare to speak under such conditions, or, if they did, would speak to deaf ears. This time there was none of the hesitation and delay that had marked the departure for Italy. Dispensing alike with Louise Compoint, Fortuné, and baggage, Josephine flew forward on the road to Burgundy.

Bonaparte, however, had taken the Bourbonnais route, and while Josephine was urging on her postillions, and straining her eyes to catch sight of the expected carriage, her husband was already in the Rue de la Victoire. She hastened back, but she had been obliged to travel as far as Lyons, where the two roads, which divide at Fontainebleau, re-unite. Three days had passed, during which Bonaparte, his determination to break with Josephine confirmed by the stories he had heard in Egypt, had questioned his brothers, his sisters, and his mother. No possible doubt remained as to her conduct in Milan, and the even more scandalous proceedings of the last seventeen months. Anxious to spare either her or their brother, the Bonapartes seem to have withheld a good deal; possibly they did not know all. However, what they told was sufficient. Napoleon announced his decision. It seemed irrevocable, and was entirely approved by his family.

It was in vain that friends, to whom he confided his wrongs, begged him to put aside his private griefs in the presence of a people's acclamations, reminding him that the country who looked to him for salvation, should be spared a scandal which touched his honor; that the reconstruction of the State was his first duty, and that his divorce was no such pressing matter; that to proclaim himself an outraged husband was to court ridicule, and that ridicule is fatal in France. But Bonaparte was immovable. "She shall go," he protested; "what do I care what people say? They will gossip about it for two days, and on the third it will be forgotten." No consideration availed to touch or soften him. His own interests weighed as nothing in the balance against his just indignation. To avoid an interview which might shake his resolution – for he knew full well how great was Josephine's power over his senses, he still feared her power over his heart – he caused her clothes, jewels, and all her personal property to be removed from the house, and lodged with the concierge. Making an appointment with his brothers for the next morning, when he proposed to go into the necessary formalities, he shut himself up in his own room on the first floor, and waited.

At last Josephine arrived, in a state of mind bordering on frenzy. Her all was at stake, and the game was more than half lost. For the first time in her life, perhaps, she had reflected seriously during her journey, and all the terrors of her position forced themselves upon her. If she failed to see him, to make her peace with him, what would become of her? Where would she find shelter? Flirtations such as that with M. Charles were all very well for a month, a year. But how could she have been so foolish – not as to have had a lover, but as to have allowed herself to be found out! Then there was Barras, and others, and the open warfare with the Bonapartes, and her debts, above all, her debts!

Her brain reeled at the thought! Incapable of the simplest calculations, always buying, never paying, or perhaps imagining, as frequently happened, that she had discharged the whole debt when she had merely paid some trifling sum on account, she was already harassed, as she continued to be throughout the Empire, and to the end of her days, by a long train of creditors who were always tempting her to some fresh extravagance, and whose accounts she was perpetually swelling, heedless of the inevitable day of reckoning. When this at last overtook her, she would lose all selfcontrol, weep, sob, make the most extraordinary proposals, invoke the help of Heaven or the devil, and, if she managed to gain a little time, would imagine her difficulties at an end. Such a crisis was upon her at this very time. She is said to have been twelve hundred thousand francs in debt to her tradespeople alone! It is very possible; her bankruptcies were generally on this Homeric scale. There were besides other secret transactions. She had bought "national property" to the value of 1,195,000 francs in the canton of Glabbaix, Department of Dyle, and still owed two-thirds of the sum; the other third was to have been furnished by her aunt, Madame Renaudin, afterwards Madame de Beauharnais, who could not produce a sixpence. Josephine had also bought from Citizen Lecouteulx, on Floréal the 2nd, year VII., the estate and domain of Malmaison – 225,000 francs for the main purchase, 37,516 francs for mirrors, furniture, and domestic utensils, and 9,111 francs in stamp duties, fees, etc. She finally paid the 37,516 francs for the furniture with "her diamonds and jewels." But the rest was still owing, and who would pay?

She could say with truth that Bonaparte had visited Malmaison before his departure, and had offered 250,000 francs for the property, very nearly the price she had paid for it. But after this, Bonaparte had seen Ris, to which he had taken a still greater fancy, abandoning it, however, in favor of an estate in Burgundy.

Besides which, Josephine had no powers to represent her husband in any business transaction. He had left his money in the hands of his brother Joseph; Josephine's annual allowance of 40,000 francs was paid by Joseph; and to Joseph alone he had confided his plans; at this time his letters to his wife had entirely ceased. Joseph indeed paid an advance of 15,000 francs to the Lecouteulx, but the receipt, dated Messidor 17, year VII., was made out to the General, and Josephine was still responsible for the 15,000 francs, as she had elected to be married on the system of separate estate.

Nothing was her own, not even the house in the Rue de la Victoire; it had been bought and paid for by Bonaparte. Her last resource was her jewelcasket, filled to overflowing during the Italian sojourn. She is said to have delighted in exhibiting its contents, which, as a feminine contemporary declared, were worthy to figure in the *Arabian Nights*. She had also the pictures, statues, and antiquities gleaned during the Italian campaign. But what were all these as compared with the sums she had to pay? What, indeed, as compared with those she had forgotten?

The case was truly a desperate one, for she was now too old for further conquests. Years had left their traces on a skin that had been ruined by paint. Her figure was graceful and supple as ever, but her face was losing its charm. A Creole, married at sixteen, fully matured at twelve, (Tercier relates how in 1776 or 1778 he paid his court to her,) she was much older than a woman of the same age in our latitudes; at thirty-seven she was almost an old woman. It is her last chance therefore. And realizing to the utmost the desperate nature of her fortunes, she clung passionately to the hope that Napoleon would see her, and that she should be able to soften him.

She succeeded in forcing an entrance into the house, but now Bonaparte's personal stronghold had to be stormed. After knocking repeatedly at the door in vain, she knelt down, sobbing aloud. Still the door remained shut. The scene was prolonged for hours, for a whole day, without any sign from within. Worn out at last, Josephine was about to retire in despair, but her maid, Agathe Rible, led her back to the door, and hastily fetched her children; Eugène and Hortense, kneeling beside their mother, mingled their supplications with hers. Hereupon the door opened; speechless, the tears streaming from his eyes, his face convulsed with the terrible struggle that had rent his heart, Bonaparte appeared, holding out his arms to his wife.

It was pardon, no grudging pardon, to be rescinded at leisure, or at best to be turned as a weapon against the sinner upon occasion, but reconciliation generous and complete, forgiveness, nay, oblivion of past errors. Bonaparte possessed the rare faculty of being able to forget at will, and, his confidence once restored, of ignoring crimes and faults he had been pleased to overlook, of wiping them out of his imperturbable memory. Not only could he forgive the faulty wife, he showed the rarer virtue of magnanimity to her accomplices. "He was never known to deprive any of them of life or liberty." He scorned to injure them, even in their fortunes; but it is recorded that on meeting any of them suddenly he would turn very pale.

The fault, he argued, lay not so much with these men as with himself. He should have kept a stricter watch over his wife. A man had been allowed to enter the harem. Obeying the instincts of his sex, he had persuaded; and she had yielded, as it was her nature to yield. If the erring wife were no longer beloved, the husband would do well to repudiate, to cast her off. But he loves her still. Then what remains but to pardon, and take her back to his heart? Reproaches will avail nothing. In the face of accomplished facts, Bonaparte is disarmed. He bows to the inevitable. He is able to take things as he finds them, and his fellow creatures as they are, and ceases to exact from a woman the purity she has ceased to possess. But henceforth he will be more vigilant; knowing, or at any rate believing he knows, what woman's virtue and morality are worth, he will make it a fundamental rule that no man shall ever be alone with his wife on any pretext whatever. She shall be watched and guarded night and day; such surveillance he takes henceforth to be the sole condition of marital safety; and if we find him occasionally relaxing this rule in the case of Josephine, by whom he no longer had any hopes of offspring, we shall see that it was rigorously enforced with his second wife.

Josephine was triumphant; she had crushed the Bonapartes, who had not only opposed her marriage, but had planned, and almost succeeded in bringing about, its dissolution. A crowning gratification was the association of Napoleon with herself in her triumph over his brothers. The morning after the great scene and the reconciliation, Lucien, the most eager advocate of the divorce, presented himself according to arrangement for an early interview, and was received in Josephine's apartment, where Napoleon was still in bed.

It is hardly necessary to speak of the debts, for after what he had brought himself to forgive, Bonaparte was not inclined to be severe about money transactions. On Brumaire the 21st, he paid off the 1,195,000 francs on the "national property" in the Department of Dyle. The estate served eventually as a dowry for Marie Adelaide, called Adèle, a natural daughter of the late M. de Beauharnais, when Josephine married her on Frimaire the 8th, year XIII., to Francois-Miche-Augustin Lecomte, captain of infantry, who was appointed special Receiver at Sarlat on the occasion. He also paid the money owing on the purchase of Malmaison, a comparative trifle of 225,000 francs; and he paid the 1,200,000 francs due to decorators and upholsterers, or rather, after going into the accounts, deducting goods never delivered, and extortionate over-charges, he brought the sum total down to about half, and compounded with the creditors for 600,000 francs.

Here was indeed food for reflection, had Josephine been capable of it. A husband who pays off two million francs of debts is a *rara avis* who may fairly claim certain concessions, and Josephine resolved to make them. Her *superficial* conduct, at any rate, gave no occasion to her enemies from this time until her divorce. She had, as she herself said, a wholesome fear of risking her position.

To the Gohiers she gave substantial proof of her gratitude. On the evening of Brumaire the 17th, she invited them to breakfast the following morning; Gohier being unable to attend, she begged Madame Gohier to urge her husband's acceptance of a prominent post in the new Government. Gohier, austere as ever, refused it indignantly; but when, after holding sulkily aloof for two years, he came to the First Consul for a place, Josephine obtained for him the post of Commissary-General at Amsterdam, a position so much to his taste that he held it for ten years, and would no doubt have retained it till his death, but for the suppression of the office in 1810. He is said to have refused the offer of transfer to New York after this, but he accepted a comfortable pension, which was continued to him under the Restoration. He maintained his pose of virtuous Republican, however, to the last, and was buried, by his expressed desire, without religious ceremony.

Chapter 7
Grassini

BONAPARTE had found it possible to forgive; he had even forced himself to forget. But his attitude towards Josephine in the year VIII. was very different to that of his first meeting with her, when the possession of the woman and the lady flattered his inexperience of love and of the world, intoxicated his awakening senses, and appealed with irresistible force to his newly-developed temperament. His *liaison* with Madame Fourès had given him a taste for the freshness of youth, the incomparable bloom of eighteen, and comparisons unfavorable to Josephine could not but present themselves. He had learned the charm of novelty, and henceforth he neither wished nor intended to be a faithful husband.

The part he would fain have assigned to Josephine in the future was that of friend rather than mistress, of confidante rather than wife; he sought in her the tender counsellor, to whom, in quiet evening hours, he might confide the thoughts that agitated him, and to whom he might turn for guidance in the usages of a society with which he had had no time to become familiar; the affectionate nurse, who would tend him in illness with almost maternal care, watch over him, pity and console him, on whose lap he might lay his aching head, and whose slender hands would soothe its pain with caresses, as if he were a child once more.

And yet there were still to be times (for she could never wholly lose her charm in his eyes) when she would be the wife, and even the mistress, but a mistress with whom he could be perfectly at his ease; who accepted his melancholy or his gaiety with the same apparent equability; who never showed signs of fatigue, but was always ready for journeys, expeditions, perpetual movement from place to place; who was always willing to wait, and never kept him waiting; who, without his own feverish activity, contentedly took part in all his occupations, sat beside him when he drove his four-in-hand, joined in the romping games he affected, followed him in the hunt, or accompanied him to the theatre with the same soft smile on her lips, the same sweetness in her voice.

In his political schemes, a more important part was reserved for Josephine. The nation he had determined to reconstruct lacked, he considered, two of its essential elements – the nobility and the clergy. The latter he undertook to conciliate; he looked to Josephine to rally the former. Ignorant of the mystic hierarchy which governed the French society of the monarchy, the minute gradations distinguishing one set from another, the impassable gulfs dividing them, Napoleon proposed to deal with this society in the mass. Josephine, he argued, had belonged to it. She could restore it. She would be a fit and natural intermediary between himself and the emigrants, courtiers, and nobles, all who had formed part of the old order. She should dispense favors and benefactions, inquire into wrongs, repair injustices, and gradually detach from the opposing camp all those deserters whom Napoleon wished to bring back into France; later on, she would be the link between the remnant of the old *régime* and the representatives of the new.

The part thus marked out for her was a brilliant and dignified one. Josephine had many of the qualities essential to its success – ease of manner, courtesy, elegance. She had to a remarkable degree the gift of well-chosen and appropriate speech, generosity, a charming grace in conferring favors or bestowing gifts, a politeness tinged with respectful deference towards a guest, and an adaptability of character which made her at home in every circle she entered. As a fact, she was far from possessing the interest and influence in the society of the past ascribed to her by Napoleon; the intimacies she had formed since the Revolution were of little use, and might, indeed, have materially damaged the new Government, had not the First Consul exacted their discontinuance.

Her position was consequently a very isolated one at first. But as Bonaparte's power increased, social obstacles seemed to disappear; fine distinctions were no longer insisted on, as new ambitions sprang into being. Both in the emigrant colony and in Paris, there were many eager to establish some chance connection with the Beauharnais or Taschers; distant kinships and alliances, hitherto ignored, were now ostentatiously proclaimed. Old servants, and underlings of every grade, were used as stepping-stones; and soon all the needy and importunate survivors of the former order were setting in a steady stream either towards the yellow saloon of the Tuileries, or the stuccoed reception rooms of Malmaison.

It must not be supposed, however, that this current flowed towards Josephine as the scion of the Taschers or the Beauharnais. Her prestige was due to the fact that Bonaparte had made her the partner of his fortunes. Her attraction lay in her position as the wife of Bonaparte, a possible intermediary with the master. The ambitious would have gathered round her whatever had been her name, her origin, or her past history, for was she not the satellite of that planet to whom they looked for light? Josephine, however, perhaps honestly enough, attributed the result to her own personality. She persuaded Bonaparte that she was rendering him the most important services, and strange to say, he believed it implicitly. Confident that he himself had conquered the clergy, he was easily convinced that his wife had won over the nobility.

What woman might not have been content with such a measure of honors, and gratified by the performance of duties so important and so varied? Had not the Consul some right to expect that Josephine, bearing in mind her own lapses, and grateful for the generosity that had condoned them, realizing with advancing years the disparity of age between herself and her husband, and judging leniently of weaknesses from which she herself had not been exempt, would have shown some indulgence to fancies that left her position and Bonaparte's affection for her untouched – fancies which the Consul's dread of scandal, and his sense of what was due to himself, combined to veil in decorous secrecy?

Such a view of the situation was far enough from Josephine's mind. Not that she was moved by a renewal of passion for her husband, nor that admiration and gratitude had awakened in her an affection so tender and entire that she could not restrain her jealousy. Her thoughts were all of herself, of her *position*. She imagined that Bonaparte's gradual detachment from her would culminate in her divorce. Hence she lived in a state of perpetual terror, spying upon him, and paying others to spy upon him, abasing herself by the most unworthy devices, wearying him by stormy scenes, tears, hysterics, confiding her suspicions to any one who would listen, and in default of evidence, inventing misdemeanours which she declared she had herself witnessed, and was ready to attest on oath.

The Consul's first infidelities were, nevertheless, of slight importance. A day or two after his triumphal entry into Milan, a concert was improvised on Prairial the 14th or 15th, in which the two most famous of Italian artistes, Marchesi and Grassini, took part. Grassini was twenty-seven (she was born at Varese in 1773), and her beauty was no longer what it had been two years before, when, in that very city, she had used her utmost art to attract Bonaparte, and win him from Josephine.

Her figure had become somewhat heavy and over abundant. Her face, always of a massive cast, with strongly-marked features, jet-black eyebrows, and quantities of dark hair, had lost its refinement. She was still beautiful, but with a beauty to be met with in every street in Italy: brilliant eyes, a rich olive skin, and an air of southern warmth and passion that her actual temperament is said to have by no means justified. She had had scores of lovers – not from mercenary motives, for she was far from venal – but in consequence of misconceptions acted upon in all sincerity on either side. There was not one among them whom she had failed to proclaim "an angel" at first, but her honeymoons rarely lasted beyond the first quarter.

Though Grassini's beauty was already on the wane, her voice was at its best, and the purity and expressive power of her singing was incomparable. She was not a great musician, and had no very logical conception of the principles of her art. But she herself was an embodiment of that art. Her voice, a contralto of extraordinary sweetness and pathos, pure and equal throughout its compass, was in itself a system of harmony.

To hear her was to listen, not to a singer, but to a Muse. Her phrasing was inimitable. As an interpreter of serious opera she was without a rival (in *opera bouffe* she was less successful), and none of her contemporaries came within measurable distance of her in breadth and grandeur of tragic sentiment, or in the magnetic power with which she could thrill a whole audience and hold it spell-bound. Bonaparte throughout his life was peculiarly sensitive to music, especially that of the human voice. Of all the arts, music was the only one for which he had a personal taste and predilection. The rest he encouraged, partly from policy, partly out of his passion for the grandiose, and his yearning for immortality. But in music he found a real enjoyment; he loved it for its own sake, and for the sensations it awoke in him. It calmed his nerves, glorified his day-dreams, soothed his melancholy, and warmed his heart.

It mattered little that he sang out of tune himself, had a bad memory for an air, and did not know his notes. Music moved him so deeply that he was no longer master of himself under its spell, as, for instance, on that occasion when he bestowed his Order of the Iron Crown on the tenor Crescentini. Does not such an act show a comprehension of music deeper than many whose technical knowledge is unassailable?

It was the singer far more than the woman who fascinated him in Grassini. She, for her part, had been waiting two years for his notice. Her resistance, as may be supposed, was not very protracted. The day after the concert she was breakfasting in the First Consul's room, with Berthier as a third, and it was then arranged that she should precede Bonaparte to Paris, and that an engagement should be offered her at the Théâtre de la République et des Arts.

The episode, with certain modifications as to its details, figures in the fourth bulletin of the army of Italy, so worded as to disarm Josephine, and forestal her objections to the arrival. "The Commander-in-Chief (Berthier) and the First Consul attended a concert, which, though improvised, was very enjoyable. Italian singing has a charm that is ever new. The famous Billington, *Grassini*, and Marchesi *are expected shortly at Milan. It is said that they will afterwards proceed to Paris, where they intend giving a series of concerts.*"

The trick is somewhat clumsy; but in this bulletin, which was evidently written solely for Josephine's benefit, we are struck by the pains Bonaparte was at to conceal his infidelity, his dissimulation in the matter of the dates, and the introduction of Mrs. Billington's name to mask that of Grassini, the only one of importance to him!

During this sojourn at Milan, immediately before and after the battle of Marengo, Napoleon spent every leisure hour in listening to Grassini.

Her miraculous voice possessed him, as it were. He looked upon it as one of the most glorious trophies of his campaign, and resolved that it should celebrate his triumph and sing his victory. To this end he directed that Grassini should be in Paris for July 14, the Feast of Concord, to sing an Italian duet with Bianchi. The Minister of the Interior was directed forthwith to procure the composition of an ode "on the deliverance of the Cisalpine peninsula, and the glory of our arms – some fine verses in Italian," insisted the Consul, "set to good music."

Twenty-three days later, official France met in solemn assembly in the Church of the Invalides, a Temple of Mars "splendidly and appropriately decorated." The First Consul, taking his place on the platform, was greeted by Grassini's voice, leading off the duet with Bianchi – or rather duets, for the first was followed by a second. "Who," exclaimed the *Moniteur*, "should more fittingly celebrate the victory of Marengo than those whose peace and happiness are thereby assured?"

It was audacious enough of Bonaparte to make his mistress sing at this official function, and loud would have been the outcry had the *liaison* been suspected. But no one seems to have surprised the secret so far, not even Josephine, who accepted the statement of the bulletin in all good faith. The fancy, too, was not long-lived. Intoxicated by a conquest she had long sighed for in vain, Grassini, before quitting Milan, imagined that she was about to play as great a part in politics as on the stage. She supposed her influence to be unbounded, and as she was good-natured and obliging, she left Italy laden with requests and petitions from her compatriots.

But Bonaparte was not the man to tolerate business discussions when he was in the vein for love-making. He further insisted that Grassini should live in great retirement, occupying a small house in the Rue Chantereine, and rarely showing herself abroad. Such conditions were ill-suited to the taste of the lady, who had planned a very different existence for herself, and had dreamed of such public marks of favor from the conqueror as should make her name, her beauty, and her talent the talk of Europe. Constancy was never her strong point at the best of times; she was bored to extinction, and had not even the distractions of her profession, for the terrible jargon she made do duty for French closed the doors of the opera against her, and there was no Italian opera company at Paris in the year IX. In desperation she took a new lover, Rode the violinist. Bonaparte's discovery of the intrigue caused a definite rupture between himself and the prima donna; but Rode's fears as to the consequences of his own success proved groundless, and neither he nor his mistress was ever called to account by Bonaparte. The Consul even gave them the use of the Théatre de la

République for concerts on two occasions (March 17, and October 10, 1801). The second was particularly brilliant. The receipts amounted to 13,868 francs, and Suard's descriptive notice in the *Moniteur* rose to flights of almost lyric eloquence.

After this, Grassini resumed her eventful career as a star of the opera, going and coming between Berlin, London, Milan, Genoa, and the Hague, feted and flattered wherever she appeared, and receiving 3000 pounds sterling for an engagement of five months. When passing through Paris she frequently knocked at the secret door of the Tuileries, which never failed to admit her. Her visits were perfectly unimportant, though they alarmed and incensed Josephine beyond measure. "I find," she writes to one of her confidantes, *"that Grassini has been in Paris for the last ten days. She, it appears, is the cause of all my sorrow. I assure you, my dear, I would tell you frankly if I had the least reason to reproach myself. You had better send Julie [the maid] to find out whether any one is admitted. Try to discover where that woman is living."*

This letter is a complete index to Josephine's character. There could be no question of rivalry between Grassini and herself. She knew that a serious *liaison* between the singer and the First Consul was impossible, and that his relations with her were the outcome of memories rather than of passion. Nevertheless, she could not master her curiosity, her inclination to play the spy, and arm herself with an additional weapon against her husband; nor could she refrain from complaints and lamentations to a woman Bonaparte hated, and had all but turned out of the Tuileries.

She seems, however, to have come to a more reasonable frame of mind in 1807, when the Chamber of Music was in process of organization, and Napoleon recalled Grassini to Paris. He offered the singer – the singer and not the woman – a salary of 36,000 francs, an annual bonus of 15,000 francs over and above such occasional benefactions as might accrue to her, and a pension of 15,000 francs on retirement. She was further to give a concert once a year, either in the Opera House or at the *Italiens*, for her own benefit, and to be at liberty to appear wherever she chose during her holidays, and to announce herself by the imposing title of First Singer to His Majesty the Emperor and King.

Her title availed little, however, to protect her against the robbers who infested the highways, and on October 19, 1807, near Rouvrai, on the borders of Yonne and the Cote d'Or, her post-chaise was attacked by four deserters from a Swiss regiment. The unhappy traveller was most barbarously treated, outraged, and stripped of all she had. Two days afterwards, however, the offenders were brought to justice, and the Emperor bestowed the Cross of the Legion of Honor on one Durandeau, commandant of the National Guard at Viteaux, who killed two of the ruffians with his own hand, and arrested a third.

A story has been told in this connection which relates that when the robbers snatched from her a portrait of Bonaparte, set in brilliants, Grassini implored them to keep the diamonds, and give her back the picture of her "*cher gouvernement!*" It was she who exclaimed in a drawing-room where the gift of the Iron Crown to Crescentini was the subject of much indignant criticism, "Eh bien! mais vous oubliez sa *blessoure!*" She could be witty upon occasion, with the artist's wit – as a man of the world who knew her has remarked in reference to that audacious humour, intensified by her Italian accent, which seemed curiously in harmony with her freedom of speech, and set all the rules of what Boileau calls propriety at naught.

From 1807 to 1814 the arrangements we have described were adhered to. Grassini received from the Emperor 70,000 francs a year, in addition to what she received from the public. As years went by Napoleon's enthusiasm cooled; he was present at the *Italiens*, however, in November 1813, when Cimarosa's *Horatii and Curiatii* was given with great magnificence. At the Court theatre her success was as great as ever, and was acknowledged by the Emperor with a like generosity and courtesy. All his favors failed, however, to compel her gratitude. After the fall of the Empire she consented to sing for Wellington, and her complaisance, it seems, did not end here. She was addicted to gambling, and may have been in want of money. Or it may be that she was moved by her passion for attracting the notice of famous men, and attaching herself to them.

The Duke had a curious fancy for Napoleon's leavings. He wished to have his portrait painted by David, who declined, on the grounds that he painted only *historical* pictures. He had better luck with Grassini, who, at forty-two, became his diva and his mistress. But the cricket is a proverbially irresponsible creature.

Chapter 8
Actresses

GRASSINI'S influence on Napoleon was transient, and jealous as Josephine was for a time, her fears were soon allayed. But other actresses were admitted into the secret apartments at the Tuileries, whose visits became more or less habitual. Here again, however, there was no cause for alarm. They were young women of easy virtue, for whom it was impossible that Bonaparte should have any serious feeling. All he asked of them was that they should be beautiful and amiable in the brief intervals he spent in their company. The presence of one of these visitors, nevertheless, excited Josephine's fears to the verge of frenzy. Candle in hand, she would wander about the corridors, trying locks and bolts, possessed by the idea of surprising her husband, and bringing his enormities home to him in an effective scene.

Many of the scandals in this connection would have been unknown but for Josephine. She it was who unearthed them, noised them abroad, repeated them *ad nauseam*, and even invented them at will, for she was incorrigibly untruthful. Trivial as these interludes were in general, they were part of the life of Napoleon, and as such we must glance at them, for they give certain indications of his character not to be found elsewhere.

The only singers who attracted him were Grassini, as we have seen, and perhaps Madame Branchu, a woman so singularly plain that the idea of his having distinguished her would seem almost grotesque, if it were not that the dilettante in him may have been fascinated for the moment by the expressive power and tenderness of the tragedian who re-created Dido, Alcestes, and the Vestal.

No dancer caught his fancy, though dancers had a great vogue at the time. Those were the days when Clotide, to whom Prince Pignatelli made an allowance of a hundred thousand francs a month, was offered an additional four hundred thousand a year by Admiral Mazaredo; when Bigottini, gathering the golden harvest on every side, accumulated millions wherewith to dower her descendants, who became in due time very desirable prizes in the matrimonial market.

Neither do we find him looking with favor upon any of the comedy actresses of the day, though these included Mademoiselle Mars, who, however, was hardly beautiful at her *début*, owing to her excessive thinness; Mademoiselle Devienne, the incomparable soubrette, whose bright face sparkled with humour, but who nevertheless was overcome with bashfulness when the Emperor made some courteous remark to her out hunting; Mademoiselle Mezeray, who, to tell the truth, was fully occupied with Lucien Bonaparte; and Mademoiselle Gros, who had captivated Joseph.

There is room for doubt, perhaps, in the case of Madame Leverd who was made a member of the *Comédie Francaise* in 1808, after a single performance at St. Cloud. It was certainly not Monsieur Rémusat, the comptroller of the theatre, who procured her admission; he had an inveterate dislike to her, and persecuted her later on relentlessly, in defiance of requests, orders, and even decrees from the Emperor. To whom then did she owe her promotion? She is said to have been charming; with a grace, a coquetry, a gaiety that gave her a dangerous fascination more serviceable than her somewhat mediocre talent.

If Napoleon had really a passing fancy for her – and it is by no means certain – it was unique. His tastes and temperament inclined him to an almost exclusive admiration of the tragic school.

It was the golden age of tragedy at the *Théatre Francais*. The company, selected with marvellous judgment, and trained to exceptional proficiency, were fit exponents of an epic literature to an audience as exceptional as themselves – an audience made up of men of letters, prompt to resent any derogation from their ideals, and of soldiers, responsive to every lofty sentiment of the drama. Bonaparte, an enthusiastic patron of the actors, was as lavish of criticisms as of money in his dealings with them. He looked upon the drama as the school of the nation, essential less to its literary education than to its moral growth. "Tragedy," he said to Goethe, "should be the school of kings and peoples. It is the highest exercise of the poet's art." The oft-quoted sentence – "If Corneille were living I would make him a prince," was the sequel to an earlier utterance – "Tragedy fires the soul, elevates the heart, and creates heroes."

He cared little for drama, which he considered "a mongrel art," and had but a poor opinion of comedy, disliking the factious element in Molière and Beaumarchais, the repulsive in Le Sage, the improbable in Fabre d'Eglantine. Farces he could not understand, nor could he find the least amusement in them.

He had no appreciation for mere verbal jingles, puns, irrelevancies, wit that played round its subject, and was not, as he expressed it, of its essence, but an embellishment; no taste for society verses, neatly turned couplets, the skilfully balanced rhythms that almost succeed in imposing themselves upon us as thoughts. All such trivialities he despised, and, indeed, knew nothing of. Tragedy, on the other hand, appealed to him by its gravity, nobility, and strength. Here there was no vulgarity. He communed with his equals, kings, heroes, and gods. He listened to his own speech, for thus he would tain be made to express himself to posterity, when in the fullness of time he too should be the poet's theme.

Wiith this passionate admiration for tragedy, he naturally addressed himself to the interpreters of tragedy. The sly glances of the soubrette, the studied fascinations of the practised coquette, the mock modesty of the *ingénue*, with all these he was familiar at his own Court, and all the actresses in the social comedy were ready to come at his nod; but Phaedra, Andromache, Iphigenia, Hermione, were something more than mortal women; they were supernatural, almost divine beings, glorious with all the treasures of poetry and history. His imagination kindled at the thought of them; the actresses who represented them attracted him, not on their own merits, but as embodiments of the characters they personated. There was no sense of degradation in intercourse with these, and thus he veiled a purely sensual satisfaction in a mist of poetic feeling.

There were times, no doubt, when prose got the better of poetry. Engrossed by great affairs, and with little leisure for dalliance, unaccustomed to the polite phrases of convention, and unable to conceal his scorn for those who came to offer themselves in obedience to a servant's message, he now and then indulged in a brutality of speech and bluntness of manner that in another man would have been profoundly cynical. At heart, however, he was anything but a cynic. "He invested all that pertains to the pleasures of the senses with a romantic aspect, and poetic terms," says one of the followers who knew him best. His very roughness was but a mask for the slight embarrassment he habitually felt with women, no matter of what class. He took refuge in bravado, and boasted of vices of which he was innocent. Thus, in conversations at St. Helena, he professed himself more intimate with sensations than with sentiments, though, as a fact, few men were more sentimental than himself.

In many instances, of course, there was little room for sentiment. It is true that his desires were the outcome less of sensual passion than of an excitable imagination. Often, when one of his facile conquests was at hand, the caprice had passed away, or his mind was fully absorbed in affairs of State. When engrossed in work every distraction was a trouble and vexation to him. The announcement of some arrival would be made by a discreet knock at the door. "Let her wait!" The knock would be repeated after an interval. "Let her go away!" And he would resume his work.

The anecdote is told in connection with Mademoiselle Duchesnois, but she was accustomed to such adventures. The story of her admission to the *Francais* is perhaps not generally known.

In the early days of the Consulate, a young dandy, who had lately inherited a fortune, invited a party of friends to celebrate his good luck at a countryhouse near St. Denis. After breakfast a hunting party was proposed, but the guests soon wearied of the amusement. "A messenger was accordingly despatched to a well-known house in the Chaussée d'Antin to fetch some ladies, of a class not remarkable for severity of manners, and generally ready to accept a good dinner." Each cavalier chose his partner. One girl, however, was left without a mate, every one declaring that she was "too ugly." Yet she had fine eyes, a well-moulded figure, much sweetness of expression, and a touching air of sad submission to disdain. The party played games in the park. She ran like a young deer, her light garments displaying the grace and freedom of her movements to great advantage. Her voice was soft and melodious; in mind she seemed more refined and intellectual than her companions. One of the young men present took compassion on her, and talked to her at some length. He mentioned her to Legouvé, who asked to see her, made her read him some verses, and was surprised in his turn at her intelligence.

Legouvé gave her good advice, introduced her to Madame de Montesson's *salon*, where she met General Valence, influenced Madame Bonaparte in her favor, and obtained permission to bring her out. She played Phedre for the first time on Thermidor the 16th, year X. Her adventure at the Tuileries is supposed to have taken place some two years later. But there are memories that nothing can efface from a woman's mind, and all her life Mademoiselle Duchesnois retained a sort of timid melancholy, a reminiscence of the days when she was a servant, and something less reputable, a perpetual apprehension of the dreaded words "She is too ugly."

Thérèse Bourgoin was another who was dismissed in very cavalier fashion. But the woman who sent the insolent missive "Neither seen nor known," signed *Iphigénie en Tauride*, in reply to an inquiry from a Duchess concerning a lost parrot, was not disposed to accept an insult with the resignation of Mademoiselle Duchesnois. The wound to her vanity was envenomed by a more material injury, the loss of a rich lover, his Excellency the Minister of the Interior. This was Chaptal. After her second appearance, which was very sharply discussed, he ordered her admission to the *Francais*. By way of gloss to the favor, he wrote a public and official letter to Mademoiselle Dumesnil, who had given the *débutante* some instruction at his request, in which he begged her acceptance of a gratification from the Ministry, and thanked her for having "employed the leisure of her retirement in forming a pupil worthy of her and of dramatic art." He put the official newspapers at Mademoiselle Bourgoin's disposal, paraded his relations with her, and was soon the talk and laughing-stock of Paris in this connection.

The Bourgoin, who was known as "the goddess of love and pleasure," was certainly a very desirable mistress for a man fifty years old. Chaptal might have been pardoned his admiration for her round face, her innocent air, her mischievous smile, her limpid eyes, so unaccountably chaste and candid in expression, her audacious speech, and highly-spiced pleasantries, had he but made a certain concession to appearances, preserved his dignity, and refrained from the gross absurdity of accepting Mademoiselle Bourgoin as a model of virtue. Napoleon was malicious enough to undeceive him. One night, when he had made an appointment with the Minister, he arranged a visit from Mademoiselle

Bourgoin, and ordered her to be announced in Chaptal's presence. Napoleon first desired her to wait, and finally dismissed her curtly enough. But Chaptal, on hearing Mademoiselle Bourgoin announced, had gathered up his papers and left the room. He sent in his resignation the same night.

Henceforth it was war to the knife on the actress' part. At St. Petersburg, where she went after the Peace of Tilsit, she amused her admirers with all the epigrams at the Emperor's expense current in Paris.

It was Napoleon's turn at Erfurt, where he regaled Alexander with stories about Mademoiselle Bourgoin, and warned him against the young lady's facile indiscretion, in terms which no doubt proved a stumbling-block to her adventurous career. After the Restoration, she was loud in her professions of loyalty. Presented to the King by the Duc de Berry, she had excellent reasons for her affection to the Bourbon dynasty. During the Hundred Days, she made an ostentatious display of the Royalist colors; her challenge passed unnoticed, however, and the Duc de Berry's neglect of her after his return from Ghent perceptibly cooled her ardour.

The Duchesnois and Bourgoin episodes were evidently unimportant. Mademoiselle Georges proved a more seductive visitor, and was not dismissed unnoticed when she presented herself at the Tuileries.

It is true, that on her first visit Napoleon bluntly accused her of concealing her feet, because they were ugly. The phrase, no doubt, escaped him involuntarily, in his dismayed perception of a defect in one so exquisitely formed.

He had a great admiration for pretty hands and feet. They were the first points he noticed in a woman, and when they were ill-formed, he condemned them in the terse and untranslatable phrase *"Elle a les abatis canailles."* Georges, who at seventeen was so magnificently moulded, whose head, shoulders, arms and body were of ideal perfection, had very coarse extremities. Her feet were especially bad. Two years earlier she was treading them out of shape in ragged slippers, as she swept the causeway in front of her home at Amiens, where her father was leader of the orchestra, and manager of the theatre.

Napoleon was just installed at St. Cloud, when, in the month of Nivose, year XL, he first received a visit from Mademoiselle Georges, in a small room adjoining the orangery. That year he made a long sojourn in his new abode, passing nearly the whole winter there, and Mademoiselle Georges was often his companion. He had a great admiration for her beauty, and was amused by her ready and lively wit.

She entertained him with all the gossip of the side scenes, and the humours of the green-room at the *Francais*, where many curious stories were to be gleaned in those clays. When he came to Paris, she visited him occasionally in the secret apartments at the Tuileries, but he never went to her house, and so was spared the embarrassment of a meeting with Coster de St. Victor and other lovers. The *liaison* lasted some two years, according to Georges' account, and she declared that she was faithful throughout. If so, it was more than Bonaparte exacted from her.

Josephine soon discovered her husband's new fancy. She was greatly disturbed, and gave way to the most violent distress and excitement. "She takes things far too seriously," said Bonaparte. "She is always afraid that I shall fall deeply in love. Can she not understand that love is not for me? What, indeed, is love? A passion that casts aside all the world in favor of some one beloved object. Such exclusiveness is not in my nature. Why then should she make herself miserable about amusements in which my affections have no part?"

The logic was unimpeachable, but Josephine had no turn for logic. She must, however, have drawn some consolation from the discretion with which the secret was kept.

There was no scandal, no public display of preference. As an actress, Georges was never distinguished above her fellows. When she failed in her attendance, the Prefect of the Palace roundly threatened to send her to prison, and she took the warning in good earnest. If she played at Court, she received the same payment as her comrades, and on one occasion, when she ventured to ask Bonaparte for his portrait, he handed her a double Napoleon, saying "Here it is; I am told it is a good likeness."

No doubt she received large sums of money from him. The entry, "Remitted to his Majesty the Emperor," occurs frequently in the accounts of the Privy Purse, against sums ranging from 10 to 20,000 francs, but there is nothing to indicate their final destination. Once only, on August 16, 1807, Georges figures as the recipient of 10,000 francs. But at this date her intermittent visits to the Tuileries had ceased for over three years, and the gift was no doubt a souvenir, presented on the Feast of St. Napoleon.

A month later, on May 11, 1808, Georges left Paris, surreptitiously accompanied by Duport, the opera dancer, who, fearing to be stopped at the barrier, had disguised himself in woman's dress. Regardless alike of her engagement at the *Theatre Francais*, and of her numerous creditors, she escaped from France to join a lover in Russia, who is said to have promised to marry her. This was Benckendorff, brother of the Countess Lieven, who had come to Paris in the suite of the Russian ambassador, Tolstoi. He had lately been recalled, and had determined to introduce his mistress to the inhabitants of St. Petersburg, and above all to the Emperor.

The project masked a Court intrigue, the object of which was to detach the Czar from Madame Narishkine by means of a fugitive *liaison* with the French actress, from which it would be easy to bring him back to the Empress. Georges, who had no suspicion of these secret combinations, extolled the virtues of her "good Benckendorff" in long letters to her mother, which she signed *Georges Benckendorff.* She was presented to the Emperor Alexander, who sent her a handsome diamond clasp, and summoned her to Peterhoff, but never repeated the invitation. A certain Grand Duke, who said, commenting on her performance of Phèdre, "Your Mademoiselle Georges does not seem to me so fine in her way as my favorite horse in his," took to visiting her daily and "loved her like a sister," as she herself declared.

He was not the only visitor who was well received; she smiled upon court and city alike. But this was hardly what the wire-pullers who had brought her to Russia had planned, nor what Napoleon had sanctioned when the stratagem was laid before him. Nevertheless, when Georges made up her mind to return to France, after 1812, and hastened to rejoin her fellow players at Dresden, whither Napoleon had summoned them during the armistice, the Emperor not only re-instated her as a member of the company, but ordered that her six years' absence should be included in her term of service, a favor her comrades never forgave her.

During the Hundred Days, she sent the Emperor word that she had papers to place in his hands deeply compromising to the Duke of Otranto. Napoleon sent a confidential servant to receive them, and on his return asked, "Did she tell you she was badly off?" "No, Sire, she only spoke of the importance of sending you the papers." "I know all about it," said the Emperor; "Caulaincourt told me; he also told me she was in want. Send her 20,000 francs from the Privy Purse."

Georges, at any rate, was grateful. There is no doubt that the attacks made upon her by gentlemen of the Chamber, and frequenters of the pit, which ended in her brutal expulsion from the *Théatre Francais*, were directed mainly against the political opinions she always frankly professed. In her last days, when she was a very old woman, retaining no vestiges of the triumphant charms of her youth, she could never speak of Napoleon but with a break in her voice, a thrill of genuine emotion, so penetrating and magnetic that the youths who listened to her – now almost old men – can never forget the impression. It was not her lover she recalled, but the Emperor. She spoke of him with a sort of timid reverence, and seemed to have forgotten that he had once thought her beautiful, and had told her so. This reticence was not the tardy modesty of old age, for she spoke freely of other lovers. It was rather that she saw in him, not the part he had played to her, but the part he had played to France, like to those nymphs of old who, honored by the embraces of a god, were so dazzled by the blinding light of his glory that they never beheld his face.

Chapter 9
Readers

MANY others, besides the famous actresses we have mentioned, climbed the dark staircase, and – guided by Constant or
Roustam – passed along the dim passage, where the oil-lamps
burnt night and day, to the small room in the half-storey formerly
occupied by Bourrienne, which communicated by means of a
secret staircase with the official apartments. Madame Bernard, the
Court florist, arranged a bouquet every morning for the secret
room, for which she received an annual payment of 600 francs a
year. But the flowers thus renewed each day faded less swiftly than
the fancies inspired by the visitors.

So numerous did these become as Bonaparte's power
increased, that it would be a difficult matter even to give the
names of the multitude, who, urged by avarice, ambition, or a love
of intrigue, flocked after him. A like experience has been the lot of
every man who has risen to supreme greatness; the conqueror of
every age has found himself beset by a like band of venal beauties,
ready to yield at his slightest nod, haunting his path, dogging his
footsteps, their very glances soliciting his notice, and craving a
profitable dishonor.

It cannot be too much insisted on that Napoleon was
thirty-one years old in 1800, and forty-one in 1810. From 1800 to
1810 he was therefore in the prime of vigorous manhood, and
though he never went in pursuit of passing distractions, neither
did he reject them when they came in his way. Broadly speaking,

he may be said to have given little time or thought to women, though two, not to mention Josephine, undoubtedly inspired him with a passion which greatly modified his normal character. But in general no woman had the power to disturb his work, distract his thoughts, retard his projects, or interfere with his course of life. Such amusements as presented themselves, however, he took without hesitation.

Was this immorality? What man in his position would not have done the same? What sovereign would not have far exceeded such limits? What mattered it that a veiled woman now and then came under cover of night to the secret staircase, so long as no woman, either wife or mistress, found her way into the council-chamber, or intruded in the study? The best of husbands are sometimes the worst of kings.

If we were dealing only with Napoleon and his idiosyncrasy, enough perhaps would now have been said on this head. But one or two of those he distinguished have not scrupled to make money in the literary market out of their souvenirs, and to this end have given piquancy to their adventures by the invention of a host of details, or by arrogating to themselves a part very different to that they actually played in events; and hence has arisen malice so clamorous, calumny so perfidious, that here as elsewhere it behooves us to search out the truth. One of these women, she who is best known as a writer, and whose obligations both to Consul and Emperor were deepest, shall be allowed to escape analysis *this time*; presumptive evidence, strong though it be, must not be allowed the weight of material proof; but a study of characters analogous to her own may suffice to indicate the place she ought to occupy.

Another, much less famous, who nevertheless furnished a text to endless pamphleteers, was a certain Madame de Vaudey, who, on the proclamation of the Empire, was appointed Lady-in-Waiting at the earnest recommendation of M. Lecouteulx de Canteleu.

She was well-born, being the daughter of the distinguished strategist, Michaud d'Arcon, who invented the submersible batteries used in the siege of Gibraltar, furnished the plans of the Dutch campaign of 1793, took Breda, and was one of the first senators of the Consulate. She had married well; her husband, M. de Barberot de Vellexon, lord of Vaudey, captain in the *Royal-Bourgoyne* regiment, belonged to an ancient family, originally of Alsace, which settled at Gray in the fifteenth century.

She was furthermore a very lovely woman, with a lively wit, a taste for intrigue, a fine voice, and a fluent pen. She was appointed Lady-in-Waiting in July, 1804, together with Madame Rémusat and her companions, and was thus among the first on whom the honor was conferred. The Empress was on the eve of departure for Aix-la-Chapelle, and Madame de Vaudey attended her.

When, at the beginning of September, Napoleon rejoined Josephine at Aix, for the triumphal progress up the Rhine, Madame de Vaudey was a prominent figure at all the festivities, and undertook to amuse the conqueror. On returning to Paris, she felt sufficient confidence in her own position to brave the wrath of the Empress, whose jealousy had been roused. She accumulated debts as lavishly as Josephine herself, and set up the establishment of an acknowledged favorite. In the pretty little Chateau de la Tuilerie, afterwards the abode of Rachel and of Thiers, and now the Convent of the Assumption, she was the center of a brilliant circle, gave magnificent receptions, and lived in almost regal state.

After a long interview with Napoleon, she laid a statement of her debts before him for the first time; they were promptly paid. On a second occasion she was equally successful. On a third, Napoleon bluntly refused the interview she requested. "I am neither rich enough nor good-natured enough," he said, "to pay so dearly for what I can get so cheaply. Thank Madame de Vaudey for her kindness to me, and let me hear no more of her."

Hereupon followed a pathetic letter from the lady, who vowed she would poison herself if her clebts – debts of honor! – were not paid in twenty-four hours. The aide-de-camp on duty was despatched to Auteuil, where he found her not at all bent on self-destruction! She was requested to resign her post immediately, and her name consequently does not appear in any of the Imperial almanacs.

At a later period, when her brain seems to have been somewhat affected, she went to M. de Polignac, and urged him to murder Napoleon. Reduced to poverty, almost blind, and paralyzed in one arm, she hawked about her *Souvenirs of the Directory and the Empire*, mainly as an excuse for begging. She it was who furnished the publisher Ladvocat with those *Memoirs of a Lady-in-Waiting*, which served as padding for his edition of Constant's *Memoirs*. The best that can be said of her is that she was poverty-stricken and half-crazed. Others had not even this excuse.

It was Josephine who introduced Madame de Vaudey to Court, at the instance of Lecouteulx. She had a swarm of *protégées* of the same, and of an inferior order, whose social sponsors were persons even less considerable, and whose only claim to a place at Court seems to have been their readiness to amuse the master.

In all this, however, there was no premeditation on Josephine's part, and the idea that she had become so far resigned as to provide distractions for her husband, rests on a radical misconception of her character. In her Creole temperament there was a singular inclination to surround herself with dependants drawn from a sort of debatable land between the world of gentility and that of domestic service, young women whose pretty faces were pleasant to look at, who amused her by their lively prattle, entertained her with their accomplishments, and gave a certain gaiety and animation to that palace, "dreary as greatness," out of which she never set foot. She engaged them without much inquiry as to their antecedents, moved by some tale of woe, or attracted by a slim figure, a piquant expression, an unexpected answer. Of these young people, many had known adventures, all were bent on conquests. Poor and unscrupulous, they and their meagre little toilettes were suddenly introduced to the most elegant Court in the world. They had no regular occupation, and shut up in idleness in the private apartments of the Empress, they had nothing to do but to flirt with the brilliant officers, whom they dreamed of as possible husbands – for had not many no better than themselves married generals, who were now Marshals of the Empire? He who was the fountain of honors, who could make or mar fortunes by a sign, passed in and out familiarly among them at all hours. They lay in wait for him, longing for such a sign, ready to risk all for attainment – some among them had little enough to risk and, as they showed their complaisance thus plainly, as they were always in evidence, and always eager to please, as the Emperor's subordinates were always on the watch, like the valets in a comedy, to see whether the master showed a preference, a bargain was readily concluded, and things followed their inevitable course, without the least attempt at seduction on the one hand, or pretence of love on the other. However secretly such an intrigue was conducted, Josephine invariably discovered it sooner or later. Then there would be a stormy scene; the young woman would be dismissed, generally with a substantial dowry, which enabled her to make an excellent match with some not too rigid gentleman, and to rear a family of the first distinction.

Among the bevy was one Felicité Longroy, the daughter of one of the ushers of the Council, whom Josephine had engaged to announce the Imperial entry. In readiness for this office she sat all day in an ante-room leading to the private apartments, her only duty being to throw open doors before the Emperor and Empress. Her salary for this office was 3,600 francs a year, and in 1806 Josephine increased the sum by 600 francs. But Felicité Longroy was an unimportant personage, scarcely more than a servant.

Mademoiselle Lacoste was rather above this level. She was a pretty blonde, somewhat too thin, but with a graceful figure, and a refined and intelligent face. She was an orphan without a penny, brought up by an aunt who was an adept in stratagems, and who, indeed, brought about her introduction to Josephine by a series of ingenious contrivances. The Empress received her kindly, and bestowed on her the somewhat vague title of Reader. No very severe tax was made upon her in this capacity, for immediately after her nomination the Court left for Milan, where the coronation was to take place. Mademoiselle Lacoste followed the Court, without, as it were, belonging to it. As reader, she was not associated with the suite, nor could she fraternize with the ladies'-maids, next to whom she lodged in solitude, much oppressed with the loneliness of her new life. At Stupinitz, the Emperor glanced at her; at Milan, he remarked her. The subsequent negotiation was neither difficult nor prolonged; but Josephine discovered that it was concluded. A terrible scene followed; the reader was dismissed; her aunt was summoned from Paris to take her away. Before her departure, however, the Emperor stipulated that she should appear once at the Empress's reception. Here was a fresh scandal; for it was against etiquette for a reader to be seen outside the private apartments. Josephine had, nevertheless, to yield. After his return to Paris, Napoleon arranged a marriage for Mademoiselle Lacoste. She became the wife of a rich financier, proved an excellent wife and mother, and was seen no more at the Tuileries.

At Genoa, during the same Italian tour, on the occasion of the festivities held to celebrate the union of the Lugurian Republic with France, a certain Madame Gazzani, or Gazzana, was designedly thrown in the Emperor's way. Her maiden name was Bertani, and she was the daughter, some say of a singer, others of a dancer, at the Grand Theatre. She had been summoned to Milan as one of the very mixed company which received Josephine, that company in which, side by side with great ladies of the Negrone, Brignole, Doria, and Remedi families, was to be found that

Bianchina La Flèche, for whom was reserved such a brilliant career in Westphalia.

Carlotta Gazzani was tall, somewhat too slight for perfect beauty, but very gracefully formed, save that her feet and hands were ugly, a defect she concealed to some extent by never appearing without gloves. Her face was exquisite, a perfect type of Italian beauty in its absolute purity of outline. Her dark eyes were large and beautiful, and the delicate harmony of her features was enhanced by an arch smile that displayed the most beautiful teeth. Every woman who saw her praised her loveliness – a proof that she was unquestionably beautiful, but that she lacked the supreme charm that rouses the envy of other women. M. Rémusat, the Grand Chamberlain, was Madame Gazzani's social sponsor. "He persuaded the Emperor to make her one of the Empress's readers." We quote from Madame Remusat herself. It seems that Talleyrand was not alone in having "his pockets always full of mistresses," as Napoleon said.

Madame Gazzani, who was usually styled Gazzani Brentano, and who at a later period took the title of Baronne de Brentano, on what grounds we know not, accordingly became reader in the place of Mademoiselle Lacoste, at a salary of 500 francs a month.

From 1805 to 1807 little was heard of her. The Emperor was constantly on the march. Austerlitz was followed up by the Prussian and Polish campaigns. After his return she began to marshal her forces, first at Paris, afterwards at Fontainebleau. Six thousand francs was not exactly the income she considered adequate to meet her own expenditure, advance her husband's interests, and give her daughter such a dowry as to enable her to make a brilliant marriage. Her opportunity came, and she seized it. She was so lodged that she could answer a summons from the Emperor at any hour, and when such a summons came, she responded with alacrity. She showed no arrogance, however, never posed as a favorite, and accepted her equivocal honors with due humility. The Empress, whose jealousy had been roused at first, was reassured when Napoleon himself confided the whole history of his ephemeral weakness to her.

Towards Josephine, Madame Gazzani's attitude was uniformly respectful and submissive. She kept in her proper place, and was perfectly unpretentious. She was accorded the privilege of joining the Imperial circle, and was admitted to the society of the Empress's suite. With this exception, however, Napoleon showed her no particular attention in public. He allowed the ladies-in-waiting to treat her as they pleased, a liberty they took advantage of to isolate her on all possible occasions, withdrawing from the corners in which she seated herself, and pointedly ignoring her presence.

This state of affairs was not of long duration. In time many, and these not the least haughty of the band, relented, and received Madame Gazzani into their midst. She had obtained something more substantial than Court honors – namely, her husband's appointment as Receiver-General for Evreux. After the divorce, she joined him there, and being within easy distance of Navarre, where Josephine was living, she became one of the intimates of the house. Her chief bond of union with Navarre was her *liaison* with one of the Empress's equerries, M. de Pourtalès, who contributed largely to her expenditure until his marriage with Mademoiselle de Castellane. After the Fontainebleau episode, the Emperor never met her but by chance. He never professed any love for her, and seems scarcely to have mentioned her name in after years.

Madame Gazzani was not inconsolable. Her daughter, Charlotte-Joséphine-Eugénie-Claire, styled Baronne de Brentano, married M. Alfred Mosselman, by whom she had a daughter, who became the wife of M. Eugène Le Hon. [1]

On the other hand, Napoleon frequently recalled a certain Mademoiselle Guillebeau, the daughter, it was said, of an unsuccessful banker, who in 1808 was appointed to share Madame Gazzani's duties as reader. Madame Guillebeau, her mother, an Irishwoman by birth, had three daughters, two of whom had been trained to dance in drawing-rooms, playing tambourines, and striking attitudes. The eldest was taken up by the Princess Elisa, who married her very well, and the younger of the two, whom, said scandal, neither Murat nor Junot had found inflexible, managed to

---

[1] I have been unable to trace the Gazzani family, but they boast a fine coat of arms. In an *ex libris* of M. Alfred Mosselman's, I find two shields, dissevered: one, that of the husband, surmounted by a count's coronet, has beautiful quarterings, one of which is a shower of *fleurs-de-lis* on an azure field; but the wife's shield is still more imposing; the quarterings, surmounted by a ducal coronet, are as follows: the first, an Imperial eagle, sable, crowned, on a field, or; the second, barry of eight pieces, argent and gules; the third, an adder, sable, crowned, on a field, gules; the fourth, a lion rampant, or, armed and crowned, on a field, sable; in the center, a shield of pretence, charged with a cask, or some measure for liquids, on a field, azure.

attract the notice of Queen Hortense, who was fascinated by her pretty face and graceful dancing.

At a masked ball given by the Princess Caroline at the Elysée, Hortense, who was to lead a quadrille of vestals, took it into her head to dress Mademoiselle Guillebeau as Folly, and to make her head the procession; tambourine in hand. Caroline, who had double cause for jealousy, rushed forward as soon as she recognized her rival; after a stormy scene between the sisters-in-law, the obnoxious Folly was finally ejected.

By way of avenging her favorite and herself at once – for the above was an episode in the struggle that was constantly maintained between Bonapartes and Beauharnais – Hortense presented Mademoiselle Guillebeau to her mother, who retorted on Caroline by appointing the young lady her reader. This was shortly before the journey to Bayonne.

After the installation of the Court at Marrac, Mademoiselle Guillebeau, whom Court etiquette excluded from the drawing-rooms during the day, and who only entered them occasionally in the evening to entertain the company with her music, passed most of her time in what was called her room, a mere garret in reality, for the Chateau de Marrac was a small building, by no means adapted to the bestowal of a Court.

Mademoiselle Guillebeau was vain and coquettish; she had ambitious dreams; she was bored to death at Marrac. Needless to say that she was by no means recalcitrant when a servant – the Mameluke in fact – came to announce a visit from the Emperor. Things were going on very much to her satisfaction, when Lavallette, who, in his capacity as Postmaster-General, kept an eye on the correspondence of the Imperial household, sent Napoleon a letter addressed to the young lady by her mother. "The document gave her careful instructions as to the part she was to play, recommending her above all to secure such evidences as might best enable her to retain her hold on the Emperor, and either to confirm her position or to retire with advantage therefrom." The baseness of this intrigue, in which Napoleon afterwards declared he had detected the influence of the Prince of Benevento, so disgusted the Emperor, that the young woman was invited to step at once into a post-chaise, which conveyed her back to Paris under the charge of a servant. M. de Broglie saw her as she passed through Les Ormes, where he was visiting his father-in-law, M. d'Argenson.

After her return to Paris, Mademoiselle Guillebeau married a certain M. Sourdeau, who was given a Receivership at the Emperor's instance. He acquitted himself ill in this office, squandering the funds entrusted to him. The Restoration came very opportunely to extricate him from his difficulties. Madame Sourdeau procured a presentation to the Duc de Berry, who pronounced her "charming," and her eyes "the most beautiful in the world," and marked his appreciation of her beauty by getting her husband appointed French consul at Tangiers.

Enough has been said to show of what slight importance were these transient caprices in Napoleon's career. They made little impression on his senses, none at all on his heart. They give no insight into his affections, and are mainly interesting from the side-lights they throw upon his habits and upon such characteristics as his hatred of intrigue, and his generosity. Other adventures of a like nature might be cited, the history of which has no further interest. They all deal with such facile garrison conquests as might have fallen to the share of any captain in his army. He met with these – or rather they were thrown in his way – at Berlin, Madrid, and Vienna. Like the marshals and soldiers who served under him, he had the weaknesses common to humanity. But he was in no sense the slave of his senses.

At Vienna he was struck by the appearance of a young girl, who professed an enthusiastic worship for him. By his orders a message was sent to her, summoning her to an interview at Schonbrunn. She obeyed, and was brought into his presence. She could only speak German and Italian. The conversation was opened in Italian. Napoleon soon discovered that she was the daughter of respectable parents, and that her passionate admiration for himself was of the most innocent and ingenuous description. He gave orders that she should be at once conducted to her home, undertook to find her a suitable husband, and gave her a dowry of 20,000 florins.

Such an instance of respectful chivalry was by no means unique in Napoleon's career. It was thrice repeated, the last time at St. Helena!

Chapter 10
Josephine's Coronation

JOSEPHINE'S life had become a round of perpetual anxiety and ceaseless agitation within very narrow limits. It was a life at once without occupation and without repose, spent in spying upon her husband, watching all comers and goers, and questioning servants and attendants – pursuits varied only by five toilettes a day, visits from lady friends, and the purchase of useless and costly trifles from every dealer who approached her. This existence, which resembled nothing so much as that of some sultana, grown old in the indolent luxury of the harem, lacked the elements of stability; and she felt that there was but one thing which could assure her future, vindicate her position, and protect her against all mischances, namely, the birth of a child.

During the first Italian campaign she had, as we know, feigned to be *enceinte*, but this was merely a pretext to defer her departure from Paris. Seeing how readily Napoleon swallowed the bait, Josephine, though far from grasping the full significance of the situation, felt a vague consciousness in her butterfly brain of her husband's passionate desire for posterity.

On more than one occasion she played upon this desire for her own ends, using it to gratify her taste for journeys and prolonged absences, which would scarcely have been permitted in the ordinary course of things. Among such pilgrimages was the journey to Plombières when Bonaparte sailed for Egypt. But as the First Consul's power increased, she felt more and more strongly that in her case maternity was not so much a convenient pretext, as an urgent necessity. That throne, the steps of which he was steadily ascending, would be but insecure without an heir. Bonaparte, Consul and head of a democratic Republic, or Bonaparte, the restorer of the Bourbons, content with a life tenure of some brilliant office under the reinstated monarch, might dispense with a son. But the contingent splendours of one who should play the part of Monk to the exiled dynasty had little attraction for him, neither could he emulate the disinterested simplicity of a Washington. A force invisible and extrinsic, one of those popular currents that no power can stem, those great tides of public opinion that carry all before them, was sweeping away the obstacles in his path, and bearing him on, first to the Consulate of the year VIII., still a Republican institution, then to the Consulate of the year X., a purely autocratic organization, separated from the monarchy only by a name, and by the thorny question of heredity.

Around this question, the solution of which rested with her, Josephine saw that all the ambitions of the one faction, all the anxieties of the other, now centerd. She saw that each of Bonaparte's brothers aspired to the succession; that his sisters were not without hopes as to the possible claims of their respective husbands; that every general and senator who had risen to greatness in the Revolution dreamed of possibilities still more splendid; and that the nation itself, after the convulsions through which it had passed, longed for a stability that should rest on some less temporary basis than the life of one man, and should ensure its security for a prolonged, an indefinite lapse of time.

If a monarchy were re-established, to whom should the reversion be assigned? To the Consul's brothers? And if so, on what grounds? Hereditary monarchy, in its Christianized form, as derived from Hebraic institutions, implies divine sanction. But this sanction applied only to the founder of the dynasty and to his descendants in a direct line, and was never extended to collaterals. To create a claim for Bonaparte's brothers to the succession, it would have been necessary to have recourse to a fiction familiar in ancient law, and assume that the late Charles Bonaparte had been Emperor of the French. But who would have accepted such a fiction? An alternative suggested itself, that of abandoning the Hebraic institution, or divine right, in favor of the Roman law of adoption, the Consul choosing him he deemed worthiest to succeed him, either from among or beyond the members of his own family. But such a resolution would have been the signal for endless competition and intrigue. And would the nation have understood it? Could it have cast aside its prejudices touching the predestination of race, the divine vocation of a dynasty? The only solution, both in law and fact at once simple and unimpeachable, the only one which could crush ambition on the one hand and satisfy legitimate aspirations on the other, was the birth of an heir to Napoleon. But this longed-for child was not forthcoming. Whose was the fault – his or Josephine's?

On this point Josephine felt that her position was vulnerable. She racked her brains for remedies. One after the other, she visited all the mineral springs reputed to be of special virtue in such cases – Forges, Plombières, and Luxeuil. She assiduously followed the treatment indicated by Corvisart; she consulted quacks; she visited charlatans; she made pilgrimages. At Plombières she betook herself to the Capuchin's Cave, where Frère Jean, its guardian, vainly promised her the fulfilment of her wishes. Deluded by false hopes, she repeatedly inspired Napoleon with joyful anticipations, which he could not refrain from communicating to his intimates. When these proved illusory, his vexation would master him, and find vent in cutting sarcasms. One day, when he had arranged to hunt in the forest at Malmaison, Madame Bonaparte came to him in tears. "How can you think of such a thing? All our animals are with young!" "We must give it up then," was the retort; "it seems that everything here is prolific, except Madame."

In public he persistently cast the blame upon her; but in his secret thoughts doubts had arisen which Josephine took care to foster. Perhaps the fault lay with himself. He remembered Madame Fourès, among others. Josephine had borne her first husband children. On every possible occasion she brought them forward to prove that the common misfortune was not to be laid to *her* account. Her incessant harping on this theme exasperated Madame Bacciochi, who silenced her at last by the caustic remark, "But, my dear sister, you were a good deal younger in those days."

Nevertheless, she contrived to imbue the whole family more or less with this idea. Napoleon himself tacitly accepted the imputation. Often he would say to his brother Joseph, "I have no children, and you all say I shall never have any; Josephine is not likely to have any more at her age, though she has all the will in the world to prove the contrary. Therefore I say, after me the deluge!" When, after his return from Spain, Lucien suggested a divorce, and a marriage with one of the Infantas, a variety of motives led the Consul to reject his propositions. But it is not improbable that the chief among them was his distrust of himself.

Marriage with a Bourbon would be a decisive step towards the throne; but would such a stake be worth playing for if children were denied him? Nevertheless the idea had been mooted, and by Lucien, for whom Josephine had little love already, and who had suggested the divorce on Bonaparte's return from Egypt. Napoleon was fond of declaring that his wife was as "incapable of resentment as a pigeon," but this was only true of her when her position was not attacked. From this time forth she did her best to estrange the brothers; she enlisted her friends in the cause, and did not scruple to repeat doubtful slanders, and to insist on damaging facts. She felt no regret when the rupture was finally brought about. It was an enemy the less.

The doubts with which she had succeeded in inspiring Napoleon in 1801 had served her by banishing the idea of a divorce for a time; but chance might dissipate these doubts, and Josephine felt herself completely at the mercy of such a hazard. There was certainly little danger to be feared from the actresses he had hitherto met. Had any one of them given birth to a child, Bonaparte had hardly a sufficient stock of simplicity to claim a paternity so many might have disputed with him. Neither was there much ground for uneasiness in his intrigues with the married ladies of the Consular Court. Here again it would be impossible to affirm the paternity of the child, difficult even to have any conviction on the subject, unless on the evidence of some striking physical resemblance, which so far had not proclaimed itself. But it needed only some such adventure as the *liaison* with Madame Fourès to convince Napoleon of the possibility of his becoming the father of an heir to the throne. And this consummation once arrived at, Josephine felt that the downfall of her fortunes would be imminent. For Bonaparte now claimed equality with any ancient dynasty in Europe, so much more might he consider himself the peer of the noblest families among the old French aristocracy. And there was no lack of intermediaries such as Talleyrand, "the accursed cripple," ready to tempt him with suggestions of names, and promises of help.

Failing a child – the only thing, as Napoleon himself said, "that would have tranquillized Josephine, and put an end to the jealousy with which she harassed her husband" – how should she contrive to attach him to her so closely that it would be impossible for him to break his chain? Her position was in itself a strong one. From the year XI. onwards, she had been associated with Bonaparte in all his public and official acts. She had been received like a sovereign at the gates of cities, had held her receptions in the galleries of St. Cloud and the Tuileries, surrounded by what was a court in all but name; at Napoleon's express command, she had taken precedence of every woman in France, his mother not excepted, even in the privacy of the family circle. Placed thus prominently before France and Europe as the greatest lady of the Republic, her humiliation could not be accomplished without a public scandal, and the divorce would certainly be ill received by the majority. Napoleon had not yet climbed so high that he could safely dispense with her help. Gifts and honors had been allowed to flow so freely through her hands that she had necessarily many adherents among those whom Bonaparte had himself constituted her clients. But as he rose in power his wife's social prestige diminished; she might well fear lest a sudden fit of anger, provoked perhaps by some imprudence on her own part, should carry away the whole structure. She could no longer rely on her personal attractions to restrain him, for though he continued very susceptible to their influence, the frequent infidelities he now permitted himself could not fail to gradually emancipate him. As a last resource, she could only reckon on habit, on the strong affection he still bore her, and on his unwillingness to make her suffer. He himself would suffer, perhaps, more than she. But would this deter him? When a victory was at stake, did he consider the men he was bound to sacrifice, even when these were friends he loved? No; all such checks would be valueless in the crisis; the only lasting bond between them would be a child. An idea, in which there was a touch of genius, flashed into Josephine's brain. Why should not Napoleon procure himself an heir by adoption, make a son of his nephew and her grandchild – the son of Hortense and Louis Bonaparte? Here was a solution which met every difficulty; it would satisfy the Bonapartes, the heir-presumptive being one of themselves, and it would assure her own future by effectually disposing of the question of a successor. Her mind full of this project, she communicated it to Bonaparte, who accepted it favorably, and laid it before Louis. But Louis was indignant. He insisted on the claims of his brother Joseph, on his own claims, on their joint claims to their brother's heritage. In deference to these absurd pretensions, which had absolutely no foundation, which were equally at variance with historical precedent and with the monarchic theory, Napoleon, moved by family feeling, agreed to press the matter no further, and thus renounced the sole expedient by which he might have established his dynasty without violating the most sacred principles, or incurring the odium of the divorce.

What further resources were open to Josephine when this golden opportunity had been lost, through no fault of hers? True, she enjoyed the advantages of possession, she had advanced stage by stage at Bonaparte's side, as events had carried him on from glory to glory. The elevation of the First Consul to the purple had made her Empress; she had received the homage of the great State bodies, and had been addressed by the title of Her Majesty. After her triumphal progress through Aix-la-Chapelle and Mayence, her return to Paris, heralded by the cannon of the Invalides, her reception of the highest dignitaries and officials from the throne, her position had been much strengthened, and the divorce seemed to have retired into the region of improbable contingencies. Yet it needed but some unfavorable incident to destroy her hold on Napoleon. Fate might sweep her away as yesterday the wind had swept away the powder burnt in her honor on the Esplanade.

Matters were at this crisis when one day at St. Cloud she observed that a lady who had come to call on her rose and left the room. She had long had suspicions of her visitor, and immediately followed her. Passing through the Emperor's cabinet, she mounted the secret staircase, and "reached the room on the half-landing. Listening, she recognized the voices of the Emperor and the lady, demanded admission, made a scandalous scene, and roused Napoleon to fury. He vowed that he was weary of her surveillance, that he would put an end to it, that he would follow the advice of his friends, and divorce her. He sent for Eugène to arrange the preliminaries. Eugène came, and sternly refused all compensation, favor, or indemnity, both for his mother and himself. Two days went by. Josephine, violent no longer, wept unceasingly. Napoleon thought "tears very becoming to a woman." He felt himself in the wrong, and recognized that a step of such importance should not be the outcome of a fit of exasperation. Had she held her ground against him he would have insisted. But he was not proof against her tears. A final conversation took place on the subject.

"I have not the courage," he said at last, "to carry out my resolution; if you show me so much affection, if you obey me in all things, I feel that I shall never have the strength to send you from me; but I confess I wish very much that you could resign yourself to the necessities of my policy, and yourself point the way out of this painful dilemma." He wept freely himself as he spoke. But Josephine was equal to the occasion. She had no taste for self-sacrifice. It was not her part to decide her fate, but his, since he had ordered it so far. She was ready to obey; but she would wait till he commanded her to descend from that throne to which he had raised her.

Napoleon himself was hard beset by his own heart, by the uncertainty of his policy, by his doubts as to the probability of his ever becoming the founder of a race, by his affection for his step-children, by his reluctance to shatter the life he had bound up with his own, by his pain at the thought of renouncing the woman he still loved. Exasperated by the triumphant air and scarcely concealed delight of Josephine's enemies, and profoundly touched by the resignation of the Beauharnais, he once more put aside the idea of a divorce, and, as if to cut off his own retreat from this position, he commanded his wife to make all necessary preparations for her coronation.

Her coronation! To be crowned by a Pope, to share the triumph of the modern Charlemagne, to realize – she, a little Creole, brought from her native island by the whim of M. de Beauharnais' mistress – the dream of splendour imagined by all the Queens of France, and achieved by so few; to receive the triple unction from the Supreme Pontiff, and the crown from the Emperor! Was not this enough to satisfy, not ambition, for what ambition could have aimed at such glory? but the wildest dreams of fancy? And after such consecration and coronation, would it be possible to repudiate her? Was not this the seal of Napoleon's covenant with her, and could she desire any stronger earnest of future security?

Yet there was something more she coveted. Hitherto, that is to say, for some eight years, her conscience had in nowise troubled her on the score of her civil marriage, and she had been quite content to live with Bonaparte, dispensing with a priestly blessing on their union. She knew there would be many obstacles to overcome before she could obtain the Emperor's consent to a religious marriage. He would object that it was undesirable to draw attention to the fact that the rite had been dispensed with. Most of the men about him were in the same case as himself, and his example in such a matter would bring about a series of rehabilitatory functions which might easily be construed as an attack on the civil law, a revulsion in favor of the ancient *regime*, or, at best, as an indication that the head of the State considered the only form of marriage recognized by the State insufficient. He would find plenty of strong arguments against the measure, without revealing the determining cause of his refusal, namely, that though he had decided to abandon the divorce, he had no intention of binding himself irrevocably in the future, or ignoring possible contingencies. He knew that the Church is accommodating in her dealings with the great, and that in an extreme case she is empowered to loosen the knot she herself has tied. But if he should ever be constrained to annul his marriage, he would prefer to act on his own authority, and to dispense with priestly intervention.

Josephine knew there was little hope of moving him on this point. What could she plead in support of her request? Her conscientious scruples? They would be the laughing-stock of Napoleon and his whole Court! But the Pope would treat them with more respect.

On Monday, Frimaire the 5th, the day after Pius VII's arrival, he paid his second visit to Josephine, who had carefully prepared the ground beforehand. She had corresponded with the Pope for some years past, and had sent him a magnificent lace rochet by the hand of her cousin Tascher, in Nivose of the year XII. She now confided in him. She confessed to her spiritual father that she had not been married according to the rites of the Church; and the Pope, commending his daughter's anxiety to conform to the holy ordinance, promised to press the religious marriage upon the Emperor.

Napoleon was completely circumvented. A Pontiff of Pius's character, education, and cast of mind would, he felt, be quite capable of postponing the coronation, or of making the one ceremony a condition of the other. The coronation, originally fixed for Brumaire the 18th, had been put off first to Frimaire the 1st, afterwards to Frimaire the 11th. Each delay had entailed immense expenditure, and had provoked much discontent and anxiety. All the civil and military deputations had arrived; Paris was full of them; they had been accommodated with great difficulty. What a scandal if the Pope, after coming to Paris to crown the Emperor, should return to Rome without having performed the ceremony! Napoleon accepted the inevitable. On the morning of the 9th, Cardinal Fesch pronounced the nuptial blessing over the pair. If ever there was a case of compulsion it was here, and Napoleon did not scruple to affirm at a later period that he had no choice in the matter, and that in default of consent on his part, the religious ceremony was not binding. Josephine was Empress, married by a priest, on the eve of her consecration by the Pope, her coronation by the Emperor. Surely she might now sleep in peace!

Chapter 11
Madame X

INTRIGUES of a purely material nature, such as many of those we have touched upon, provided occasional distractions, and served as interludes in the drama of Napoleon's career. But there was a side to his character which demanded satisfaction less gross than was afforded by a venal and transient connection. There was a fund of unsuspected melancholy in his nature, a longing for solitude in the midst of the crowd with one beloved companionship, a craving for sentimental affection which increased as he grew older, and as his opportunities for mere sensual gratification multiplied, while at the same time his lofty destiny raised him more and more above his fellows, to heights of isolated greatness.

The dawn of such a sentiment may be traced towards the close of the Consulate. From that period onward it gradually developed. It had little in common with the tempest of youthful passion evoked by Josephine, but its periodic ebullition shows Napoleon as a being whose stormy soul, ever athirst for the unknown, cherished a dream of happiness side by side with dreams of ambition.

While the sentiment was as yet vague and confused, possession, which he had ardently desired – the more ardently in proportion to the obstacles that intervened – had the immediate effect of suppressing desire, for reality fell short of the anticipation of his senses. But these in their turn were chastened and spiritualized; physical possession ceased to be the sole object of his thoughts. In this phase of his passion we recognize a new Napoleon, differing altogether from him whose material aspirations sought satisfaction in the veiled visitors of the secret staircase – a Napoleon full of delicate sentiment, whose thoughts found utterance in language worthy of a hero of the *Astraea*.

Such an aspect of his character is, of course, an unfamiliar one, and one which we should hesitate to attribute to him without abundant evidence of the most precise and authentic nature. But, supported by such evidences in connection with a later period of his life, we may fairly apply the inductive method to earlier episodes, and confidently interpret indications which appear insignificant at the first glance.

It is obvious that we can hardly expect to find direct proofs in this connection, and the difficulties of investigation are great. The women to whom Napoleon revealed this phase of his character were not eager to tell the story of their conquest; they were rather careful to destroy every trace that might betray them. They had husbands to consider, reputations to protect. Their descendants have carefully guarded their secrets. Those indiscreet enough to babble of the romance suppressed the real names of the characters, and even after the lapse of a century it would not be well to lift the slight veil that shrouds them. Nor can we be certain that this veil always conceals the same woman; raising it, we should perhaps discover several where we looked for one.

In one instance, however, we are able to trace an identity of many physical and mental features throughout; there are characteristic facts which scarcely allow of misconception, especially when the impression of a certain face has been clearly and indelibly impressed on one's mind from childhood. But I am no longer dealing with documents here, and I can only proceed with the utmost caution; even at the risk of seeming obscure, I must leave many details in the shade.

Among the ladies of the Consular Court there was a young woman of twenty, married to a man thirty years her senior.

The husband, a man of the highest character and the most indefatigable industry, who had served the State with credit in a variety of capacities, was one of those admirable public servants who, under the old regime, were made heads of departments, and under the new, directors-general. He had particularly distinguished himself in a special matter of great importance in its bearing on national finance, and had himself organized the department over which he presided to such good purpose, that its present administration is based upon his precepts and traditions.

His wife was charming, a creature all grace and sweetness, with a pretty face, beautiful teeth, and abundant fair hair; her nose was aquiline, and though somewhat too long, delicately arched, and full of character; her foot was very small, her hand perfectly modelled. Her features were irregular, but her smile was bewitching, and combined with the long glances of a pair of deep blue eyes, gave an expression of peculiar harmony to her face.

Those blue eyes, indeed, conveyed any sentiment their mistress chose to affect, and limpid as they were, they lacked sincerity; but it needed a woman and a rival to discover this. Their owner danced and sang exquisitely, played the harp, could read or listen with equal grace, and at this time made no great display of the remarkable intellectual powers she afterwards developed. She was amply endowed with strength of will, ambition, and worldly acuteness, and was troubled by few scruples when her interests were at stake; but this hardness of character was veiled by a grace and distinction no less remarkable than her beauty, and though of middle-class origin, she excelled many of the greatest ladies of her day in the perfect courtesy of her manners, the elegance of her toilettes, and the stately dignity of bearing proper to Court etiquette. "She had a natural aptitude for the graces and refinements of good society, and an instinctive knowledge of that art which, as has been truly said, may be divined, but cannot be taught." She had withal a superb and lofty air, as if her forefathers had been dukes and peers, rather than provincial citizens of very humble rank.

When did Bonaparte fall in love with this young woman? Certain evidences seem to indicate Brumaire, year XII. (November, 1803). But the rapidity with which the preliminaries had been conducted in the case of the woman whom Josephine surprised in the Orangery at St. Cloud, seems hardly to agree with this hypothesis, in spite of the additional probability it derives from the fact of a birth which took place exactly nine months later (August 5, 1804).

True, the child then born developed no very significant traits either of mind or person; but features so characteristic as those of the Bonapartes not unfrequently pass over a generation, and lay the tell-tale impress of their sovereign beauty on some descendant. Such was, no doubt, the case here; and this freak of nature, while inspiring Napoleon with doubts as to his own paternity of the child, left the husband's confidence unshaken, secured the wife's safety, and, after the lapse of a generation, revealed a secret that had been kept with almost complete success hitherto.

Was this lady of St. Cloud the mysterious unknown who, towards the close of the Consulate, inhabited a small house in the Allée des Veuves, to which Napoleon paid frequent secret visits? Was she the same woman to whose house in the middle of Paris he occasionally found his way, alone and disguised? It is impossible to decide. The St. Cloud adventure seems to have been one of those trivial intrigues which have no sequel; but the nocturnal expeditions are very significant in the case of one who so seldom quitted the shelter of his own roof as Napoleon. They seem to point to an impetuosity by no means normal. The subject is shrouded in a mystery we cannot undertake to solve at present, a mystery that chroniclers or their publishers have been careful to preserve in deference to the reputation of the woman, and the susceptibilities of her descendants. But there is one point at which all evidences converge, all testimonies reinforce and corroborate one another. If material proofs are still lacking, the very strongest presumptions may at least be adduced.

The Emperor proceeded to Fontainebleau to receive the Pope on the Pontiff's arrival from Rome for the coronation. He was attended by the Court. It was soon evident that his temper had become more serene, his manner more affable. After the Pope had retired into his own apartments, he remained with the Empress, conversing with the ladies of her household. Josephine became uneasy, her jealousy was aroused; such proceedings seemed to her unnatural, and she suspected some hidden intrigue. Who was the offender? Whom should she accuse? At last she fixed on Madame Ney, who defended herself vigorously to Hortense, her former schoolfellow. She declared that the Emperor paid her no attention whatever, that he was entirely absorbed in a lady of the household, whom Eugène de Beauharnais also greatly admired, and to whom Josephine had shown favor in consequence. Eugène was only a blind; the lady might return his glances, and seem to take pleasure in his conversation, but, as a fact, she was the sworn ally of the Murats, or rather of Caroline, for it was she who was the moving spirit in such machinations. Hating her sister-in-law, and always ready to annoy her, she directed this intrigue, as she afterwards directed many others.

The Court returned to Paris; nothing decisive had happened so far. Napoleon was obviously in love; he had great difficulty in tearing himself away from the Empress's apartments when a certain lady was in attendance. He joined Josephine at the play if a certain lady accompanied her. He arranged parties in the smaller boxes, though he generally insisted that his family should appear at the theatre in state. Josephine, yielding to her growing exasperation, attempted expostulations, which were very ill received. Though gayer, franker, and more gracious in public than he had ever been, Napoleon was irritable and gloomy in private when a certain lady was not of the company. "Not a day passes without some outbreak from Bonaparte," writes Josephine; "and always without the least cause. Life is not worth living under such conditions."

The Emperor had taken to playing cards in the evening, or at any rate to a pretence of playing. Every night he summoned his sister Caroline to his table, and two of the Court ladies, of whom the favorite was always one. Holding his cards negligently, and making the proposed game a mere screen for conversation, he would discourse on the various aspects of Platonic and ideal affection, or deliver himself of violent tirades against jealousy and jealous women.

At the other end of the room, Josephine, engaged in a dreary game of whist with certain Court dignitaries, would glance sadly from time to time at the favored table, listening eagerly to the words of the sonorous voice that penetrated to the farthest extremity of the apartment, amidst the respectful silence of attentive courtiers.

At a fête given to the sovereigns by the War Minister in honor of the coronation, the ladies only were seated at supper, as was customary. The Empress, with some of her ladies, and the wives of the great Crown officials, presided at the table of honor. Napoleon had refused to take his place. He passed along the room, addressing each of the ladies in turn, gay, courtly, and gracious. He served Josephine, taking a dish from one of the pages to present it to her. "He wished to charm one woman only, but was anxious that others should not perceive it. This in itself was a sign of love."

After having perambulated the whole room, with a word or two to every one of the ladies, he felt he had purchased the right to speak to the real object of all his gallantry. Approaching her, he began, in some embarrassment, by addressing her neighbour. Leaning between the two chairs, he soon drew her into conversation, anticipating her wants, and handing her the dishes she pointed out. One of these contained olives. "You ought not to eat olives at night," he remarked; "they will make you ill." Then, turning to her neighbour, "I see you do not eat olives. You are quite right, and doubly right not to imitate Madame _____, for she is inimitable."

Josephine was fully alive to all these manoeuvres. If any doubts had lingered in her mind, they had been dispelled by a recent pilgrimage to Malmaison, undertaken in the depth of winter at the sudden desire of the Emperor. All her arrangements had been upset by this inopportune journey, in addition to which there had been no time to heat the stoves, and the first night had been spent in a veritable icehouse. But Napoleon, indifferent to the cold, was not deterred from a midnight expedition through the flagged corridors, as Josephine ascertained by concealing herself behind a glass door, from which hiding-place, after a long spell of waiting, she surprised her husband's secret unobserved.

The Court returned to Malmaison after the ministerial fete, and on the following day the Empress found a pretext for summoning the lady who had refused the olives. After some desultory conversation, she asked her what the Emperor had said to her the night before, and finally, what he had said to her neighbour. "He advised her not to eat olives at night," was the reply. "Well," retorted the Empress, "while the Emperor was advising your friend, he might have told her that it is ridiculous to attempt the part of Roxalana with a nose as long as hers." Then, turning over the leaves of a book upon the chimney-piece, *La Duchesse de la Vallière*, by Madame de Genlis – "This is the book," she said, "which turns the heads of all young women with fair hair and slender figures."

There was a good deal of truth in the stricture, for *La Duchesse de la Vallière* was to be found in the room of every lady at Malmaison. Its extraordinary success stood the test of ten editions, and many aspiring La Vallières no doubt profited by its lessons.

But the Emperor had no intention of establishing a favorite. "There shall be no petticoat government at my Court," he said. "It was the bane of Henri IV and Louis XIV. My mission is a graver one than that of either sovereign, and Frenchmen have become too serious to tolerate recognized favorites and official mistresses." His true mistress, as he often said, was power. "Its conquest has cost me too dear," he would add, "for me to allow of its being snatched from me, or even coveted by another." He felt that insidious advances had been made. The lady was too clever and too well-tutored to formulate demands on her own account. She could not have accepted marks of distinction that would have given rise to comment, or roused the suspicions of a husband by no means disposed to be complaisant. The utmost she had ventured to solicit on her own behalf was the post of Lady-in-Waiting, a dignity from which her youth, her birth, and her position seemed to preclude her; nor was it possible to justify her preferment on the grounds of any former connection with the Bonapartes. The appointment, therefore, caused some discussion, and many a covert smile. But the favorite's moderation in her own case put her at greater advantage in furthering the cause of others, her patrons of yesterday, her *protégés* of today.

Murat, already Marshal of the Empire, was promoted to the dignity of Prince High Admiral, which admitted him to rank after Cambacérès and Lebrun among the Serene Highnesses. But at the same time Napoleon, on his own initiative, appointed Eugène de Beauharnais Prince Arch-Chancellor of State, of equal rank with Murat. By this measure the balance was struck between Bonapartes and Beauharnais, with some slight inclination in favor of the latter. There is a striking difference between the terms in which the Emperor announced the two decisions to the Senate; every turn of expression seems to mark the space that divided his step-son from his brother-in-law in his affections.

In the one case, we feel that he yields to outside pressure, to family expediency, to selfish solicitations; in the other, the words gush from a fount of pure feeling, and give an echo of his best self — "Amidst the cares and trials inseparable from our high rank, we have sought and found solace in the tender affection and faithful friendship of this dear child of our adoption. . . . Our paternal blessing will follow the young Prince throughout his career, and, with the help of Providence, he will not fail to deserve the praise of posterity." And Eugène had asked for nothing. He had seemed perfectly content with his honors as grand officer of the Empire, and his command as Colonel-General of Chasseurs, and was already on his way to Milan, at the head of the Cavalry of the Guard. His new position was a distinguished one, and there is a curious fatuity in Madame Remusat's contention that this, the highest compliment the Emperor could have bestowed on a general of twenty-three, was, in fact, a punishment.

In any case, this punishment, which she supposes to have been the result of an outbreak of jealousy on the Emperor's part, was of brief duration. Eugène set out on January 16, in obedience to an order dated January 14, that the Guard should proceed to Milan in readiness for the coronation. A fortnight later, he received a private letter from the Emperor, enclosing a copy of the message to the Senate, and his nomination as Prince Arch-Chancellor of State.

No more significant proof could have been given that Napoleon was reconciled to Josephine, that he was no longer to be played upon, and that the passion on which so many hopes had been built had died out. When no longer quickened by restraints, it had perished of satiety. The intrigue began at Malmaison in the depth of winter; it closed at Malmaison, before the spring.

During a sojourn of a week or two made there by the Court, on which occasion the usual formalities were much relaxed, Napoleon was able to walk and talk constantly with the lady, and to visit her whenever he pleased. Josephine kept her own room, and spent her time in tears, growing thinner and more melancholy every day. One morning the Emperor came to her apartments, addressed her with all the kindness of former days, acknowledged that he had been very much in love, but that it was all over, and begged her to help him out of his entanglement. Josephine readily undertook the task; she summoned the lady, who showed herself equal to the occasion, betrayed no emotion, and met the Empress's attack in haughty silence, with a face of marble impassibility.

She always retained a faithful attachment to the Emperor, though he seems never to have renewed his homage after Austerlitz. If he ever yielded to a passing return of his former fancy, the feeling was so fugitive that it was barely noted by the most observant. He invariably treated her with the greatest consideration, was prodigal of such privileges and favors as were compatible with her husband's position, and always included her among the first recipients of Court honors and distinctions. In return, she showed herself one of the most faithful adherents of his fallen fortunes. Her beauty graced the fetes of the Hundred Days, and when the victim of Waterloo was about to quit his country for ever, she was one of the last to visit him, on June 26, 1815, at Malmaison, the scene of the dawn and eclipse of their brief romance, offering the discrowned Emperor the tribute of her respectful attachment and imperishable devotion.

Chapter 12
Stéphanie De Beauharnais

EVEN before Austerlitz was lost and won, Napoleon determined to strengthen the political alliances he had entered into with the reigning houses of Germany by a network of domestic contracts. He was convinced that his system would never be firmly established in Europe until the blood of the Napoleonides had mingled with that of more ancient dynasties. In default of such hopes as he might have entertained in his own person, he gathered all the marriageable youths and maidens of his family round him, and awaited his opportunity for the formation of the ties he considered all-important, because he judged them to be beyond the hazards of political fortune. In this way he hoped to bind the princes to him by means of family interests and affections.

The first result of this policy was the marriage of Eugène de Beauharnais and the Princess Augusta of Bavaria, immediately after the conclusion of the campaign. She was betrothed to the Prince of Baden, but this was an obstacle of slight moment. As a set-off to the husband he had bestowed on the Princess, Napoleon was quite prepared to find a wife for the Prince. His choice fell on another Beauharnais, Stéphanie-Louise-Adrienne, daughter of Claude de Beauharnais, Comte de Roches-Baritaud, and of Adrienne de Lezay-Marnésia, his first wife, cousin in the sixth degree to Hortense and Eugène. Born in Paris, August 26, 1789, she was left an orphan at four years old, and was educated for a time in the Convent of Panthémont. A friend of her mother's, Lady de Bathe, took her in hand after the suppression of the religious houses, and entrusted her further training to two of the expelled nuns of Panthémont, Mesdames de Trélissac and de Sabotier. These ladies carried her off to their native district, and she lived with them first at Castelsar-rasin, then at Périgueux, and perhaps at Montauban. Her paternal grandmother, Fanny de Beauharnais, was entirely occupied with Cubières, society verses, and affairs of gallantry. Her father had emigrated. Her grandfather, the Marquis de Marnésia, was travelling in Pennsylvania. But for Lady de Bathe, the child would have been dependent on public charity. One day, in the early part of the Consulate, Josephine happened to mention her little cousin. Bonaparte, always keenly alive to family claims, was indignant that a relative of his wife's should have been left to the chance kindness of a stranger, and that stranger an Englishwoman! He despatched a messenger, with orders to bring the child back with him. The nuns refused to give her up, whereupon a second messenger arrived, empowering the Préfet to seize Stéphanie in the name of the law! Resistance was useless, and she obeyed the mandate, not without tears and terror. On her arrival, the child was placed under the care of Madame de Campan, and henceforth made one of that little band of young girls who were wont to assemble at Malmaison on the Tenth Day (*Décadi*) and brighten the shade of the great chestnut trees with the flutter of their white dresses. Josephine and Hortense received her with great kindness, but she was treated with no sort of special distinction. She never appeared on gala days; no rank was assigned her, and it seemed probable that she would make some such marriage as had been arranged for her cousin, Emilie de Beauharnais, Madame Lavallette. The little lady, however, had other views for herself. She affected regal airs, and treated those among her relatives who did not dwell in Imperial palaces with scant courtesy.

Such was the situation when Eugène's marriage made it necessary to provide for the Prince of Baden. Napoleon's first thought was of Stéphanie Tascher, another ward of Josephine's. He finally fixed on Stéphanie de Beauharnais. The preliminaries having been arranged by him when he passed through Carlsruhe on January 20, 1806, the negotiations were formally ratified by a treaty signed in Paris on February 17.

Stéphanie was then seventeen. She had a pleasing face, much natural wit and gaiety, a certain childishness of manner that was very attractive, a sweet voice, a lovely complexion, a pair of sparkling blue eyes, and beautiful fair hair. On the Emperor's return to Paris, she was at once removed from tutelage at the Tuileries, and lodged in an apartment adjoining that of the Empress. In a very short time she became the delight and amusement of the whole Court. Her gay sallies, her youthful high spirits, her lively prattle relieved the tedium of Court ceremony. Far from showing any timidity before the Emperor, her animation seemed to derive an added piquancy from his presence. She amused and charmed him, and the consciousness of her power to please gave her increased confidence. The interlude scarcely bordered on love-making, its elements being rather coquetry on Stéphanie's part, flirtation on that of Napoleon. The Emperor may have felt inclined to go further; but his little *protégé* only wished to amuse herself, and to profit as far as possible by the situation. She had no idea of compromising herself. She was perfectly aware that not Mademoiselle de Beauharnais, but a Napoleonide had been chosen to wed the Prince of Baden. On what footing was she to enter the family? What were to be her titles, her rank, her honors? All this depended solely on the Emperor; and Stéphanie was not averse to furthering her prospects by means of the fancy she had inspired.

Josephine, though her jealousy may have begun to take alarm, showed no hostility to Stéphanie. She had at least the consolation of knowing that the future princess had been provided by herself. The struggle was between Stéphanie and Bonaparte's sisters, who had no idea of making way for the favorite. Both, but more especially Caroline Murat, defended their position with great acrimony, and did not spare the little interloper. Stéphanie held her own with gallantry, parrying the thrusts of her opponents with jests and laughter, which displayed her pretty teeth to much advantage, as she was well aware. Exasperated beyond measure, Caroline had recourse to open insult. One evening, when the Court was awaiting the Emperor's arrival, Stéphanie seated herself on a folding stool. Caroline ordered her to rise, and to remember that she was expected to stand in the presence of his Majesty's sisters. Stéphanie obeyed, no longer laughing. She burst into a flood of tears. At this moment the Emperor appeared, and noting her distress, which perhaps became her as well as her smiles, he inquired the cause of her emotion. "Is that all?" he said. "Well, come and sit on my knee. Then you will be in no one's way." We will not vouch for the authenticity of this anecdote, but it seems to be confirmed by the following instructions sent to the Grand Master of the Ceremonies on the arrival of the Prince of Baden — "Our intention being that our daughter, the Princess Stéphanie

Napoleon, should enjoy all the privileges proper to her rank, we wish her to take her place by our side at all receptions, fetes, and banquets; in the event of our absence, she shall be placed on the Empress's right hand." By this decree Stéphanie took precedence of Julie, the future Queen, of Hortense, of all the Emperor's sisters and sisters-in-law, and even of the Princess Augusta, the wife of his adopted son.

It was followed on the next day by a message to the Senate, announcing the adoption of the Princess Stéphanie Napoleon, and her approaching marriage; and further, by an order to all the great State bodies to send deputations to the ceremony. Among the delegates of the Senate was M. Claude de Beauharnais, the Princess' father, a returned émigré, who had been a member since the year XII., with a salary of 25,000 francs. He was further rewarded for being the father of his charming daughter by the Senatorship of Amiens, with an income of 25,000 francs, by a pension of 25,882 francs in 1807, to say nothing of the post of Chevalier d'Honneur to Marie Louise, with its accompanying 30,000 francs a year, and an award of 200,000 francs on September 22, 1807.

But these were trifles as compared to all that was lavished on Stéphanie herself. The Emperor himself inspected her trousseau, and passed her dresses in review. Notable were such items as a long tulle robe embroidered in gold and precious stones, the price of which was 2,400 francs; and twelve dresses furnished by Lenormand at prices varying between 1900 and 1200 francs. He further presented her with 45,178 francs' worth of millinery and knickknacks from Leroy's; and with 2,574 francs' worth of artificial flowers from Roux-Montagnat. He gave her a dowry of 1,500,000 francs, a magnificent parure of diamonds, a quantity of jewels, and a thousand louis from his privy purse as pocket-money.

The marriage itself, more especially the religious ceremony, was celebrated with the utmost pomp, all the resources of imperial processions and sovereign splendours adding lustre to its solemnity. Napoleon could have done no more for a daughter of his own. The festivities were not confined to the palace; they overflowed into the town, which was illuminated by the blaze of fireworks in the Place de la Concorde.

But when the last sparks were extinguished, when the last notes of music had died away, and the Emperor and Empress had conducted the bridal pair to their apartments, according to ancient custom, Stéphanie absolutely declined to admit her husband to her room. She wept, and sobbed, and insisted that her school-friend, Mademoiselle Nelly Bourjolly, should be allowed to spend the night with her. The Court removed to Malmaison on the following day; at night the same scene was enacted. Some one suggested to the Prince of Baden that it was the manner in which his hair was dressed which inspired the Princess's repugnance, and that she had a great dislike to a queue. The Prince at once had his hair cut short and curled in classic fashion all over his head. But when he appeared in this guise, Stéphanie burst into a peal of laughter, declaring that he was even uglier than before. Every evening the Prince presented himself with fruitless entreaties and supplications, falling asleep at last in an armchair, utterly wearied out. In the morning he carried his complaints to the Empress, and Napoleon watched the progress of the comedy with secret amusement. It soon became the talk of the household. The magnificent fete given by the Emperor at the Tuileries in honor of the marriage seems to prove conclusively that he took a certain malicious pleasure in the situation, and showed no signs of anger against Stéphanie. Not only the entire Court, but all the town was invited to the first great ball, at which two thousand five hundred guests were present. Such sights had never been seen as the two quadrilles led by the Princess Louise and the Princess Caroline, one in the Galerie de Diane, the other in the Salle des Maréchaux, or the sideboards, loaded with a hundred large joints, sixty *entrées*, sixty roasts, two hundred *entremets*, at which a thousand bottles of Beaune, a hundred of Champagne, a hundred of claret, and a hundred of various dessert wines were consumed.

At last the question became one of policy, and Napoleon made up his mind to intervene. Mademoiselle de Beauharnais' coquetries had amused him, and he had taken a certain pleasure in teasing his wife. He had gone somewhat further than he intended in the disproportionate rank he had bestowed on the young girl, and the splendour with which he had celebrated her marriage. But he saw that the Prince of Baden was losing patience; a war with Prussia was imminent, and it was highly important to conciliate all such of the German princes as might become allies, or at least furnish information. Added to which, he was anxious to put an end to a flirtation ill-suited to his dignity, his age, and his temperament. He had respected Stéphanie before her marriage, and had no intention of burdening himself with a mistress in the person of an hereditary princess, whose head was already turned to a considerable extent by her elevation. She was becoming a nuisance in Paris, whereas at Carlsruhe she might be made useful, if only to counterbalance the influence of the Margrave Louis, and the hostility of the whole petty court to France.

Napoleon barely allowed himself time to inquire into some story of intercepted letters which showed what opposition awaited his adopted daughter. Before seeking any satisfaction, he hurried on the departure of the Prince and Princess. Stéphanie went off in despair, though accompanied by three of her schoolfriends – Mademoiselle de Mackau, Mademoiselle Bourjolly, and Mademoiselle Gruau. Immediately on her arrival in her father-in- law's dominions she addressed the following letter to the Emperor – "Sire, whenever I have a moment to myself, I think of you, of the Empress, of all that is most dear to me. I imagine myself in France once more, I dream that I am with you, and I even find a certain mournful pleasure in dwelling on my sorrow." Napoleon's answer is marked by a certain severity. His tone is admonitory, but he refrains from any parental formula, or tender expression "Carlsruhe is a lovely spot. . . . Do your best to please the Elector, he is your father. . . . Love your husband; his attachment to you deserves such a recompense." When she wrote again to say that she was happy at Carlsruhe, he unbent, and wrote to her as *his daughter*, but continued to lay down rules of conduct, with a certain commanding austerity. He did not resume his tone of familiar affection until the Grand Duke offered him his support in the forthcoming campaign, and at the same time announced that Stéphanie was about to become a mother. "I hear nothing but good news of you," he wrote. "Be good and gentle to every one, as you have shown yourself hitherto." And he gave her leave to join the Empress and Hortense at Mayence, while her husband was with the army. In subsequent letters to Josephine, Napoleon rarely omitted some mention of Stéphanie. But these were mere passing remembrances, and had no deeper meaning here than in any other case.

In 1807 Stéphanie and her husband were invited to the fetes given in honor of Jerome's marriage with Catherine of Wurtemburg, and Stéphanie joyfully hailed the opportunity of revisiting Paris.

Great must have been her chagrin, if she had retained any illusions as to her power over Napoleon's heart, the prestige conferred by her adoption into his family, and the position he had assigned her only a year before! Now her place was last among the princesses; she seemed to be admitted into the Imperial circle on sufferance rather than by right. She was recognized only as one of the princesses of the Germanic Confederation, and had any German queens been present, they would have taken precedence of her. In the Imperial presence she was allowed a folding-stool as a favor, whereas the other princesses of the family had a right to chairs. She seems to have hardly realized the change in her circumstances at first, and was absorbed in a flirtation with Jerome, the new King of Westphalia. But her aunt undertook to put the matter plainly before her. She soon perceived that her position was only to be consolidated by means of her husband's affection, and she made him so desperately in love with her that his jealousy became unbearable.

His devotion stood her in good stead, however, in 1814, when he defended her against the combined attack of all his kindred. After the fall of the Emperor, an attempt was made to oust her from the house of Zaehringen. Her presence was a perpetual reminder of broken faith and forgotten benefits, and the ducal family eagerly demanded her repudiation by her husband. Was there any direct connection between his resistance and the mysterious illness by which he, a robust man of thirty-two, in vigorous health, was suddenly attacked? He lingered for a year, and died in strange agonies in 1818.

Among all the children born to her, Stéphanie had never succeeded in rearing a son. When she lost her second, or at least supposed him to be dead, her despair found utterance in the following letter to the Emperor – "I was so happy to tell your Majesty that I had a son, and to implore your love and protection on his behalf! A son would have made me forget many of my sorrows, and was most essential to me in my position, the duties of which are often very difficult.... But I have been forced to relinquish all my hopes!" She mourned unspeakably over the fatality which seemed to single out her sons, and spare her daughters, branding her race with political sterility, and cutting it off from the succession.

Ten years after the death of the Grand Duke, between five and six o'clock in the evening of May 26, 1828, a citizen of Nuremburg discovered in the Tallow-market of that city, a youth about seventeen years of age, who had never stood upon his feet, or seen the sunlight, and whose stomach would not digest any animal food, a being whose organs could only have been thus atrophied by imprisonment in darkness from his birth. Stéphanie was the first to calculate, reason, and compare dates. She became convinced that the mysterious unknown, who went by the name of Caspar Hauser, was her son – her son, for whom a dead child had been substituted; her son, the victim of the Margrave Louis's hatred and the Countess of Hochberg's ambition, who had expiated the crime of having a Napoleonide for his mother by sixteen years of darkness and suffering. But Stéphanie was powerless.

Her enemies had triumphed. One was on the throne; the other, raised to unexpected honors, had secured the succession for a family that courtesy might call morganatic, but which truth can only describe as bastard. Stéphanie could but tremble for Caspar Hauser, and weep for him when he was at last murdered, after three unsuccessful attempts upon his life. Was her conviction a pathetic illusion, born of a mother's grief, or one of those mysterious intuitions which have thrown more light on certain great crimes than all the machinery of law and justice? To her last hour (she died January 29, 1860), she declared to the small French circle who visited her dilapidated palace at Mannheim, that her son had not died in 1812, but had been stolen from her; she named the principals and accessories of the crime, and detailed her suppositions and conjectures. Certain German writers have endeavoured to show that she was the victim of a delusion! If so, we may congratulate the reigning family of Baden!

**Désirée
Queen
of Sweden**

**Giuseppina
Grassini**

**Josephine
de Beauharnais**

**La Comtesse
Bertrand**

**Madame de
Ranchoup**

Madame Walewska

Mademoiselle Georges

Marie-Louise

Reine Hortense

Chapter 13
Eléonore

JOSEPHINE had comparatively little cause for anxiety, so long as Napoleon was in doubt as to the possibility of his ever becoming a father. A concatenation of circumstances which should convince him absolutely of this possibility was in the highest degree improbable. It was nevertheless brought about, and in the most unexpected manner, the revelation being the result of an adventure to which the Emperor attached very little importance, and from which a momentous sequel could never have been predicted.

Mention has already been made of the school established at St. Germain-en-Laye towards the close of the Revolution by Madame Campan, formerly Lady-in-Waiting to Marie Antoinette. Josephine had taken it under her special protection from the first; her daughter Hortense, her nieces and cousins, Emilie and Stéphanie de Beauharnais, Stéphanie Tascher, Félicité de Faudoas, her sister-in-law, Caroline Bonaparte, and even Lucien's daughter Charlotte, had all been confided to Madame Campan at her instance. The daughters of most of those who had, or desired to have, some footing at the Consular Court, soon clustered round these more notable pupils. Among the satellites were Mesdemoiselles Barbé, Marmois, Leclerc, Victor, Clarke, and MacDonald. After the successful marriages made by Mesdemoiselles Augier, Madame Campan's nieces, as a result of their intimacy with Hortense, many were the applicants for admission to Madame

Campan's fold, even among families of small means and smaller pretensions.

Madame Campan was supposed to be a power at Court. She had obtained a reversal of the decrees against many *émigrés*, and restitution of their confiscated estates. In short, it became the fashion to be educated by her, and side by side with the glorious but brand-new names of many of her pupils, her registers make mention of Noailles, Talons, Lally-Tollendals, and Rochemonds, of many representatives of the financial world, and finally, of a swarm of nobodies.

There was one young girl in particular of whose origin the mistress would have been puzzled to give an account, had she kept up the standard of exclusiveness she had at first adopted. But the prestige of her establishment having suffered some eclipse after the Consulate, she was reduced to filling up vacancies without too close a scrutiny of her candidates' claims. The young lady in question was Mademoiselle Louise-Catherine-Eléonore Dénuelle de la Plaigne. Her father, who gave himself out to be a gentleman of independent means, was given to speculations, not invariably of a successful nature. Her mother, still a very pretty woman, had figured in a variety of scandalous stories. The pair lodged in sumptuous apartments in the Boulevard des Italiens, where they entertained a numerous and very mixed company. They lived from hand to mouth on the dubious profits of the one or the other, looking forward to the time when their daughter, who was seventeen in 1804 (she was born September 13, 1787), should have found a rich husband, or at any rate should be fairly launched on the quest.

But time passed on. The lady began to grow old, the gentleman was deeply in debt; admirers fell off. The quarterly payments were not easily scraped together for Madame Campan, and the parents began to realize that chances of marriages like those of Madame Ney and Madame Savary had been reduced to a minimum since the Beauharnais had left the school.

In default of the drawing-rooms from which she was excluded, Madame Dénuelle determined to show off her daughter's charms in the theatres. One evening, a good-looking officer entered the box they occupied, and took the vacant place behind them. The two ladies showed no signs of austerity; the officer was enterprising; and the trio soon became acquainted. He whispered of love, and the pair discoursed of marriage. No alternative presenting itself, he agreed to the conditions.

He was invited to the Boulevard des Italiens, and duly present-ed himself to pursue his conquest. The father made an attempt to borrow money of him, which roused his suspicions as to the solvency of the household. His doubts, however, were laid at rest by a conversation he had with Madame Campan. He stipulated only that the marriage should be at St. Germain, where it took place on Nivose 25, year XIII. (January 15, 1805).

The bridegroom, who gave himself out as a captain in the 15th Regiment of Dragoons, in General d'Avrange d'Haugrauville's division, was a scamp of the first quality. He had formerly been quartermaster in the regiment, and had just resigned his commission with the intention of becoming an army contractor. Meanwhile, he was living on credit at an inn, relying apparently a good deal more on his wife's beauty than on his own resources for escape from his embarrassments. Two months after the wedding, he was arrested on the charge of having forged a bill he had paid over to his regiment, and was condemned to a term of imprison-ment.

Eléonore then bethought her that she had been at school with Caroline Murat (her Imperial Highness the Princess Caroline), and, warmly recommended by Madame Campan, she went to implore her protection. Caroline placed her at a boarding-house at Chantilly, where young women in distressed circumstances were received. But yielding to Eléonore's entreaties, she eventually took her into her own household, very much against the advice of Madame Campan, who wished her to retire from the world for a time, and then to find a fresh husband in the provinces.

Eléonore was a beautiful creature, tall, graceful, and finely formed, a brunette with magnificent dark eyes. She had great vivacity of manner, and was a born coquette. Her youthful training had not taught her to be over-scrupulous, nor had the two months she had spent with Revel tended to increased rigidity of morals. Her duty at first was the announcement of visitors to the Princess, from which office she was promoted to the rank of reader. Chance brought her under the Emperor's notice, when he came to see his sister towards the end of January, 1806, after his return from Austerlitz. She took every possible opportunity of attracting his attention, and when his overtures were laid before her, she responded with alacrity. She consented to visit him at the Tuileries, and it soon became her habit to spend two or three hours there from time to time.

On the 13th of February in this year, she lodged an application for a divorce on the grounds of her husband's misconduct, and obtained a decree in her favor almost as a matter of right, Revel having been condemned to two years' imprisonment by the Criminal Court of Seine-et-Oise. The decree was made absolute on April 29, 1806. It was time, for in the month of March Eléonore was *enceinte.* On Saturday, December 13, 1806, she was delivered of a son, at No. 29, Rue de la Victoire. The child was registered as Léon, son of Eléonore Dénuelle, spinster, of independent means, and of an unknown father.

There was no possibility of doubt as to its paternity. Eléonore, who in the deed of divorce was described as "attached to the household of her Imperial Highness the Princess Caroline," had lived since her return from Chantilly at the Hotel du Gouvernement, in the Rue de Province, purchased by Murat on the 22nd Nivose, year X., and formerly known as the Hotel Thélusson. She had never left it save for her visits to the Tuileries, the secret of which was perfectly well known to Caroline. But evidence even more conclusive was to be found in the child itself, which bore the most striking likeness to Napoleon.

The news of the accouchement reached the Emperor at Pulstuck on December 31. The spell was broken, and he knew now that he might reasonably hope for an heir of his own blood. Thus, the clandestine birth of a nameless child determined his future more directly perhaps than any other influence, and undoubtedly was the secret cause of the momentous decision he made shortly after Tilsit, and carried out some two years later.

Léon was first placed under the care of Madame Loir, Achille Murat's nurse; but in 1812 a family council was convened, which appointed two guardians, Monsieur Mathieu de Mauvierès, Mayor of St. Forget, Baron of the Empire, and the Baron de Méneval, the Emperor's private secretary and trusted confidant. Not content with the provision he had already made for the child, Napoleon, before starting to join the army in January, 1814, directed the Duc de Bassano to augment it by a sum of 12,000 livres; this he supplemented on June 21, 1815, by ten shares in the Canals Company, valued at 100,000 francs. In a codicil to his will, he further assigned him 320,000 francs for the purchase of an estate, and, solicitous for him to the last, he mentions him in the thirty-seventh paragraph of his *Instructions* to his executors — "I should be glad for the little Léon to enter the magistrature, should his inclinations lie in that direction."

But what were all these benefits as compared with those he dreamed for a moment of conferring on this child? There seems to be no doubt that he entertained the idea of adopting his natural son as his successor, that he broached the subject to Josephine, and sounded several of his intimates. Such an expedient seemed to offer a means of escape from the proposed divorce, from a rupture with Josephine, to whom he was sincerely attached, and whose very faults had a certain attraction for him, while at the same time he saw in it a sufficient concession to the law of heredity. He cited examples, invoked precedents, invented justifications; if he drew back at last, it was because he recognized the difficulty of imposing his own view of the case on others, and realized that the days were past when a Louis XIV conferred the rights of succession on a Duc du Maine, or a Comte de Toulouse. But while the project was in his mind, he liked to have the child about him, and showed considerable affection for him. He often sent for him at the Elysée, when he visited his sister Caroline, or even at the Tuileries, while he was dressing or breakfasting, and would play with him, and give him sweetmeats, amused by his lively prattle.

The disasters of later years of course affected Léon's position considerably. No longer able to watch over his fortunes himself, the Emperor in 1815 commended him to the good offices of Madame Bonaparte and Cardinal Fesch.

The Emperor's mother had already shown some interest in him, and seemed inclined to do considerably more. But Léon's character was not such as to inspire affection.

In 1832, when he was twenty-five, he seems to have already ruined himself by gambling. We find him applying to Cardinal Fesch, and promising never again to lose 45,000 francs in one night, in the true gambler's vein! A year later he was dipping alternately into speculation, politics, and mesmerism, and challenging his acquaintances very freely to duels (1833 and 1834), for he had plenty of courage, and was somewhat of a swash- buckler. In 1834 he was chosen to command the St. Denis contingent of the National Guard, during his canvass for which post he advertised himself and his claims by incessant references to "that great man to whom I owe my being." He was temporarily suspended for some dereliction of duty, and finally dismissed, after which he published a series of apologetic pamphlets, the contentions of which are very difficult to follow after this lapse of time. In 1840 he took part in the official reception of his father's remains in Paris. He was then completely ruined, and made attempts to mend his fortunes by various lawsuits with his mother.

Eléonore had preserved her own fortune intact. The Emperor had never seen her after 1806, and had refused to receive her when she presented herself at Fontainebleau the following year. He acknowledged her claims on him, however, by the gift of a house, No. 29, Rue de la Victoire, and by a permanent settlement of an income of 22,000 livres, on February 8, 1808. That very day she married Monsieur Pierre-Philippe Augier, a lieutenant of infantry, the son of Monsieur Augier de la Sausaye, who had been successively Deputy of the Third Estate in the Constituent Assembly, Sous-préfet of Rochefort, and, from the year XII. onwards, the representative of La Charente in the Legislative Body. Lieutenant Augier took his wife to Spain, and died in captivity after the Russian campaign. His widow was soon consoled, and took a third husband at Seckenheim, May 25, 1814, in the person of Charles-Auguste-Emile, Count Luxburg, a major in the service of the King of Bavaria. Returning to Paris with this new partner, she was immediately attacked by her first husband, Revel, who tried to blackmail her, taking advantage of the fall of "the tyrant" to pose as a victim, and trade upon his wrongs. Madame de Luxburg, however, resisted his extortions; whereupon Revel avenged himself, and made a few francs by the publication of innumerable pamphlets with sensational titles of a scurrilous description. He was unsuccessful, however, in all the various lawsuits he brought against his ex-wife.

Léon was somewhat luckier in his proceedings against his mother. He was defeated in an action in which he charged her with fraud, and demanded a general audit of accounts. On the other hand, he gained the cause in which he claimed recognition as a natural son, and in default of alimony, obtained a settlement of 4000 francs by a decree of July 2, 1846. He seems to have somewhat improved his financial position by 1848, for he then had some idea of offering himself as a candidate for the Presidency of the Republic in opposition to Prince Louis Napoleon, with whom he had been anxious to fight a duel eight years before, in March, 1840. The whole story is so strange, that Léon's conduct is only to be explained as the result of some mental derangement. In 1849 he took an active part in the legislative elections, and published a manifesto, entitled – *Citizen Léon, sometime known as the Comte Léon, son of the Emperor Napoleon, Director of the Peace Society, to the French Nation.*

When the Second Empire was established, Leon obtained from Napoleon III, whom he had wished to kill, a pension of 6,000 francs, and the payment of Napoleon I's legacy – altogether a capital of 225,319 francs. Not content with this, he made a further claim in 1853 for 572,670 francs, which he alleged to have been assigned him by decrees of April, May, and June, 1815. In 1857 he sued the Minister of Public Works for 500,000 francs, which he declared to be due to him for draught plans of the Northern Railway.

Not a year passed without a mass of claims, proposals, and petitions on his part. His debts were paid out of the Civil List no less than six times. His brain was in a perpetual state of ferment with schemes for railways, public roads, proposed law-suits, commercial speculations, etc. His pamphlet, published in 1859, *Peace, the Solution of the Italian Question*, is a sort of ultimatum, in which Coessin is extolled as the prophet of his times. "To him, and to him alone, we owe the solution of all difficulties, past and to come." Coessin, it may be necessary to explain, was the author of the *Nine Books* (1809), the founder of the *Gray House* (1810), the *New Gray House*, and *Spiritual Families*. It is not unlikely that the Peace Society, of which Léon styled himself Director in 1849, was an emanation from the *Spiritual Families*, which every one but himself had probably forgotten by 1859.

Leon died at Pontoise, April 15, 1881, certainly deranged.

Many romances have been built up on the hypothesis of a natural son of Napoleon's having survived him. But what romance could rival that true history, of which we can only glean fragments from law-reports, civil registers, circulars, and electoral addresses? Strange and startling would be such a history, given in its entirety!

Chapter 14
Hortense

THE beginning of the year 1807 was an epoch of moment in the life of Napoleon. In January he heard of the birth of Léon; in May, of the death of Napoleon-Charles. The birth of Léon convinced him that he need not despair of posterity; the death of Napoleon-Charles, the son of Louis and Hortense, dispelled a vision of heredity he had long nourished, a vision which external circumstances rather than his own inclinations had hitherto prevented him from realizing by a solemn act of adoption. The boy was the child of his heart, the son of the young girl to whom he had been father and guardian, and for whom his affection had been so strong from the beginning that her tears had moved him to grant the pardon he had refused to his own love for Josephine. He was the son, too, of his favorite brother, the little brother who had been almost a son to him, whom he had brought up and educated out of his own scanty pay as lieutenant of artillery, whom he had made his aide-de-camp, who had witnessed the first of his great achievements, and whom he had raised, in his own upward course, to a throne. In this child he recognized the very characteristic type of the Bonapartes, neither disfigured by Louis's thick lips and ill-shaped nose, nor emasculated by Hortense's slender Creole grace, yet softened and etherealized by a halo of golden hair. To this child, the first boy of the new generation, Napoleon gave his father's name, Napoleon-Charles. So warm was his affection for the boy, and so openly was it manifested, that malicious tongues soon began to insinuate that he was its father, and that his stepdaughter had been his mistress before her marriage. We will now inquire into the truth of this rumour.

Hortense's marriage contract was dated Nivose 13, year X. (January 3, 1802). The wedding took place on the 14th (January 4), and her son was born on the 18th of Vendémiaire, year XL (October 10, 1802). Clearly, then, she was not *enceinte* at the time of the marriage, and it was no "case of necessity," as Lucien Bonaparte hinted, seeing that a period of two hundred and eighty days elapsed between the marriage and the birth of the child, the normal interval in such cases being two hundred and seventy days. Now on Nivose the 18th (January 8), at midnight, the First Consul started for Lyons. He did not return to Paris until Pluviose the 12th (February 1). These material proofs may be corroborated by others.

Louis, the most jealous and suspicious of husbands, who had tyrannized over his wife from the first to such an extent that he had forbidden her ever to spend a night at St. Cloud, who never left her, and kept her surrounded by spies, had not failed to make his own calculations. Every waiting-woman who seemed to attach herself to her mistress was promptly dismissed, and the most scandalous accusations were formulated against Josephine by her son-in-law. Taking these things into account, it becomes a strong presumption in Hortense's favor, that Louis himself had no doubts as to the child's paternity. In his *Documents historiqties sur la Hollande*, he expressly declares that he knew himself to be the father of the three children, whom he and his wife loved, he says, "with equal tenderness." This statement he repeated both in prose and verse, for he prided himself on his poetic gifts. When Napoleon proposed to adopt Napoleon-Charles, Louis very possibly alluded to the rumours that were rife; not that he believed them, but they gave him a pretext for opposing his brother's plans. The very fact of his having discussed the subject with Napoleon, even by implication, tends to prove that he himself had no misgivings. During the child's lifetime, Louis was much attached to him, though the manifestations of his affection were often held in check by the caprices of a melancholy and distorted mind. As far, however, as he was capable of loving anything, he loved the child, and he was unaffectedly grieved at the death. It was on this occasion that he became reconciled for a time to Hortense, with whom he had been on such terms that the Emperor was obliged to intervene. He wrote affectionate letters to the mother-in-law he detested, and accompanied his sick wife to Cauterets, where, under circumstances familiar to all students of history, Hortense became *enceinte* with her third son, Charles-Louis Napoleon, afterwards the Emperor Napoleon III.

It is evident that Louis never for a moment believed his wife to have been Napoleon's mistress. We have not only his written testimony to this effect; the fact is most fully borne out by the whole tenor of his conduct from 1800 to 1809. As to Hortense, no whisper of the calumny ever reached her till 1809.

Her mother's marriage with General Bonaparte had been a severe shock to her. Even before it took place she was living at St. Germain-en-Laye with her grandfather, the Marquis de Beauharnais, and her aunt, Madame Renaudin, whom the Marquis had married a short time before. She was then sent to school with Madame Campan, whence she was not transferred to the Tuileries till about the time of the First Consul's departure for Marengo. It was not, therefore, until after Bonaparte's return from Italy that she was brought into constant and familiar intercourse with him. Napoleon became attached to her, treating her with fatherly indulgence and tenderness, but she could never conquer her awe of him. He inspired her with a sort of respectful dread that made her tremble when she spoke to him; she never ventured to make him any request; if she had a favor to ask, she always sought the help of some intermediary. "Little fool!" Napoleon would say, "why doesn't she ask me herself? Is the child afraid of me?'" When Josephine was negotiating her daughter's marriage with Louis Bonaparte, Napoleon refrained from any action in the matter, partly because he hoped the union might bring about greater harmony between his own family and his wife's, partly because he foresaw certain political advantages to be derived therefrom, and partly from a feeling of delicacy towards Josephine and the children of her first marriage. But whenever, in the unhappy sequel, he was able to calm and soften Louis, or to admonish him as to a proper course of conduct towards Hortense, he never failed to carry out the task with admirable tact, delicacy, and patience. He pitied his stepdaughter profoundly, and had the greatest respect for her, restraining his freedom of speech in her presence. "Hortense forces me to believe in virtue," he often said.

He was well aware of the rumours current. He knew, and was perhaps not altogether indifferent to the malicious gossip which affirmed that he had married Hortense to his brother when she was already *enceinte* by himself, and that her child had been born before nine months had elapsed. The calumny had crossed the

Straits, and had come back to Paris amplified and embellished by the English newspapers. Determined to give the lie to his assailants, the Consul had contrived a scene which reflects little credit on his ingenuity, and even less on his sense of delicacy. He gave orders for a ball at Malmaison; Hortense was present, though then in her seventh month. Bonaparte invited her to dance with him. She pleaded fatigue, and refused. She knew that her step-father usually inveighed in the strongest terms against women in her condition who danced, especially when dressed in the clinging garments of the period, which revealed every contour of the figure. On this occasion, however, he persisted, begging her to take part at least in a country-dance. Again she refused. Whereupon he brought "so many cajoleries" to bear upon her that she at last consented. The next morning one of the newspapers published a copy of scurrilous verses on the incident. Hortense, greatly incensed, lodged a complaint, but without effect. The ball indeed had been given with no other object than to furnish an occasion for these verses, which might be produced at some future day to prove that Madame Louis Bonaparte was in the orthodox stage of her pregnancy. A like precaution was taken in the case of the *Moniteur*. This journal, which had never made any allusion to the Consul's family heretofore, published the following notice in its issue of Vendemiaire the 21st – "Madame Louis Bonaparte was safely delivered of a son on Vendemiaire the 18th, at nine o'clock in the evening."

Napoleon clearly did all in his power to circumvent the calumny, but it survived in spite of his efforts, and gained credence in many quarters. Outrageous as it was, he felt that it could not seriously affect either Hortense, Louis, or himself; he therefore accepted it as a move in the political game, and at once saw how it might be turned to account. He loved the child scandal had fathered upon him almost as fondly as if it were indeed his own. He had a genuine parental weakness for the boy, and showed a tender and charming playfulness in his treatment of him. He was enchanted when the child exclaimed to some grenadiers he saw passing in the garden – "Long live Nonon the soldier!" He often sent for him when at dinner, and would perch him on the table beside him, laughing when he touched every dish, and upset all within his reach. He took him to give snuff to the gazelles, set him astride one of them, and smiled to hear himself addressed as "Uncle Bibiche." Or he would have him brought into his dressing-room, and after having kissed him, pulled his ears, or made faces for his amusement, he would finally go down on all fours to play with him. He reflected, that if he adopted the boy, and proclaimed him his heir, the world would be convinced that he was his father. But what of that? They would recognize his blood, his race, his genius, in his chosen successor. The heredity thus established would be no spurious heredity, at variance with all popular constitutions, but a claim based on direct descent, the only hereditary claim admitted by popular logic. The idea was offensive from the moral standpoint; but Napoleon had no prejudices. He held his destiny to be so far above that of the crowd, that the nation would not judge his actions by the moral formula applicable to ordinary mortals, and believed that the national desire to ensure a stable form of government might be relied on to excuse the suspected lapse from domestic virtue. At the worst, the accusation rested on mere suspicion and hearsay; it was impossible to bring it home; and Napoleon himself knew it to be entirely baseless.

It may be urged that we are attributing ideas and opinions to the Emperor, wholly in the air. But it is not so. Two years later, in a conversation recorded by Hortense in her unpublished memoirs, he discussed the consequences of her son's death at some length, adding that he himself had been commonly reputed the child's father. "You know," he said, "the utter absurdity of such a suspicion. But I can assure you that at one time all Europe believed him to be my son." He paused a moment at Hortense's movement of surprise, and then continued – "No one thought the worse of you. The world has always respected you, but the story was believed." He paused once more, and then added – "I thought this belief might be turned to good account, and the child's death was a great misfortune." "I was so startled," writes Hortense, "that I stood by the fireplace unable to utter a word. I heard nothing more that he said. That speech, 'I thought this belief might be turned to good account,' seemed to lift a veil from my eyes. It threw all my thoughts into confusion, and, above all, it wounded my heart most cruelly. 'What!' I exclaimed to myself, 'when he treated me as his daughter, when it seemed to me so sweet and so easy to find in him the father I had lost, were all his solicitude, all his marks of preference, the outcome, not of affection, but of policy?'"

Hortense was wrong. There was as much affection as policy in the matter. But the indignation she felt, a perfectly legitimate indignation from the feminine point of view, made it impossible for her to appreciate that philosophical view of the situation that presented itself to Napoleon's masculine mind. If he had heaped kindnesses on Hortense, it was not with the intention of confirming the rumour that he was the father of the child, for we know he took effectual steps to discredit it. But finding that the rumour persisted, and was accepted by the majority, he determined to make it subservient to his own interests, and to the consolidation of his dynasty. It was the sudden inspiration of a skilled tactician on the field of battle, for it was one of the most extraordinary of his faculties to be able to recognize a situation at a glance, to accept its conditions, and to act at once on the impulse it inspired.

Hence it was, that although, as he himself said, he looked upon the death of Napoleon-Charles as a great misfortune, he bowed to the inevitable. "I have no time to feel or to regret like other men," is a dictum ascribed to him. He may have uttered it. The death of the little Napoleon moved him deeply; he wrote of it to all his correspondents, twenty times to Josephine, five or six times to Hortense, to Joseph, to Jerome, to Fouché, to Monge. But it was "his destiny," and useless tears over the irrevocable decrees of fate were contrary to Napoleon's nature, and to the philosophy he had learnt from long contemplation of the terrible chances of war, that game in which death is the partner of every player, but in which only the living are of account in the gambler's combinations.

This particular combination had failed. Napoleon-Charles had been one of the external links that bound the Emperor to Josephine. That link was broken. The only ties now remaining were those personal bonds of affection and tenderness woven during the years of a companionship disturbed by long absences, frequent quarrels, and strange misunderstandings. Could those ties stand the strain of such a test as that to which they were subjected in 1805 by the intrigue with Madame _____?

Chapter 15
Madame Walewska

ON January 1, 1807, the Emperor, on his way from Pulstuck to Warsaw, stopped to change horses at the little town of Bronia. A crowd had gathered to welcome the Liberator of Poland, a shouting, gesticulating, excited multitude, which dashed forward at the sight of the Imperial carriage. The carriage drew up; Duroc, the general officer in attendance, alighted, and made his way to the posting-house. As he entered, he was greeted by despairing cries; clasped hands were raised to him in supplication, and a voice exclaimed in French – "Ah, sir! help us to get away from here, and let me see him, if but for a moment!"

He paused at this appeal; the supplicants were two ladies, lost in the crowd of peasants and workmen. The one who had addressed him seemed hardly more than a child; she was dazzlingly fair, with large blue eyes, peculiarly sweet and candid in expression, and sparkling with a fire as of some sacred frenzy. Her delicate skin, pink and fresh as a rose, was flushed with nervous excitement. Somewhat small of stature, her figure was so exquisitely moulded, so supple and undulating, that she was grace itself. She was very simply dressed, and wore a dark hat with a long black veil.

Duroc took in all these details at a glance. Extricating the two ladies from the crowd, he gave his hand to the beautiful blonde, and led her to the door of the carriage. "Sire," said he to Napoleon, "here is one who has braved all the dangers of the crowd for your sake."

The Emperor took off his hat, and bending towards the lady, began to address her. But she, beside herself with excitement, agitated almost to the verge of delirium by her emotions, cut short his speech, and greeted him in a kind of transport, "Welcome, thrice welcome to our land!" she cried. "Nothing we say or do can adequately express our attachment to your person, and our delight at seeing you tread the soil of that country which looks to you for deliverance!"

Napoleon gazed at her attentively as she uttered these words. He took a bouquet which was in the carriage and presented it to her. "Take it," he said, "as an earnest of my good-will. We shall meet again, I hope, at Warsaw, when I shall look forward to thanks from your beautiful lips."

Duroc took his place by the Emperor's side. The carriage drove off rapidly, Napoleon waving his hat from the door by way of farewell.

The young woman was Marie Walewska. Her maiden name was Laczinska. She belonged to an ancient but impoverished family, and was one of six children. M. Laczinska died when Marie was still a child, and his widow, who was fully occupied in managing the small estate which constituted their sole fortune, sent her daughters to school. They learnt a little French and German, a little music and dancing. When she was fifteen and a half, Marie returned to her mother's house, not very learned, but perfectly chaste, her heart divided between two passions, religion and patriotism. Her love for her country was only less strong than her love to God. These were her sole springs of action. Her temper was usually calm and gentle, but she could be roused to sudden fury in a moment by the suggestion that she should marry a Russian or a Prussian, an enemy of her nation, a schismatic or a Protestant.

She had scarcely returned to her mother's roof, when a strange series of circumstances provided her with two suitors, either of whom would have been a great match for her. Madame Laczinska gave her to understand that she must choose one or the other of these unhoped-for *partis*. One was a charming young man, possessed of every quality that could call forth a girl's admiration; he pleased her at the first glance. He was enormously rich, very well born, and remarkably handsome. But he was a Russian, the son of a general who had been one of Poland's most rigorous oppressors. Never would she consent to become his wife.

She was therefore obliged to take her other suitor, the aged Anastase Colonna de Walewice-Walewska. He was seventy years old, had already been married twice, and his eldest grandchild was nine years older than Marie. This, however, mattered little, for he was very rich. He was the great man of the Laczinski's district, the owner of all the land, the lord of the castle, the law-giver, the princely dispenser of hospitality to his humbler neighbours. He had been Chamberlain to the late King; on great occasions he wore the blue cordon of the White Eagle across his coat. He was the head of one of the most illustrious families of Poland, a family allied to the Colonnas of Rome, and therefore of greater antiquity than any family of kingdom or republic. It was natural that Madame Laczinska should be well-disposed towards such a suitor. Marie did not attempt to resist openly, for her first objection had been met with a very uncompromising response. But she fell ill of a fever that kept her hovering between life and death for four months. Directly she was convalescent she was married.

Three years passed away, which the young girl spent drearily enough, in constant ill-health, at the lonely castle of Walewice, finding her only consolation in religious exercises and pious rhapsodies. At last she became a mother. With the birth of a son her whole being seemed to revive; her son should live the life that had been denied her, he should taste the happiness she had never known. But must this child grow up, like herself, on conquered territory, no longer a fatherland or a nation? Should he bow his neck to the yoke, like herself, and, like his father, hold his lands and titles by favor of the victor? She longed to see her child a Pole and a free man, and therefore prayed that Poland might rise and deliver herself.

The man who had laid Austria low, who had measured himself against Russia at Austerlitz, was now about to engage Prussia and her allies. Napoleon was the adversary raised up by Providence against the powers concerned in the partition of Poland. He had taken the field, and each stage of his advance had been marked by some fresh victory. The Prussian army melted away like a phantasmal horde before him. He had entered Berlin, he was now approaching the frontiers of the former kingdom. A sort of fever seized on its inhabitants, a frenzy of enthusiasm and expectation. Walewice was far out of the track of tidings; but at Warsaw she would know all that was passing.

Her husband, a patriot like herself – as who was not in those days of exaltation? – proposed that they should go to the capital. They arrived, and installed themselves on a scale of some importance, for the husband had his rank to maintain, and wished his young wife to make her *début* in society. She, very much alive to the defects of her education, shy of speaking French lest she should make blunders, naturally timid and retiring, and conscious of standing alone, without the support of friends and relatives, dreaded the social ordeal, and especially disliked appearing at Prince Joseph Poniatowski's palace, La Blacha, the rallying-point of the leaders of society. In obedience to her husband's commands, she made up her mind to such visits as were obligatory in her position, but eschewed all others. Hence she was practically unknown, and excited little attention, in spite of her remarkable beauty.

When the Emperor's approaching visit was announced, the excitement became intense. It was resolved to give him a reception at Warsaw that should eclipse even that he had met with at Posen, The ordinary course of affairs was suspended for the time. The great preoccupation of high and low was to gratify Napoleon. The fate of Poland might depend on his first impression. Marie Walewska determined to be the first to bid him welcome. Little dreaming of the consequences of her act, she persuaded a cousin to accompany her, ordered her carriage, and hastened, regardless of difficulties and dangers, to Bronia.

After the Imperial carriage had disappeared, she remained for some time where she had been left, gazing into space, as if in a dream. Her companion recalled her to herself by shaking her, and calling her, whereupon she carefully wrapped up the bouquet the Emperor had given her in her handkerchief, and got into her carriage, arriving late at night at her home.

It was her own intention to keep her journey a secret, to excuse herself from presentation to the Emperor, and to appear at none of the festivities. But her companion was too proud of the adventure to keep silence, in spite of her injunctions. One morning, Prince Joseph Poniatowski presented himself, inquiring at what hour she would receive him. He came in the afternoon, and with a significant laugh, evidently meant to establish some secret understanding, invited her to a ball he was about to give. As she blushingly put his innuendo by without any sign of comprehension, Poniatowski went straight to the point. He explained that at one of the banquets given in honor of the Emperor, Napoleon had seemed much struck by a certain Princess Lubomirska, since which the lady had been constantly thrown in his way. Whereupon Duroc had revealed that his master had noticed the princess merely on account of a certain resemblance between her and a lovely unknown he had seen at Bronia. Who, Duroc inquired, could she have been? He gave all the details of the adventure, with minute descriptions of the lady's features and style of dress. Poniatowski, however, had not guessed the truth, until the confidante's indiscretion had put him on the right scent, which he had at once followed up.

The Emperor evidently admired her greatly; she *must* come to the ball. Madame Walewska repeated her refusal. Poniatowski insisted "Who can tell? Heaven has perhaps marked you out as the instrument by which our country is to be restored."

Even this appeal failed to move her, and Poniatowski retired in dudgeon. He had scarcely left her when the principal representatives of Poland arrived in rapid succession – "statesmen whose authority was based on the consideration, esteem, and deference due to their conduct and wisdom." Every one of them was fully aware of the situation, and, like Poniatowski, was lavish of compliments and insinuations. To crown all, the husband appeared on the scene, and threw his influence into the scale against her. Knowing nothing of the adventure at Bronia, he took the attentions of his compatriots as a recognition of his own rank, and a courteous acceptance of the young girl he had chosen from a lower social sphere for his third wife. He was more insistent than all the rest, treating her scruples as absurd timidity, and even as a breach of due etiquette. Finding persuasions of little avail, he at last commanded her to accept the invitation. Further resistance was impossible. She yielded, but on one condition. All the ladies had already been presented to the Emperor, and she stipulated that she should not be further embarrassed by a solitary presentation.

The great day came; her husband hastened her toilette, fearing to arrive after the Emperor's departure. When she was dressed, he was full of objections and criticisms. He thought her dress was not sufficiently rich and elegant. She had chosen a plain white satin, with a gauze tunic; the only ornament in her hair was a simple wreath of foliage. A murmur of admiration greeted her arrival, and followed her across the reception rooms as she passed. She was given a seat between two ladies, both unknown to her, and Joseph Poniatowski immediately took up his station behind her. "Some one has been expecting you with the greatest impatience," he whispered. "He was overjoyed when you appeared. He asked your name again and again until he had it by heart. He looked attentively at your husband, shrugged his shoulders, and muttered, 'Poor victim!' He sent me to engage you to dance with him."

" I do not dance," was the reply. "I do not wish to dance."

The Prince explained that the request was, in fact, an order, that the Emperor was watching them. If she would not dance, he himself would be deeply mortified. The success of his ball depended on her. Madame Walewska refused even more positively. Poniatowski felt that he had but one resource left. He went to Duroc, and confided in him. Duroc reported his confidence to the Emperor.

Meanwhile, several of the brilliant officers of the staff had begun to flutter round the fair unknown.

What was no longer a secret to the Poles was still ignored by the French. Napoleon determined to scatter his unconscious rivals by heroic measures. The most ardent among them seemed to be Louis de Périgord; the Emperor made a sign to Berthier, and ordered him to despatch the aide-de-camp at once to the 6th Corps, on the Passarge. Then Bertrand took up the running; another signal from the Emperor, and Bertram was immediately despatched to Prince Jerome's head-quarters at Breslau.

Meanwhile dancing was suspended. The Emperor passed through the rooms, making what he meant to be complimentary speeches on every side. Such, however, was his preoccupation, that these were uttered at random, and were singularly inappropriate in many cases.

One young girl was asked how many children she had; an old maid beside her was rallied on the jealousy her beauty must cause her husband; while a prodigiously stout dame was questioned as to her love of dancing. He spoke without thinking, without hearing the names of his various interlocutors, which seemed to suggest none of the details in which he had been schooled beforehand. Eyes and mind were riveted on one woman, the only one present to him.

At last he paused before her; her neighbours hurriedly signed to her to rise. Pale as death, she stood with downcast eyes before him. "White upon white is a mistake, Madam," he said aloud. Then, almost in a whisper, he added – "This is not the sort of reception I expected after – ” She was silent. He looked at her for a moment, and passed on. A few minutes later he left the house. The circle was at once broken up. The ladies began to compare notes as to what Napoleon had said to each. But the absorbing topic of conversation was what he had said to *her*. What was the meaning of the phrase all had heard? And above all, of the whispered remark, the last word of which alone had been audible? Madame Walewska took advantage of the excitement to slip quietly away. In the carriage her husband again plied her with questions, and finding her unresponsive, told her he had accepted an invitation to a dinner to meet the Emperor. He desired her to prepare a more elaborate toilette, and briefly bade her good-night at the door of her room. A moment more, and the impulsiveness which had carried her away at Bronia would have urged her to a full confession of the pursuit with which she was threatened, and the fears by which she was harassed.

Scarcely had the door closed upon her, when her maid handed her a note. With some difficulty she deciphered the following –

I saw but you, I admired but you, I desire but you. Answer at once, and calm the impatient ardour of

“*N.*”

She crushed the paper hastily in her hand, disgusted at the tone of its contents. Prince Poniatowski was waiting her reply in the street. “There is no answer,” she bade the woman tell him. But, determined not to be beaten, the Prince followed the messenger back to her apartment. She had only just time to double-lock the door, from behind which she declared to him that her determination was not to be shaken. She declined to send an answer, just as she had declined to dance. The Prince tried prayers, persuasions, threats. He remained some half-hour outside the door, at the risk of causing a scandal in the house. At last he went away in a fury.

As soon as she awoke the next morning, her maid was at her bedside with a second note. This she left unopened, and enclosing the first with it, gave orders that both should be returned to the bearer. What was she to do? She was alone, without guide or counsellor. She defended herself to the best of her ability, but what chance had she in the struggle? Throughout the day she was besieged by a crowd of visitors, among them all the great personages of the nation, the members of the Government, and the Grand Marshal Duroc. She refused to appear, pleaded a headache, and retired to a chaise longue in her own room. Greatly enraged at her mysterious behaviour, her husband, bent on proving that he was not jealous, as had been asserted, forcibly introduced Prince Joseph and the chief of the Polish visitors. He insisted, in their presence, that she should agree to be presented to the Emperor, and appear at the dinner to which she was invited. The Poles supported him warmly. The Nestor of the band, the most respected and influential among them, looked fixedly at her, and said severely – "All private inclinations, Madam, must yield to circumstances of such overwhelming importance to the nation. We must hope, therefore, that your indisposition will have passed away by the date of the dinner, at which you must certainly appear, if you would not be accounted a bad patriot."

She was then obliged to rise, and, by command of her husband, to go to Madame de Vauban, Prince Joseph's mistress, for advice as to her toilette, and instruction in the etiquette of the court. This was a master-stroke of diplomacy. To hand her over to Madame de Vauban was, in fact, to give her up to the moving spirit of the whole intrigue. Madame de Vauban, indeed, played her part in perfect good faith, and with no touch of malicious intention. By birth a Pugot-Barbentane, she had lived at the Court of Versailles, and had fled to Warsaw at the time of the emigration. Finding a former lover ready to receive her, she had since lived openly with him, and was of opinion that the provision of a mistress for his sovereign, were that sovereign Louis XV or Napoleon I, was one of the most important functions of a courtier. Chastity, duty, wifely fidelity, she looked upon as old-fashioned prejudices which no woman of the world could weigh in the balance against obvious advantages. In the case with which she had now to deal, she recognized, however, that material gains would prove an ineffectual bait. She felt that the tactics to be relied on for the sapping of her *protégé's* virtue were of a kind with which she was unfamiliar, and after lavishing compliments and professions of friendship on her guest, she handed her over to a young lady who lived with her more or less in the capacity of a companion. She had been divorced from her husband, and had no private fortune; but she was pretty, quick-witted, high-spirited, and impulsive; about the same age as Madame Walewska, who was attracted to her at once, more especially as she combined with all these sympathetic qualities a patriotism, real or feigned, as exalted as her own. "All,

all for the sacred cause!" was the constant burden of her argument.[1]

She very soon gained Madame Walewska's confidence, learning all the secrets of a heart that had never known friendship hitherto – a heart that yearned for sympathy, and revealed itself all unconsciously. She insinuated herself into the good graces of the husband, and hardly ever left the wife. When she judged the latter to be sufficiently shaken by her representations, her reasoning, her patriotic rhapsodies, she laid before her the following letter, signed by the foremost men of the nation, among them many members of the provisional government.

"Madam, great events have often sprung from trifling causes. Women have in all times had an immense share in shaping the policy of nations. This truth is certified by the history of the most ancient times, as by that of our own day. As long as man is swayed by his passions, women will continue to wield a formidable power.

"Had you been a man you would gladly have given your life to the sacred cause of your country. But you are a woman; you cannot serve her by force of arms. Your natural instincts disqualify you for the task. There are, however, other sacrifices open to you, and those you should be ready to make, painful as you may feel them to be.

"Did Esther, think you, give herself to Ahasuerus out of the fulness of her love for him? So great was the terror with which he inspired her that she fainted at the sight of him. We may therefore conclude that affection had but little to do with her resolve. She sacrificed her own inclinations to the salvation of her country, and that salvation it was her glory to achieve!

"May we be enabled to say the same of you, to your glory, and our own happiness!

"Are you not the daughter, the mother, the sister, the wife, of devoted Poles, all of whom make part with ourselves of the

---

[1] The documents in my possession are silent as to this young woman's actual name; but I am strongly inclined to identify her with that Madame Abramowicz who was commissioned by Napoleon to present the ladies of society to him when he visited Wilna in 1812. Madame Abramowicz, who became very intimate with Madame Walewska, is supposed to have drafted the letters written by the latter to the Emperor at Warsaw in 1807, a practice Napoleon is said to have reprobated in these words "Write to me just as you please; but I will have no third person intervening between you and me."

national fasces, the strength of which can only be augmented by the number and union of its members? Learn, Madam, how a famous man, the sainted Fénélon, briefly summed up the present situation. 'Men, in whom all ostensible authority is vested, are powerless to work any lasting good by their deliberations, without the practical aid of women.' Listen to this voice, mingling with those of your countrymen, and your reward will be the happiness of twenty million souls."

Every force seemed now arrayed against her. Her country, her friends, her religion, the Old and the New Testament, all conjured her to yield, all combined for the overthrow of a simple and inexperienced girl of eighteen, who felt herself unable to confide in her husband, and had neither parents to counsel nor friends to save her. The impression made by the above letter was at once followed up. Her friend proceeded to read Napoleon's second missive, the note she had returned unread.

Have I displeased you, Madam? I had hoped otherwise. Was it a delusion on my part? Your ardour has cooled, while mine burns more and more fiercely. You have destroyed my peace! Oh, give some little joy and happiness to the poor heart that longs to worship you. Is it so difficult to get an answer from you? You owe me two.

"N."

Just as the officious confidante concluded, the husband entered. Proud of his wife's success, which he thought due in great measure to himself, for he was a man of honor, and had no suspicion of the real state of the case, he began once more on the subject of the proposed dinner-party. The unhappy girl felt that the step was a decisive one, and would be taken as a pledge of further concessions. But since they all insisted, she would go. The stream of visitors, all the bearers of unuttered congratulations, continued to flow till the evening. And lest she should waver and change her mind before the morning, Madame de Vauban's ambassadress remained on guard throughout the night.

As she stepped into the carriage that bore her, an unwilling captive, to meet the Emperor, Madame Walewska comforted herself with the thought that there could be no real danger for her, since she did not love Napoleon. On her arrival, her disgust with her so-called triumph was increased a hundredfold by the flatteries of certain among the guests, eager already to secure her protection; she had taken refuge in a cold impassibility of manner, when the Emperor made his entry. He was more master of himself than on the night of the ball, and more happily inspired in the courtesies he distributed as he passed rapidly along the circle. When he paused in front of her, and she was presented in her turn, he said simply, "I heard Madame Walewska was not well. I hope she has quite recovered?" The commonplace nature of the phrase, the triviality of which was so evidently calculated to baffle suspicion, approved itself to her as singularly delicate.

At the table she found herself next to the Grand Marshal, and almost opposite the Emperor, who at once began to question one of the guests in his usual concise manner on the history of Poland. He seemed to listen attentively to the answers, following them up in each instance by further discussion; but speaking or listening, his eyes never left Madame Walewska, save when he turned them on Duroc, with whom he seemed to keep up a system of silent communication. Indeed, every phrase addressed by Duroc to his neighbour was inspired by a look from the Emperor, or by some perfectly natural gesture of which he made use almost mechanically from time to time, while apparently absorbed in a grave discussion of European politics. Once he laid his hand for an instant on his left side. Duroc hesitated, looked attentively at his master, and catching his meaning at last, uttered an "Ah!" of satisfaction. It was the bouquet he had in his mind, the bouquet he had given her at Bronia. "What had become of it?" asked Duroc.

She assured him that she had carefully set aside the Emperor's gift as an heirloom for her son. "Ah, Madam," rejoined the Grand Marshal, "deign to accept others more worthy of you!" Annoyed at the insinuation she detected in this speech, she colored, and retorted with some warmth that she preferred flowers. Nonplussed for the moment, Duroc soon recovered himself, and gallantly replied: "Then we must gather laurels on your native soil, and lay them at your feet." This was a more skilful shot, and went home, as he saw from her evident agitation.

How describe the tumult of her feelings when, on leaving the table, the Emperor took advantage of the momentary confusion to approach her in the crowd, and take her hand, which he pressed passionately in his own? Fixing on her that keen and brilliant gaze, the mysterious power of which no human eye could withstand, he whispered, "No, no! with those soft, sweet eyes, that gentle expression, you cannot be inflexible, you cannot delight in torturing me, unless you are the most heartless of coquettes, the cruellest of women!"

He retired; all the men followed him, and she allowed herself to be carried off by Madame de Vauban. Here she found awaiting her several of her late fellow-guests, and others, a privileged company of the initiated, who surrounded her, with flatteries and congratulations – "He saw no one but you; his eyes flashed fire as he looked at you." She alone might hope to plead the cause of the nation to him; she alone could touch his heart, and induce him to restore Poland to her place among the nations. Gradually the guests dispersed, as if in obedience to some preconcerted signal. When Duroc entered the room, she found herself alone with the confidante who had become her shadow. Closing the doors, Duroc took a seat beside her, laid a letter on her lap, and taking her hand, began to plead his master's cause in soft, persuasive tones. "Can you," he asked, "repulse him who has never brooked a refusal? Ah! the lustre of his glory is dimmed by sorrows, which you might brighten if you would by a few hours of happiness." He continued in this strain for some time, but she remained silent. Snatching away her hand at last, she hid her face, and burst into tears, sobbing aloud, like a child in distress. Her friend took upon herself to answer for her, and promised she would come at the hour appointed. In reply to Madame Walewska's indignant protest, she reproached her with her want of patriotism, declaring that no Polish woman could do enough for Napoleon. Dismissing the Grand Marshal with further promises, she opened the letter he had brought, and read it aloud.

> *There are times when all splendours become oppressive, as I feel but too deeply at tke present moment. How can I satisfy the desires of a heart that yearns to cast itself at your feet, when its impulses are checked at every point by considerations of the highest moment? Oh! if you would . . . you alone might overcome the obstacles that keep us apart. My friend Duroc will make all easy for you.*
>
> *Oh! come, come! your every wish shall be gratified! Your country will be dearer to me when you take pity on my poor heart.*
>
> *"N."*

It rests with her, then, to decide the fate of Poland! He himself confirms what others have maintained. The belief that all around her have diligently instilled into her for the last five days seems to crystallize in her brain. If she so wills, her country may be regenerated, the shame of its partition wiped out; the scattered limbs may be knit together again, and the White Eagle rise once

148

more in glorious flight! What a vision! What dazzling hopes! But what is she, and how is she fitted for the task? Her counsellors have their answer ready; she has only to carry out the instructions that will be given her. She still resists. What, shall she consent to dishonor? Her modesty rebels at the thought! They laugh at her provincial virtue, her absurd scruples. Does she not know how many there are who would gladly accept the place offered her? Why should she leave it for them? How can she question the good that may result from her influence? Emperor though he be, Napoleon is, after all, a man, and in love. Sooner or later, the woman he loves will hear the words, "Do as you will with me," from his lips.

She gave way at last, stipulating only that she should not be made to write an answer to the note. She was by this time, in fact, physically incapable of the effort. They left her alone for a time to consider the matter, but took care to lock the door of the room, fearful lest she should change her mind, and attempt to escape. She had no such intention. Left to herself, she reflected; or rather, exhausted by emotion, she lost herself in dreams.

Might she not consent to an interview, without danger? Would it not be possible for her to win the Emperor's respect and friendship, obtain his confidence, incline him to listen to the voice of her people? He would not use violence against her. She would tell him she had no love to give him. She would offer him admiration, enthusiasm, grateful devotion.

Her youthful imagination, uncontaminated as yet, ignorant of anything more impassioned than the almost Platonic affection of a septuagenarian husband, carried her away into a land of dreams, a land where the modesty of woman had nothing to fear from the chastity of man, where the senses were vanquished and fettered, and soul communed with soul, and mingled in a harmony complete and almost divine.

Her advisers returned. The final arrangements were made. She refused to write or to speak; but she agreed to remain all day in the palace, and to follow the messenger who would be sent to fetch her in the evening. The hours passed wearily away, and sitting in expectant terror, the poor girl kept her eyes fixed alternately on the swift hand of the clock and at the door, now closed and silent, through which the harbinger of her doom would enter.

At half-past ten there was a knock. She was hastily muffled in a cloak. A hat with a thick veil was placed on her head, and she was led, bewildered and half unconscious, into the street, where a carriage awaited her. Into this she was hurriedly thrust. A man in a long coat and round hat, who held the door open for her, pulled up the step, and seated himself by her side. Not a word was exchanged on the way. The carriage stopped at a secret entrance to the Great Palace. They got out, and her companion half led, half carried her to a door, which was eagerly opened by some one from within. She was placed in an arm-chair.

She found herself in Napoleon's presence. But she could not see him for her tears. Kneeling at her feet, he began to speak reassuringly to her. But presently the words, "Your old husband," escaped him. She uttered a cry, sprang from the chair, and tried to escape, her sobs choking her utterance. At the words, the fault she was about to commit rose before her in all its horror, all its degradation, all its ignominy, and as by a sudden inspiration, she realized its infamy. He, for his part, gazed at her in astonishment, understanding nothing of what was passing in her mind. Never had he found himself in such a position. What sort of a woman was this, whose virtue had yielded, after some persuasion certainly, but no very great pressure (for he knew nothing of the means employed), who had come to a midnight assignation, and who was now sobbing wildly, and flying to the door? Was she a coquette of marvellous histrionic powers, or a simpleton of phenomenal ignorance? Was it all a piece of acting, meant to increase his ardour? No; these are cries that cannot be simulated, impulsive movements that cannot be feigned, especially by a girl of eighteen.

With gentle violence, he brought her back from the door to which she was clinging, and placed her again in her chair. Then, in a voice full of caressing kindness, in spite of the habitual note of command that rang in it occasionally, almost against his will, he questioned her, carefully avoiding words or suggestions that might wound her, and choosing such paraphrases as he judged least offensive, yet, by the irresistible logic of his method, drawing from her faltering replies, each of which he presently turned to account against her. Was her union with the man whose name she bore a voluntary act on her part? Was it his wealth and title that had tempted her? What could have induced her to mate her youth, her fresh beauty, with the decrepitude of advanced old age? Her mother had arranged the marriage!" Surely, then, you can have no scruples in the matter!" he cried. Whereupon she took refuge in her religion: "What God hath joined together, man may not put asunder." Napoleon laughed. Her indignant tears burst forth afresh.

Truly, this was no ordinary woman! He thought of her as of some strange fruit, the flavour of which was unknown to him. A woman who clung desperately to her marriage vows, her religious principles, and yet had come in response to his summons, to this midnight assignation! He determined to clear up the mystery, and plied her again with questions – questions about her education, the sort of life she led in the country, the society to which she was accustomed, her mother, her family; he wished to know all about her, more particularly her baptismal name, Marie, the name by which he always addressed her henceforth.

At two o'clock some one knocked at the door. "What, already!" he exclaimed. "Well, my pretty, plaintive dove, go and rest. You must not fear the eagle; the only power he claims over you is that of a passionate love, a love that will be satisfied with nothing short of your whole heart. You will love him in time, for in all things you shall command him, in all things, do you hear?" He wrapped her cloak about her, and led her to the door. Then, placing his hand on the latch, he vowed he would not lift it unless she would promise to return the next day.

She entered her own house calmer and more assured. Her dream seemed to her not impossible of realization. He was kind and gentle to her, he had shown no violence. He had spared her once; would he not spare her again?

By nine o'clock the next morning the confidante was at her bedside, a large parcel in her hand, which she unpacked after carefully closing the door. She discovered several red Morocco cases, a bouquet of hot-house flowers mingled with laurels, and a sealed letter. But when she unclasped the cases, and taking out a magnificent parure of diamonds, held it so as to catch the light, Madame Walewska snatched the gems from her, and hurled them across the room. She insisted that they should be sent back at once. Did he think she was to be bought with jewels? The messenger seemed little concerned at this outburst. She broke the seal, and read the following letter –

Marie, my sweet Marie, my first thought is of you, my first desire to see you again. You will come, will you not? You promised. If you fail, the eagle will fly to you himself. I shall see you at dinner, my friend tells me. Deign to accept this bouquet. Let it be a secret link, binding us to each other in the midst of the crowd. It will enable us to communicate, under the very eyes of the multitude.

When I press my hand upon my heart, yon will know that it is dreaming of you. Touch your bouquet in reply. Love me, my Marie, and keep your hand constantly on your bouquet.

"N."

In spite of the letter, she declined to accept either diamonds, flowers, or laurels, her excuse in the case of the bouquet being that it was not usual to wear flowers, except at balls. She felt that it would be useless to try and escape the dinner. All around her were in a fever of expectation, self-interest, and ambition; her relatives intoxicated by her successes, her husband absolutely unsuspicious. Unconscious of the drama in which he was an involuntary actor, he was delighted at the numerous invitations they received.

On her arrival, the whole company clustered round her. Those who were unknown to her begged to be presented. She felt as if her adventure of the night before must be known to all the guests. The Emperor was already present. He frowned, and looked displeased, flashing the keen light of an offended eye upon the newcomer.

Suddenly she saw him advancing abruptly towards her, and trembling at the thought of some public scene, some irreparable scandal, she remembered, and laid her hand on the spot where her bouquet should have been. In a moment his features relaxed, the flame died down in his eye; he made an answering sign with his own hand, and before passing into the dining-room, he called Duroc, and whispered a few rapid words in his ear.

Scarcely had she taken her usual seat by the Grand Marshal, before he attacked her on the subject of the bouquet. She retorted by a counterattack upon the present of the diamonds. Let it be understood once for all that she would accept no such gifts. How indeed could they suppose that she would dare to appear in such ornaments? The only offering her admiration and devotion led her to look for from the Emperor was a ray of hope for the future of her country. "Has not that offering already been made?" inquired Duroc. And he recalled a long series of actions which he declared to be infinitely more significant than promises. And as to his love for her, was it possible that she could question it? She might see that he had no eyes for any one but herself. Apparently absorbed in general conversation, asking questions and listening attentively to the answers, he laid his hand perpetually on his heart. When the Emperor had spoken to Duroc before dinner, he had desired him to remind her of her promise, and implore her to come without fail as before. Then the Grand Marshal launched out into a dissertation on the miseries of greatness, the longing of such a sovereign as his master for a heart that should beat in sympathy with his own, the glory of a mission which any woman might envy....

Having gone once, she could not refuse to go again. The same precautions were observed; she was conducted to the same place. As she entered, she saw that Napoleon looked gloomy and ill at ease. "At last!" he exclaimed. "I hardly hoped to see you again!" He took off her hat and cloak, placed her in a chair, and standing over her, asked her harshly how she could justify her conduct? Why had she come to Bronia? Why had she tried to inspire in him a feeling she could not return? Why had she refused his flowers, even his laurels? What had she done with them? He had hoped for so many *interesting moments* in connection with them, and she had robbed him of these. His hand had scarcely left his heart all the evening, but she had made no sign; only once had she responded. And, striking his forehead with a passionate gesture, he exclaimed, "You are a true Pole. You have fully confirmed my former opinion of your nation!"

Greatly troubled by this reception, and utterly overcome by these last words, she could only murmur, "Ah! Sire, tell me what that opinion is."

He declared that all Poles were capricious and impulsive. All their actions were the result, not of principle, but of whim. Their enthusiasm was impetuous, noisy, and easily awakened; but they could never control nor sustain it. Was not this a portrait of the Poles in general, a true likeness of herself in particular? Had she not rushed to meet him on his entry like one possessed? His heart had been ensnared by her sweet glances, her passionate expressions, and then she had vanished. He had sought her everywhere, in vain; and when she had appeared, one of the last to welcome him, she had become an icicle. But she must understand him. The thought of impossibilities only nerved him to renewed effort. Nothing could turn him aside from a quest in which he had once engaged. Difficulties only spurred him on. Long accustomed to ready submission from all with whom he came in contact, her resistance challenged him to put forth all his strength.

His excitement grew as he talked. Anger, perhaps real, perhaps only feigned, glowed in his words. "You *shall*, yes, I repeat it, you *shall* love me! I have restored the name of your country. It owes its very existence to me! I will do more than this for it. But look at this watch in my hand. Just as I dash it to fragments before you, so will

I shatter Poland and all your hopes if you drive me to desperation by rejecting my heart, and refusing me yours."

Terrified by these threats, and the violent gesture with which he threw the watch from him, the unhappy woman sank helpless on the floor.... When she recovered from her swoon, the long conflict was over, and the victor was beside her, wiping away the tears that rolled slowly from her eyes....

The *liaison*, if we may give the name to the habit she now contracted of a daily visit to the Palace, was an accomplished fact. With passive resignation she endured caresses, the price of which she still looked for in vain. The little she had obtained so far – a form of provisional government, the creation of the nucleus of an army, the enrolment of a few companies of light cavalry under the French Emperor's standard – was not the indemnity she had promised herself for her surrender, or rather her capture. The restoration of Poland as a state and nation was the only boon which could either satisfy her aspirations or justify her in her own eyes. Incapable of feigning what she could not feel, or of simulating a passion from which her modesty recoiled, she had none of the qualities by which a more wily mistress might have played upon her lover. She was not even astute enough to conceal the true motive of her compliance from him. Every evening she brought the conversation round to the one subject that filled her mind, and always to be met with vague hopes and promises of action in the future, that future in which she now began to foresee a long-drawn agony of indefinite duration.

Not that she suffered from any social degradation among her compatriots. With the one exception of her husband, from whom she had separated, all the members of her former circle were assiduous in a homage offered, not to the favorite, but to the victim, for her sufferings were known to all, and inspired universal pity and respect. Her husband's two sisters, Princess Jablonowska and Princess Birginska, had constituted themselves her chaperons. Had she been so minded, she might have occupied the first place in society at Warsaw, and any other woman would have exercised all but sovereign powers. Such an one would have made enemies; whereas she, modest, retiring, and unpretentious, was neither feared nor hated, and in default of flattery, tasted sympathy.

Her position, indeed, created no scandal in a society where the simplicity of Oriental polygamy was complicated only by the elegant scepticism borrowed from Versailles, where the moral lessons of Catherine the Great had been learnt and assimilated, and where divorce readily gave legal and even religious sanction to extra-conjugal fancies.

There was not one among the great Polish nobles of the day without either an acknowledged mistress, who took her place in the same society with his wife, or some two or three Georgians in his countryhouse.

In the eyes of these nobles, Napoleon was a peculiarly chaste sovereign, for he made war, and brought no harem in his train; he had disregarded all the women who would gladly have accepted his advances; he had desired but one among them, and even for this one he had been content to wait until she came to him of her own free will.

Their own conduct in the matter seemed to them not only natural, but becoming. A companion was necessary for the Emperor's happiness when he took up his residence in Warsaw, and it was their business to provide him with the woman who pleased him best.

Fortunately for them, this woman happened to be one in a thousand. Simple, sincere, modest, disinterested, animated in all she did by a passionate love for her country, capable of inspiring both ardent passion and lasting affection, a type of all that was most lovable and generous in her nation.

She would be no temporary mistress to Napoleon, but a kind of supplementary wife, who, though she would not share the splendours of his throne nor the dignities of his crown, would hold an unique position as the ambassadress of her people to the Emperor, *his Polish wife*! She would knit Napoleon's heart to the destinies of Poland with a bond which, though as yet intangible, her hand would strengthen by degrees.

This reasoning was by no means extravagant. Almost every evening the national problem was pressed upon him by the woman whose one absorbing thought it had become.

He felt, and often said to her, that she loved, not him, but her country. Far from evading the charge, she frankly admitted its truth, and he, who would have distrusted any woman he suspected of a desire to lead or make use of him, gave his full confidence to the simple girl. He recognized her absolute detachment from the ambitions of ordinary women. He longed to satisfy her! And yet, bankrupt debtor that he was, he could not pay the price she had a right to expect!

" You may rest assured," he would say to her, "that my promise shall be kept. I have already forced Russia to disgorge her portion, the rest must be the work of time. We must be patient; the supreme moment is not yet. Policy is a cord that snaps if strained too tightly. Meanwhile, you will be forming your politicians. How many can you count at the present moment? You are rich in patriots, I allow; every arm is ready to strike a blow for the cause; courage and honor are the very breath of your heroes; but this is not enough. You lack unity of purpose."

No man had ever shown himself more hostile to feminine influence in politics. Yet strange to say, he returned to these subjects incessantly, and almost involuntarily, in his evening interviews with Madame Walewska, discussing schemes for the amelioration of social conditions, the revival of prosperity, and the promotion of some great unanimous movement among the people. Such a movement he deemed indispensable to the future of the nation, even should it prove inimical to the dominant aristocracy.

" You know," he said, "that I love your nation, that my inclinations and political convictions alike point to its redintegration. I am willing to second its efforts and maintain its rights; all I can do for it without prejudice to my own duties and the interests of France I am ready to undertake. But you must remember the great distance that divides us; what I build up today may be destroyed tomorrow. My first duty is to France; I cannot shed French blood in a foreign cause, nor send an army to your aid every time you are threatened."

Often, to the amazement of his companion, he would pass from some weighty speech of this sort to the discussion of society gossip, scandalous anecdotes, family secrets. He liked her to tell him the private history of every one he met. His curiosity was insatiable, and he insisted on the utmost minuteness of detail. It was his method, here as elsewhere when great interests were at stake, of forming an opinion upon the governing class.

From all these trivialities, none of which ever escaped his memory, and in which he showed an interest that astonished his informant, he drew his own conclusions, and she found that she had provided him with a weapon it amused him to use against herself. She protested, indignant at the inferences he drew from her facts; and the quarrel ended in his tapping her on the cheek, and exclaiming, "My dear Marie, you should have been a Spartan woman; you deserve a country of your own."

Loving her as he did, he was naturally much interested in her dress. It was a subject in which he considered himself an authority. "You know I am a connoisseur of costume," he wrote to Savary. Even under the Consulate it was he who always chose the presents sent to sovereigns such as the Queens of Spain or Prussia. No badly dressed woman ever escaped his criticisms at his own Court. Even Josephine, who had accustomed him to the greatest luxury, the most perfect elegance, the utmost refinement of taste, was not always exempted. He had a special dislike to dark dresses, and Madame Walewska observed the utmost simplicity in her attire, always wearing either white, black, or grey, a fancy which caused him much annoyance. "A Polish woman," she said in answer to his remonstrances, "must wear mourning for her country. When that is restored to life by you, I will wear nothing but rose-color."

Thus every discussion seemed to lead him back to the one topic. But it neither angered him nor wore out his passion. In a letter of this date to his brother Joseph he writes – "My health has never been so good, nor my material enjoyment so complete." Such confidences are the more significant that they were unusual with him.

Not content with seeing his mistress every evening in private, he insisted on her appearance at every dinner, and every fete he himself attended during his sojourn at Warsaw before the campaign of Eylau. During their presence at such festivities, he conversed with her incessantly through the medium of that secret and silent language he had taught her, in the use of which she had become more expert than Duroc himself. She was able to follow and interpret signs addressed to her alone, and to divine a love-message from the gesture accompanying some animated remark, or grave discussion, some precise enunciation of fact, or solemn pronouncement.

"This surprises you," he said. "But I must fill the great position that has been assigned me worthily. It is my high privilege to lead nations. I was an acorn, but I have become an oak. I stand on an eminence, and far and near I am noted and observed. This position obliges me to play a part not always natural to me, but which I must needs sustain if I would satisfy myself, to say nothing of others. Yet even when I am the oak for all around me, I love to become the acorn for you! And when we are surrounded by a watchful crowd, how can I say – 'Marie, I love you!' Whenever I look at you, I long to say it, but I could not whisper it in your ear without a loss of dignity."

When he made Finckenstein his head-quarters, he insisted on her accompanying him. Her life there was a melancholy one, very much on the lines of that she had led at Walewice with her old husband. Her solitude was only broken by *tete-a-tete* meals with the Emperor, served by a single footman. The slow hours were spent in reading and needlework, her only other distraction being to watch the parade from behind the windowblinds. It was the life of a recluse, subject only to the commands and discretion of the master, without society, pleasure, or vanities. But it was more congenial to her than the brilliant, feverish gaiety of her life at Warsaw.

In her Napoleon realized the dream of woman as he had hoped to find her in Josephine – a woman soft, tender, and submissive, without ambition, apparently without will, a creature all his own, who lived but for him, and who, if she indeed looked for some return from him, desired it in a form so vast and impersonal, that none but the loftiest mind could have conceived it, while her very confidence in his power to grant the boon raised him to the level of the gods.

Such thoughts as these stirred the inmost fibres of his being, and made him in his turn the humblest of suppliants. When he was about to withdraw from Poland, without having realized the dream for which this woman had bartered herself; when she, desperate and disillusioned, after a final appeal to him to restore her country, refused to follow him to Paris, and declared her intention of retiring into some solitude, there to await in prayer and tears the fulfilment of his broken vows, he answered her in these words – "I know that you can live without me. I know that you have never given me your heart. But you are gentle and compassionate, your heart is so pure, so noble! Can you indeed deprive me of a few minutes of happiness each day by your side? You alone can give me such moments; and yet men call me the most favored of human beings!" He smiled so sadly and bitterly that her heart swelled with a strange pity for this master of the world, and she promised to come to Paris.

She arrived at the beginning of 1808. Henceforward this mysterious *liaison*, interrupted, no doubt, by occasional infidelities on Napoleon's part, that left his genuine passion unshaken, was established on so strange a footing that, were not the proofs we hold irrefutable, and the chain of evidence forged by the collation of dates and details unconsciously furnished by a variety of witnesses complete, we should not dare to vouch for a series of facts apparently unknown to the highest contemporary authorities.

From these authorities we learn, however, that Madame Walewska went to Vienna during the campaign of 1809, that a luxurious house was prepared for her close to the Palace of Schonbrunn, where she became *enceinte*, and that after the Peace of Vienna she returned to Walewice, and was there duly delivered of a son, Alexander-Florian-Joseph-Colonna Walewska, on May 4, 1810. In the light of more recent knowledge, it is not unreasonable to suppose that Napoleon's vacillation on some points in his negotiations with Austria, and his irresolution touching the fate of Poland, may have been due to the presence of her to whom he had promised the restoration of her country.

In no contemporary record do we find any mention of Madame Walewska's return to Paris in 1810, with her sister-in-law, the Princess Jablonowska, and her infant son. She lived in a pretty house in the Chaussée d'Antin, first at No. 2, Rue du Houssaye, then at 48, Rue de la Victoire. Every morning a messenger from the Emperor attended to receive her orders for the day. Boxes at all the theatres were placed at her disposal, and all the museums were open to her. Corvisart looked after her health; and Duroc was specially charged to gratify all her wishes, and make her outward life as varied and agreeable as possible.

We may give one slight but significant instance of her power. At Spa, a young Englishman, Mr. S_, had made some joke of very questionable taste at the expense of the Princess Jablonowska. On their return, the Princess invited him to accompany Madame Walewska and herself to the Artillery Museum. The party paused in the hall devoted to ancient armour, before Joan of Arc's suit of mail, and as Mr. S_ was gazing at it, the heroine suddenly extended her arms, seized the young Englishman, and pressed him to her breast. Half suffocated, he struggled, gasped, and begged for mercy. But Joan declined to release him until Madame Walewska gave the order. Bearing in mind Napoleon's extreme jealousy of any interference with his museums, the incident is a conclusive proof of exceptional privileges.

Whenever he could escape, the Emperor came to snatch a few minutes of her society, or sent for her and her son, on whom he conferred the title of Count of the Empire immediately after their arrival in Paris. None but a few Poles among the society of the day seem to have had the slightest suspicion as to their relations. Madame Walewska indeed lived in the utmost retirement, receiving only her compatriots. Her manners were perfect, her mode of life modest and unpretentious, her conduct very reserved. When she went to take the waters at Spa, she was accompanied by her sisters-in-law. She spent the summer in the Chateau de Bretigny, a house rented by her sister-in-law at Mons-sur-Orge, the property of the Duchesse de Richelieu, nor could she ever be induced to leave it. It was her constant endeavour to hide what others were proud to proclaim.

The modest country-house was her world, and she rarely quitted it. Repeated invitations from Josephine obliged her occasionally to appear at Malmaison with her son, whom the Empress loaded with toys and trinkets; but she seems to have held aloof from habitual intercourse with the Imperial Court until 1813. Two *full dress toilettes* figure in her accounts for the first time that year, one a black velvet gown with a *cherusque* of tulle embroidered in gold; the other a costume of white tulle with a *cherusque* and a feathered turban.

Hitherto, though her dress-bills show her to have been fairly lavish in her expenditure, her evening dresses from Leroy alone amounting to some three thousand francs a quarter, she had had no Court dress. She had retained her preference for white, and for pale tints somewhat suggestive of mourning. Thus, she ordered dresses of lilac silk, of white tulle with three rows of acacia, of white tulle powdered with rose-petals; or gowns of blue and white, her national colors; a dress of shot taffetas, in blue and white; a dress of blue tulle, trimmed with white heather and daisies.

Napoleon did not require her presence at Court to keep her in his mind. We need but quote a letter written at Nogent on February 8, 1814, in all the throes of the French campaign, on the morrow of Brienne, the eve of Champaubert. He had desired his treasurer, Monsieur de la Bouillerie, to arrange for a reversion of the property settled on young Walewski to his mother, in the event of the young Count's death. Agitated by the thought that the formalities had not yet been concluded, he wrote the following note to La Bouillerie with his own hand:

> *I have received your letter relative to young Walewski. I give you a free hand in the matter. Do what is best, but do it at once. I am deeply interested in the boy, and after him, in his mother.*
>
> *"N."*
>
> *Nogent, February 8.*

Of all this she knew nothing, for no one was ever more purely disinterested than she. In those last days at Fontainebleau, when, abandoned by all, the Emperor attempted to find in death the refuge fate denied to him, she waited all night in an ante-room, expecting to be summoned. Absorbed in bitter thoughts, and exhausted by the physical crisis through which he had just passed, the Emperor never thought of asking for her till an hour after she had left. "Poor woman," he exclaimed; "she will think herself forgotten!"

He misjudged her. A few months later, towards the end of August, 1814, accompanied by her son, her sister, and her brother, Colonel Laczinski, she landed at Elba, and spent a day with the Emperor in the Hermitage of La Marciana. In 1815, when she heard of Napoleon's return to Paris, she hastened to welcome him, and we find her conspicuous among those women whose devotion survived his happier fortunes, and who gathered round him at the Elysée and at Malmaison.

After the banishment to St. Helena, however, she considered herself free. M. Walewski had died in 1814, and in 1816 she married General Count d'Ornano at Liège, where he had sought an asylum after the second restoration of the Bourbons. D'Ornano was a cousin of the Emperor's, formerly a colonel in the Dragoons of the Guard, and one of the most distinguished officers of the Grand Army. This marriage moved the captive of St. Helena deeply. "The Emperor," said one of his companions, "was greatly attached to Madame Walewska, and it was not in his nature to suffer any one he loved to love any but himself." The poor woman's happiness was very brief. She was confined at Liège, on June 9, 1817. Permission to come back to Paris having been obtained for her husband, she returned thither, and died in her house in the Rue de la Victoire on December 15, 1817.

The brilliant career of her son, of whom Napoleon wrote in his will: "I wish Alexander Walewski to devote himself to the service of France in the army," is a matter of history. His course as soldier, writer, diplomatist, and statesman is too intimately connected with contemporary history to call for comment, and too recent to be made the subject of judicial appreciation.

Chapter 16
The Divorce

THE death of Napoleon-Charles had destroyed Napoleon's plans for the succession; the birth of Léon had made it evident that he might hope for a direct heir; and his passion for Madame Walewska had shaken his affection for Josephine. It is uncertain whether any overt discussion of a possible alliance with a Russian Grand Duchess took place at Tilsit; but immediately after the Emperor's return, the first steps were taken in the matter of the divorce. It was felt that a great advance had been made when the Emperor agreed to consider the idea; but a long interval seemed likely to elapse between its inception and execution! In matters where his mind alone was engaged, he suffered no delay when once his resolution had been formed, but proceeded to act directly upon it. In this case, his judgment indeed perceived all the evil consequences of Josephine's sterility, and the advantages to be looked for from a divorce and a second marriage, but his heart cried out against his policy. Hence the delays and hesitations of two full years, from July, 1807 to October, 1809, and those strange alternations of attitude, obviously due, not to diplomacy, but to love.

Before Napoleon could steel himself to repudiate the woman to whom he was bound by a companionship of ten years, by a passionate attachment, by his ardour of character, his vanity even, – a woman he had loved sufficiently to let her share his throne, a woman whose relatives, to say nothing of herself, he had often preferred over his own flesh and blood – the tie between them was strained to breaking point, and divorce was not only prudent, but necessary. He could not at first agree to sacrifice the companion whose merits grew in his sight in proportion to his own feeling of guilt towards her. "She will not resist; she will die." He began to think that his own fortunes depended on her and on her star.

But it was not an idle superstition that restrained him, nor even a dread of the judgment of his former companions in arms, of the army and of the nation, should he repudiate the woman he had crowned with his own hand only two short years before. He gave little thought to public opinion, but he listened to his own heart, and hesitated. Weary of his vacillations, some of his most trusted agents, such as Fouché, sought to precipitate matters by adroit insinuations, which they hoped might induce Josephine herself to take the initiative in the impending sacrifice. Napoleon could not deny that this excess of zeal was born of projects he had formed, and perhaps even discussed. But feeling himself vulnerable, he became violent. He repudiated Fouché's action with every mark of anger and contempt, treating him as he had never treated any one, no matter of what condition, in all his life. What! was he the man to yield to pressure from one of his ministers? And did this minister, this ex-policeman, dare to interfere in his domestic life, and thrust his hideous face into the nuptial chamber? Josephine took advantage of his momentary rage, and acting on the sage advice of Talleyrand, who for some unknown reason was anxious to thwart Fouché, she went boldly to Napoleon. Lacking courage to declare himself, Napoleon hesitated, temporized, and finally allowed himself to be recaptured.

For a time no more was heard of the lists of marriageable princesses, compiled from almanacs, of the confidential reports of foreign agents, or of the various portraits brought together for comparison. Napoleon seemed "more devoted to his wife than ever, and was constantly in her apartments. Holding her in his arms, he wept over her, and made vows of the most ardent affection." It was in vain that fresh arguments were brought to bear upon him, which seemed for the moment to convince him. The sight of his wife roused all his former feelings, and it was she who, pressing home her advantage, questioned him on the subject, facing the idea of the divorce to all appearances more resolutely than himself. She told him openly that nothing would induce her to take the initiative; if he commanded, she would obey; but the order must come from him. And he had not courage to give it. The consolidation of his power, the establishment of his dynasty, the continuity of his mighty work, depended, as far as human wit could foresee, on the dismissal of a woman; and the "Man of Iron" could not nerve himself to the task!

It may perhaps be asked whether the revival of Napoleon's love for Josephine induced a stricter fidelity than before? By no means. Fidelity was not an essential element in the feeling with which his wife now inspired him. His love was made up of memory, pity, gratitude, and tenderness; desire was but a reminiscence; he had no illusions as to the youth and beauty of its object. When, therefore, Napoleon found younger and lovelier women within reach, and took advantage of his opportunities, his affection for Josephine suffered no decrease. The sojourn at Paris and Fontainebleau, from August to October 1807, witnessed the reign of Madame Gazzani; nor was Madame Gazzani his sole distraction. The purely physical attraction she exercised over Napoleon, by virtue merely of her extraordinary beauty, was not sufficiently absorbing to occupy him for two months. At Fontainebleau it was whispered that he was falling in love with Madame de B_, lady-in-waiting to the Princess Pauline. Madame de B_, whose husband was distantly connected with the Beauharnais, and who owed her appointment to this remote kinship, was one of the most lovely women of the Court. Her rich and luxuriantly developed beauty – she was at this time just twenty-eight – was displayed to great advantage by her unusual height of five feet six inches. There were some who thought her head too small and her features too childish for her large frame; but these cannot have seen her as the queen in a game of chess at the Marescalchi ball. She had a lively wit, no money, and no prejudices. The Emperor remarked her at one of the hunt breakfasts she habitually attended, admired her, and let her know it. He is said to have written to her. Her room was on the groundfloor of the castle, overlooking the garden of Diana and easily accessible by the window to a nocturnal visitor. A raised step in the embrasure exposed the unwary to the risk of a noisy fall, but the lady was gracious, and did her best to facilitate access. She reaped her reward, and her husband, a very old man, simple and credulous in the extreme, chuckled delightedly at the results. "My wife," he remarked one day at a reception, "is a woman of the most extraordinary resource! We are not rich, yet we seem to be, thanks to her good management! She is a perfect treasure!" Her exertions procured him the post of Chamberlain to the last-made king among the Emperor's brothers, and the title of Baron of the Empire, an honor he owed to her own desire for that of baroness. The intrigue, the existence of which has been questioned by some, so well was the secret kept, was dropped after the return from Fontainebleau, and the husband's satisfaction in his domestic economy was somewhat over-cast. He had other grievances. Madame de B_ quarrelled with her princess about a certain brilliant officer; she was struck off the Imperial register, and had to retire to the country, while the officer was ordered to Spain, where he was severely wounded. He returned, however; his cure and the lady's divorce were alike effected, and the story ended in a marriage, the date of which it would be indiscreet to reveal.

In spite of the passing amusements at which we have hinted, of the temporary revival of his passion for Josephine, of the memories that had melted and unnerved him for the moment, Napoleon was not convinced. He had not renounced the idea that haunted and possessed him; his advisers never ceased to urge it upon him; his reason and ambition seconded every such appeal. The future divorce was doubtless at the bottom of his journey to Italy at the close of 1807. One of the points that caused Josephine grave anxiety was the probable fate of her son in the event of a separation. Napoleon had, it was true, made Eugène Viceroy of Italy in 1805; he had married him to the Princess Augusta of Bavaria in 1806, and had conferred on him the title of Son of France. But these honors had never been ratified by a legislative measure; and Eugène's right to transmit the kingdom to his descendants rested only on Napoleon's verbal promise.

The Emperor was anxious to reassure both his wife and the reigning house of Bavaria. He also wished to make some inquiries as to a lady who might prove a suitable match for himself. He is supposed to have sometimes regretted not having married the vice-queen, Princess Augusta, "the most beautiful woman of the 'Circles,' as others had said before him." Would not her sister, Princess Charlotte, be the right wife to choose? Some such project was no doubt in his mind when he summoned the king and queen and the princess to Milan. But he seems to have presently reflected on the unseemliness of becoming the brother-in-law of his stepson. The young lady pleased him less than he had expected. He left her to her strange future, and threw himself into a fresh project, of marriage with a member of his own family.

Surely Lolotte, the little girl he used to lead by the hand through the Consular reception-rooms, and had not now seen for five years, must be grown up, and marriageable by this time. She was Lucien's daughter by his first wife, the Catharine Boyer whom Napoleon loved as a sister, though she was only the daughter of a humble innkeeper of St. Maximin du Var, and could not even sign her name when she first entered the family. No doubt Lolotte, who, escaping from the guardianship of her aunt Elisa, had left France with her father and step-mother, had espoused their cause, and taken up their quarrels. But she was barely fifteen; childish memories might be re-awakened. The Emperor, whose family feeling was so strong that he scrupled to bestow a share in his sovereign dignities on any but a Bonaparte, that all his relations with his brothers seemed to resolve themselves into a series of pardons, and that a reconciliation with Lucien was in his eyes a matter of the highest moment, may have had dreams of grafting his posterity on a stem of his own stock, and founding a purely Bonapartist dynasty. Failing this (for the young girl might prove hostile, he himself might feel scruples, the disparity of age was perhaps too great), how would it be to introduce the Bonapartist element by means of Lolotte into some other reigning house, that of Spain, for instance? The only marriageable girl of his own blood at the moment, she might prove an important card in his future game. He sent for her, and placed her with his mother on probation. But Lolotte's sojourn in Paris was a brief one. She amused her father by her lively accounts of the Court, and seems to have had no suspicion that her correspondence was examined. Napoleon soon decided that Lucien's daughter was impracticable, and sent her back to Italy. There she secured a coronet in default of a sovereign crown. She married Prince Gabrielli in 1815, and lived until 1865.

The journey to Italy had borne little fruit, as far as matrimonial schemes were concerned, but Fouché had again been busy spreading and encouraging rumours of an immediate divorce, nor were his machinations at all affected by the furious letters he received from his absent master. Keen and cunning as he was, he did not understand that the hour was past; the perils of Eylau, and the plot that had been hatched during his absence, may have affected the Emperor's policy for the moment; but the impression had not been deep enough to last, or to suggest the necessity of leaving a living representative of himself in Paris the next time he quitted it for a campaign. He might have made up his mind, could a suitable wife have been found at once. But the Russian Grand Duchess was a possibility of the future; the Bavarian scheme had proved abortive; and Austria, who had made overtures in 1805, had now no marriageable daughter to offer. The family marriage remained in reserve; but it might involve endless dangers and difficulties with the Luciens! It would be best to wait!

To this course Napoleon not unwillingly resigned himself during the three months after his return to Paris. His heart was fully occupied with Madame Walewska, who had recently arrived from Poland. His mind was busy with innumerable affairs of State, notably those of Spain, which he was anxious to settle before resuming the negotiations of Tilsit with Alexander. The question of the divorce only recurred to him at intervals, when it caused him the most violent agitation. He felt less capable than ever of coming to a decision, though Talleyrand had now thrown his weight into the scale, and was urging him to proceed. His nervous excitement brought on terrible internal spasms. There were times when he would draw down his wife upon his bed, as she stood beside him dressed for some Court function, and weeping over her, declare with sobs and cries that he could not give her up!

It seemed indeed as if she had bewitched him, and held him in bondage by means of some talisman. Though he sometimes complained that she had grown old and lost her beauty, throughout their stay at Marras he treated her with all the tender playfulness of a youthful lover. Who could have suspected any anxiety for the future, or any projects of final rupture, in the midst of such school-boy pranks as those that enlivened their walks on the beach, when, in the presence of the mounted escort, he chased Josephine along the shore, and pushed her into the water, with peals of laughter, or when, snatching up the shoes she dropped in her haste, he threw them away, and made her get into the carriage without them, that he might the better see and feel the feet he so greatly admired?

At other times he was touched rather by her moral than her physical graces. Josephine had never shown a finer tact, a more delicate insight, than in this journey to Bayonne. Never had she been of greater service to him, and never had she displayed her social talents to better advantage.

She seemed in her element in the strange meeting with the Spanish sovereigns, showing an instinctive skill, intelligence, and good breeding under difficult conditions then, as throughout their triumphal progress through the southern and western provinces. The heat was so intense that they were obliged to travel by night, to enjoy a little fresh air. Each halt was the signal for a fresh fete, exactly like the last, and no less tedious, and for receptions and presentations without end, which oppressed him more and more with the satiety of ovation. She, however, was always in her place, a gracious smile on her lips, in spite of headaches and discomforts, always punctual and exact, always ready with the right word, the appropriate gesture; unsurpassed in the art of unfastening jewels she had been careful to deck herself with for the occasion, and presenting them to the matrons or young girls she had been told to distinguish, with a grace that transformed a prosaic official recognition into a friendly personal gift. She charmed all who approached her by the interest she seemed to take in them and their affairs, and delighted all the mothers by her sympathetic questions about their children and households. He could not but recognize in her the complement of himself, a creature born to temper his dominant might by her caressing softness, to win the heart, while he inflamed the imagination.

And yet, fully alive as he had been to Josephine's charm throughout these four months (April to August), when he was entirely faithful to her, with the exception of a trivial lapse in the case of Mademoiselle Guillebeau, the idea of the divorce came back to him on his return, and no doubt had a good deal to do with his journey to Erfurt. He took Talleyrand with him, with instructions to give Alexander a hint that he was disposed to share his throne with one of the grand duchesses. But Talleyrand, instead of forwarding his master's interests, unblushingly betrayed him, suggesting to the Czar the means by which to evade Napoleon's request, pointing out the way to a fresh coalition against France, and laying the train for the war of 1809.

After the meeting at Erfurt, Napoleon set out in all haste for Paris and the Spanish frontier. Trusting to Alexander's ambiguities and half promises, he thought the Russian marriage might be accomplished as soon as he had put down the Spanish revolt. It proved a formidable insurrection. The two months he had counted upon to restore order prolonged themselves into three, which brought him only barren victories, discounted by plots against him among his own kinsfolk in Paris, the attitude of Austria, who was once more arming herself for the fray, the crusade of revolt preached by the archdukes to the German populace, and the successful attempts of the secret societies to fan the flame of the Holy War. At last he started at full speed for Benavente, spurring his tired horses from stage to stage, and riding as indefatigably as one of his own pages. After a sojourn of barely three months in Paris, during which he unmasked a traitor or two, put his own affairs in order, organized an army and despatched it to the Danube, he set out to meet the Austrian attack, the Archduke Charles having invaded the territory of the Confederation.

When at last he drew rein at Schonbrunn, after a breathless course of nearly seventeen months, and allowed himself to reflect calmly, the imperative necessity of the divorce became clear to him. It was not only that the question of the succession had become a pressing one, though the birth of a son would at least have put an end to the dark intrigues of the Murats; he further felt the importance of leaving some representative of himself in Paris, round whom his friends might rally in such an event as an English invasion, or a Legitimist rising. Josephine was not with him, to work upon his senses by the remembrance of youthful passion, to touch his heart with the thought of a sweet companionship, or to alarm his imagination with superstitious fears of a future from which the influences of her star should be withdrawn. Another woman, more timid and yielding, and no less amiable, younger and lovelier than Josephine, even as he had first known her, had not only realized his dreams of gentle and discreet affection, but of paternity. The child she was about to bear was unquestionably his own. No such doubts as had crossed his mind in the case of Eléonore were possible here. He knew how complete had been her self-surrender at Warsaw; he knew every detail of the secluded life she had led for two years past. He himself had prepared her prison at Schonbrunn, and was well assured of its security.

He would hesitate no longer! The struggle that had disturbed his peace and wrung his heart for two long years was at an end! Those days and nights of doubt and anguish, in which he had revolved every possible alternative his fertile brain could suggest, had taught him the necessity of the sacrifice. Such expedients as the adoption of a natural son of his own, a simulation of pregnancy on the part of Josephine, the settlement of the succession on another of Hortense's children, had all been duly weighed and dismissed. There was, in truth, but one course by which the consolidation and stability of the Empire could be assured, and this he had come to recognize as the one clearly marked out for him. Anxious to save himself and Josephine useless emotion, and to secure himself against further weakness and hesitation, he sent orders from Schonbrunn to the architect at Fontainebleau, that the communication between the Empress's apartments and his own should be closed. And when Josephine arrived to join him there – late for the first time in her life – she found him closeted with his ministers, the door locked against her. He allowed no opportunity for private conference and explanations; she never saw him but in the presence of others. Hints and suggestions were conveyed by means of intermediaries; and the situation was discussed with the few who were fully in the Emperor's confidence. He felt the need of some intervention from a third person in the final struggle, and after invoking the help of Hortense, who declined to act, he summoned Eugène from Italy. As soon as it was known that the Viceroy had started for Paris, Napoleon felt that the supreme moment could no longer be delayed, and he arranged for a private interview, in which he announced his resolution to the Empress. She had expected his decision not only since 1807, but for many years. And now the blow had fallen which all her skill had been powerless to avert, the dread of which had poisoned all her married life. She was now face to face with the terror that had threatened her after Bonaparte's return from Egypt, which had tormented her afresh when he became Consul, when he was proclaimed Emperor, at every epoch of her life when Fortune seemed to be heaping new gifts upon her. And this time she felt herself powerless. There was no remedy, no way of escape. She fell back upon swoons and tears, but rather as expedients by which something might be done to improve her position than with any hope of melting the Emperor. She demanded a settlement for her son, definite promises and documents. For herself she first stipulated that she should not be compelled to quit Paris; then that her debts should be paid; then that she should be allowed to retain the rank and privileges of Empress, and finally, that she should have plenty of money. Everything she asked was promptly granted. The Elysée was assigned her for her town residence, Malmaison for her country house, Navarre for a hunting-box. An income of three million francs was settled upon her. Her household was arranged on the same scale as before. She retained the title, armorial bearings, guards, escort, and all the external tokens of sovereignty, occupying a place in the State so strange and unique in modern history that we must turn to Rome or Byzantium for its parallel.

But money, palaces, titles, were as nothing to Napoleon; he gave her the higher tribute of his tears. The first days of the separation he spent at Trianon, vainly attempting to forget his sorrow in the excitement of play. He was haunted by a feverish anxiety concerning his wife, and the road to Malmaison was enlivened by constant relays of pages, equerries, chamberlains, and State officials, galloping backwards and forwards in hot haste to bring him the latest bulletins. He despatched letter after letter, with all the assiduity of an uneasy lover, sent daily visitors to observe and report upon her state, and eagerly devoured every detail of her life and surroundings. No deference, no attention, no graceful act of recognition, seemed adequate to express his contrition. He implored her to summon all her resolution to her aid, to accept the inevitable, to make the best of her new position, and as far as possible to spare him the misery of knowing her unhappy by his act.

When, however, he visited her himself at Malmaison, he never embraced her, nor did he ever enter her private apartments, for he wished it to be evident both to Josephine and the world that all was over between them. Such conduct was yet another token of his delicate consideration for her. None, he resolved, should have any grounds for the suspicion that his wife of yesterday might become his mistress of to-morrow. Or it may be that he was not sure, even now, of his own self-control. And if we admit this view of the case, it bears witness to something more vital than his respect for Josephine – to that fervid and lasting love of thirteen years, which, surviving the loss of youth and beauty, had proved itself, in spite of momentary infidelities, one of the most blind and imperious passions ever inspired by woman.

Chapter 17
Marie-Louise

Part I

HITHERTO Napoleon had looked upon every woman he had encountered as his inferior. The social prestige with which his fancy had invested Josephine at their first meeting ceased to dazzle him after 1806. When the great ladies of the old regime, Montmorencys, Mortemarts, and Lavals, began to frequent his Court, he recognized the true position of the Beauharnais; and acquired a more exact knowledge of social distinctions. None of his mistresses had been women of exalted rank or fashion. He had never been seriously attracted by any such; or if he had, he had soon wearied of them, and abandoned his pursuit.

At the height from which he now surveyed the world, his vanity would have found little satisfaction in any such conquests in France. The woman who should satisfy his ambition must be of a sphere as lofty as his own, the daughter of an Imperial race. This dream too was to be realized. The Emperor of Austria formally craved an alliance, and offered him his eldest daughter, Marie-Louise, in marriage.

This was no spurious entry into the Faubourg St. Germain, as in Josephine's case. It meant enrolment among a race of kings, kinship with a stock unsurpassed in antiquity and historic splendour, the dynasty of Bourbon and Hapsburg-Lorraine. This was the final step in his ascent, raising him (in his own judgment at least) to the level of his predecessors on the throne he had conquered, and even giving him the right to speak of them by titles that would establish a sort of relationship between them and him. He would be justified in speaking of Louis XVI as "my uncle," of Marie Antoinette as "my aunt." For his future wife was niece to the late King and Queen of France both by her father and her mother.

Henceforth, in addressing kings and emperors, he would no longer be reduced to the fraternal formula conventionally used by one sovereign to another. He would be really son-in-law or grandson, cousin or brother-in-law to his peers. The Napoleonic system he had established in the West, and interwoven with the ancient dynasties by the marriages of Eugène, Stéphanie, and Jerome, would now, by his own marriage, be as closely allied to the Austrian rulers as the Bourbon family had been. His dynasty would lose the improvised appearance that was now its chief source of danger, and acquire the royal quarterings which would qualify its revolutionary origin, together with the family attachments which Napoleon considered the only solid and lasting links in the chain of policy.

The marriage satisfied his ambition at every point. But would his spirit of domination brook the pretensions of a woman of such haughty lineage and supreme rank? Would not birth and instinct alike have taught her her own importance, given her an overweening love of power and prominence, and imbued her with that sense of infallibility, the attribute of princes born in the purple, which raises them in their own estimation above their fellow-mortals?

By a strangely fortunate combination of circumstances, the ground seemed to have been specially prepared for him. The young girl destined to be his wife had been trained in the belief that her father's will must be her own in all things. She knew that her future would be subordinated to the interests of her house, that her person would form an item in some treaty, and she had been so educated as to insure her acceptance of any husband imposed on her by political exigencies without repugnance.

Such was the part for which she had been trained from her earliest years.

She had been taught many languages – German, English, Turkish, Bohemian, Spanish, Italian, French, and even Latin, for it was impossible to say where her lot might be cast. But the richer her vocabulary, the more extensive her machinery for expressing ideas, the fewer ideas she had to express! A wise provision, both of nature and of her teachers!

Much care had been bestowed on accomplishments such as music and drawing, which afford dignified and suitable occupation for idle princesses wherever fate may place them.

She had been instructed in the elements of religious knowledge, and trained to a minute observance of outward forms, but all discussion of disputed points of dogma had been avoided, for the husband of the future might not improbably be a schismatic.

Her moral training had been based mainly on a system of elaborate mystification. The Archduchess was kept in ignorance of such facts as duality of sex in nature. With an ingenuity only possible to casuists of the great Spanish school, her teachers had safeguarded her innocence by refinements of prudery that verged on the obscene. The poultry-yards of the palace were stocked with hens, among which no cocks were allowed to intrude. Hen-canaries only were to be found in the cages, and only she-dogs were admitted to the Archduchess's apartments. All the books – and such books! – were expurgated by the aid of a pair of scissors. Pages, lines, and even words were cut out bodily, the operators never apparently considering that the curiosity of Archduchesses might be aroused by these mystical *lacunae*. A governess, an ayah, and lastly, a headmistress, successively held all speculation in check. The latter superintended the Princess's surroundings, was present at her lessons, directed her amusements, and overlooked servants and teachers. She never left her charge day or night. The post being an important one, and of some weight from the political point of view, its occupant changed with the ministry. Marie-Louise had five head-governesses in eighteen years; but her education was regulated by rules so strict and severe, that its course was little affected by such mutations.

Her amusements were those of a nun – flowers to cultivate, birds to tend, sometimes an *al fresco* meal with her governess's daughter. Her other distractions were visits to her old uncles, who occupied their leisure with music and painting, and with whom she was on terms of pleasant, and very homely intimacy and affection. No smart dresses, no jewels, no participation in Court ceremonial, save an occasional journey when a Diet was to be held. The events of greatest interest in Marie-Louise's career hitherto had been her flights before the French invaders. Discipline was relaxed on these occasions, and punishments fell into abeyance.

Napoleon's bride was not a woman, but a child, brought up under a system so severe, narrow, and uniform, that any discipline would appear mild to her in comparison, and the simplest pleasure a novelty.

But in this very severity there was danger. Might it not be expected that nature, so long repressed, would take its revenge? The education of Marie-Louise had been the education of Marie-Therese's daughters; its results might be studied in the conduct of Marie-Antoinette at Versailles, of Marie-Caroline at Naples, of Marie-Amélie at Parma! Napoleon admitted the facts; but he concluded that the husbands of these princesses had proved unequal to circumstances. He himself laid his account far otherwise. The school-girl about to be entrusted to him would simply pass from the convent of Schonbrunn or Laxenburg to the convent of the Tuileries or St. Cloud. The only new element would be a husband. Her life would be governed by the same inflexible rules, the same rigid surveillance. She would be allowed no liberty in the choice of friends, nor in the selection of books; no male acquaintances or visitors whatever; the ayah was to be replaced by a lady-in-waiting, and four "red women," two in the Empress's apartments, and two outside the door, were to keep unceasing watch, like sentinels in the presence of the enemy.

In his character of husband he would be obliged to enlighten his wife on subjects her whole education had tended to keep from her knowledge, but he determined to replace the ignorance he must needs destroy, by material precautions. No man, no matter what his rank or station, should be allowed to spend an instant alone with the Empress.

The elaborate etiquette of the Court of Louis XIV, which Louis XV's indifference and Louis XVI's weakness had suffered to fall into abeyance, was revived in all its rigour around Marie-Louise. But where royalty masked its distrust in the guise of traditional honors, employing the greatest ladies of the land to watch their Queen under color of keeping her company, Napoleon stamped his precautions with a quasi-military character by entrusting their execution to the widows and sisters of soldiers.

He was not jealous, for the woman whose virtue he thus safeguarded was unknown to him. But he determined to prevent the possibility of catastrophe. "Adultery is a matter of opportunity," he declared to the State Council, and he was convinced, perhaps from his personal experience, that private interviews between a man and a woman were rarely innocent in character. Such was his distrust of women, that the Oriental system must have thoroughly approved itself to him. But as public opinion in the West forbade him to lock his wife up in a harem, he substituted the "red women" for eunuchs, and etiquette for bars and gratings. Her palace was a prison in all but the name. It is true that he tried to soften its rigours by all the material pleasures a woman could desire, delights very much akin, indeed, to those a sultan bestows on a favorite odalisque.

At Vienna Marie-Louise had known nothing of fine dresses, exquisite lace, rare shawls, and dainty linen; in Paris all the costliest and most novel productions of French taste were lavished upon her, on the sole condition that no salesman approached her in person, and that all negotiations with such persons were carried out by her Mistress of the Wardrobe. Napoleon gave her a foretaste of luxury in the trousseau he despatched to her before her marriage, each article of which was examined by him, and packed under his supervision.

It included such items as twelve dozen chemises of fine cambric trimmed with embroidery and lace, at 19,386 francs; twenty-four dozen handkerchiefs at 10,704 francs; twenty-four bed-jackets at 9,060 francs; thirty-six petticoats at 6,354 francs; eighty night-caps at 5,652 francs; besides fichus, dressing-gowns, pin-cushions, towels, and chamber-linen of every description, and dresses, one of embroidery at 5000 francs. The linen furnished by Mesdemoiselles Lolive and De Beuvry cost 94,666 francs.

Eighty-one thousand one hundred and ninety francs were spent on lace, the principal pieces of which were an Alencon shawl at 3,200 francs, a dress of English point at 4,500 francs, another at 4,800, and a third at 8000 francs. Sixty-four dresses from Leroy amounted to 126,976 francs, and seventeen Cashmere shawls to 39,860 francs. The twelve dozen pairs of stockings ranged in price from 18 to 72 francs. Shoes and slippers of every color and material were made to measurements sent from Vienna, all so small and dainty that Napoleon, poising them admiringly on his finger-tips, declared them to be "of good omen."

All the treasures and rarities of the city that rules fashion and reigns supreme in taste throughout the world were scattered at her feet. The trinkets and ornamental trifles that accompanied the more useful items came to 411,736 francs. Ample means were further provided for the replenishment of this stock. Her dress allowance was 30,000 francs a month – 360,000 francs a year!

The few ornaments she possessed at Vienna were such as a Parisian tradesman's wife would have despised; hair-bracelets, a set of seed-pearls, and one of green pebbles – the few poor relics of a ruined princess. The diamonds she displayed in Paris were such as no sovereign had ever owned. The thirteen diamonds that encircled a miniature of the Emperor cost 600,000 francs; a necklace, 900,000 francs; two pendants, 400,000 francs. A magnificent parure, more costly than any of the above, consisted of a tiara, a comb, a pair of ear-rings, two rows of large single stones, and a girdle. Another parure contained 2,257 brilliants, and 306 rose diamonds. A set of emeralds and brilliants cost 289,865 francs, one of opals and brilliants, 275,953 francs. She had, further, two other parures, of rubies and brilliants, and turquoises and brilliants respectively, and yet another diamond parure from the Crown jewels, the reputed value of which was 3,325,724 francs. Her private apartments at home were severely plain and simple. The rooms prepared for her in France had been newly arranged and decorated under the Emperor's personal supervision, so that nothing might recall their former occupant. In each of the several Imperial residences, the small pieces of furniture in daily use were identical, and occupied as far as possible the same position. Thus, in passing from one to the other, the Empress's habits were not disturbed, and familiar objects stood ready to her hand. Every detail had been planned by the Emperor himself, and so proud was he of the result, that every guest was carried round on a voyage of inspection. At the Tuileries he took the King and Queen of Bavaria down the little dark staircase leading from his study to the Empress's apartments, a staircase so narrow that the King had great difficulty in squeezing his portly person through sideways; on arriving at the bottom, the door of communication was found to be locked, and the three potentates were reduced to facing right-about, and returning in inverse order, a feat by no means easy of accomplishment. At Compiègne he did the honors to the Queen of Westphalia, calling her attention in particular to a bath-room furnished and hung with Indian cashmeres, at a cost of 400,000 francs.

The governesses who had brought her up had been careful to forbid all delicacies, as injurious to the health. The Emperor, however, who knew her to be fond of dainties, like all the Viennese ladies, who love coffee and cakes, made considerable changes in his table to please her, adding made dishes, sweetmeats, fancy cakes, and pastry to the daily bill of fare.

Naturally generous, she had hitherto been unable to make any presents beyond little pieces of work done by herself. She was now able to shower gifts upon her father, her brothers, her sisters, her stepmother, and all her friends, sending them over two hundred thousand francs' worth of Parisian goods every year, dresses, china, books, and small pieces of furniture. The Emperor's indulgence in this respect was signified to her even before her arrival.

She could not say whether she was fond of the theatre, for she had never seen a play. But one of her age and nationality would naturally incline to such amusements. She should enjoy them as often as she pleased, and feast on music and the drama, either by his side at the public theatres, or in private performances at the palaces. What was there, indeed, that he denied her? She had dogs, birds, music-masters, dancing-masters, teachers of embroidery, prints and curiosities from the bric-a-brac shops, everything, in fact, that she desired, if she would but submit to the discipline of the harem, and accept a supervision that was the less irksome to her as she had never been without it from her birth. She was only allowed to emerge for great civil or religious ceremonies, for State balls, visits to the theatre, receptions, hunts, short visits to the country, and royal progresses. On such occasions she had a haughty, almost hieratic air, in her Court dresses and diamonds, guarded by a train of ladies and officers, glittering before the multitude from afar, like an idol.

It was thus he gilded her cage, and decked the walls of her prison, hoping to keep her a child, and amuse her with toys, regulating every detail of her life to enable her to pass without any sense of shock from the state of captive archduchess at Schonbrunn to that of captive Empress at Paris. It was by such means as these that he assured her fidelity, and placed the wife of Caesar above and beyond suspicion. This rigour was the outcome, less of marital jealousy, than of anxiety that there should be no question as to the title of his offspring. He was preparing for the part of founder of a great dynasty. The woman he placed under the ward of the four red sentinels had been set apart for a special, an unique function. She was to bear him a son. All his precautions were intended to demonstrate the legitimacy of the dynastic germ which it was to be her mission to develop. Napoleon's line of argument was perfectly logical; it recognized the true basis of the monarchical dogma.

He had no doubt that Marie-Louise would become a mother. He had made the most careful inquiries as to her health. She was vigorous and well-developed, and the family tradition was highly encouraging. Her mother had borne thirteen children, her great-grandmother twenty-six. On his own part, he felt equal confidence. He could hardly be deceived in the two experiences that had reassured him, and dissipated his fears. No words can describe the eagerness with which he longed for the advent of her who should secure the continuity of his sway, and give a future to his race!

Would she please him? Would she attract and win him by her personal charms? Her portrait had been sent him from Vienna. It showed him a girl with long fair hair, parted, and looped in two drooping masses over a rather high forehead. The eyes were bright blue, the complexion somewhat injured by small-pox; the nose curved inward at the root, the lips were rather thick, the chin heavy and prominent; her white, and slightly prominent, teeth were set somewhat far apart; she had a fine and very full bust; broad, white shoulders, thin arms, small hands, and exquisite feet. She was tall for a woman, only a trifle shorter than himself. A handsome creature certainly, but without grace, flexibility, or charm. These, however, might be acquired, together with ease and elegance. Her air of hauteur was not displeasing to him; he thought that there was a something imperial in her mien. The point he thought of the highest importance was that the characteristics of her race should be strongly developed in her. When Berthier's aide-de-camp, Lejeune, arrived at Compiègne, preceding the Empress by a day or two, Napoleon sent for the portrait he had received from Vienna, and closely questioned Lejeune, who, fortunately, was an artist as well as a soldier, as to the likeness. Lejeune then produced a sketch of the Empress he had himself made, in profile. Napoleon at once exclaimed "Ah! there's the true Austrian lip!" He then took some medallions of the Hapsburgs from the table where they were lying, compared their profiles with that of the portrait, and showed every sign of delight at the resemblance! Here, indeed, was the wife, the Empress, of whom he had dreamed!

Ever since the negotiations had been concluded, and the dream realized, the Emperor had been consumed with impatience. It was in vain he sought distraction in violent exercise, covering from ten to fifteen leagues daily with his harriers. The one idea took entire possession of him; he talked of nothing else. He expected the preparations for the reception to be finished before they were well begun. A chapel for the religious ceremony was to be prepared in the *Grand Salon* of the Louvre, but it was found difficult to dispose of the huge pictures on the walls. "They can be burnt," remarked the Emperor. He, whose carelessness about his own dress was proverbial, was filled with anxiety as to the effect of his proposed costume. He ordered a Court suit from Mural's tailor, Léger, so stiff with embroideries that he found it impossible to wear it. He sent for a new bootmaker; he tried to learn to waltz, and made himself sick in the attempt. As Catherine of Westphalia wrote to her father – "He behaves in a fashion neither you nor I could have imagined possible."

His impatience increased as the bridal train traversed Germany and entered France. He longed to possess the woman, or, rather, all she represented. To each of the towns in which Marie-Louise halted, according to an itinerary he had himself drawn up, he sent pages, equerries, and chamberlains, with letters, flowers, and game killed by his own hand. From each he expected bulletins and despatches, letters from the Empress herself, from Berthier, from his sister Caroline, whom he had despatched to meet his bride, from ladies-in-waiting, equerries, and prefects! He would have been pleased with the reports of the pages, grooms, and postillions!

At last he could no longer forbear! Marie-Louise slept at Vitry on the 26th March. She was to arrive at Soissons on the 27th; the first meeting with the Emperor was fixed for the following day, and a pavilion had been constructed and decorated for the ceremony. Banquets were prepared. All the towns through which the procession was to pass were astir and expectant. But all such considerations were brushed aside. On the 27th, Napoleon left Soissons with Murat in a downpour of rain, without attendants or escort. He halted in the porch of the church at Courcelles.

At last the great berlin, drawn by eight horses, came in sight. The Emperor hastened to meet it. The equerry on duty announced his approach. Caroline presented him to his bride. Napoleon opened the door, and sprang, wet through as he was, into the carriage beside her. The horses were hastily changed, and the cavalcade set out at full speed, dashing through villages in which the mayors stood ready to receive them, addresses in hand; through gaily decorated towns, in which the splendid banquets ordered by Bausset were left to grow cold. The party arrived dinnerless at Compiègne at nine o'clock in the evening. Cutting short speeches, presentations, and compliments, the Emperor carried off Marie-Louise to his private apartments.

At noon the next day the Emperor breakfasted by the Empress's bedside, waited on by her women. During the day he said to one of his generals – "My friend, marry a German. They are the most charming of all women, sweet, gentle, fresh, and innocent as roses!" He was prepared with his justification, in the event of any demurs as to his having taken the marriage by proxy so seriously, and not having waited for the final ceremonies – "I followed the example of Henri IV." Against such a precedent there was no appeal!

Part II

"I am not afraid of Napoleon," wrote Marie Louise to Metternich, three months after her marriage, "but I begin to think he is afraid of me."

Three months had amply sufficed to dispel the grief and terror which had paralyzed her during the journey from Vienna to Compiègne. Was it possible, on the other hand, that Napoleon should feel any awe of a girl of eighteen, of whom he had so unceremoniously possessed himself at the first moment of her arrival, dispensing with all the prescribed ceremonies of Church and State? Yes; for his action had been the result of a sudden impulse; and it was characteristic of him to mask his real embarrassment and timidity under a show of brutality. It was not so much the woman he desired, as the princess. His desire was born rather of his ambition than of his senses. The impossible, the unattainable, had been brought within his grasp in the person of this woman. And he grasped at it with passionate eagerness, dreading lest, even at the last moment, it might escape him. The impulse was one he had yielded to before, at Warsaw and at Cairo, under very different circumstances, when physical passion had been his sole stimulus.

But a reaction soon declared itself. The woman of whom he had taken possession took possession of him in her turn. The passion which had played so small a part in his earlier feeling for her now ruled him absolutely. He wished to be loved, and dreaded her dislike or her indifference.

No longer satisfied with possession, he longed for affection. He wished his wife to declare to all the world that she was happy, and by his means. One morning at the Tuileries he sent for Metternich, and left him with the Empress. In about an hour he returned. "Well," he asked, smilingly, "have you had a good talk? Has the Empress abused me much? Did she laugh or cry? But I must not ask. These are your secrets." He returned to the subject, however, the next morning, when Metternich declined to be questioned, quoting the Emperor's own words. "I know," said Napoleon, "that the Empress has nothing to complain of. I hope you will tell your master so, and that he will believe your report."

It was not so much the Emperor Francis he wished to reassure by the evidence of witnesses, as himself. He wished to feel convinced that his wife had learnt to love him, that no regrets or misgivings oppressed her, that she was content with what he called her "uneventful life" by his side, and that the domestic happiness he sighed for was secure.

Yet this woman had grown up from her earliest childhood in an atmosphere of hatred to him. When she was six years old, her "Mamma" had told her stories of *Monsignore Bonaparte*, the Corsican – how he had deserted his army, fled from Egypt, and become a Turk. She firmly believed that he beat his ministers, and had killed two of his generals with his own hand. The year immediately preceding her marriage - the year which witnessed the battles of Eckmuhl, Esslingen, and Wagram, and the bombardment of Vienna – she had looked upon as the "last days" foretold in Scripture. Napoleon was the Antichrist of the prophecy. "I should choke with rage," she wrote after Znaim, "if I were forced to live with one of his Marshals." When the divorce was announced she would not for a moment admit the possibility of her own marriage with the Emperor. "Papa is too kind," she said, "to coerce me in a matter of such importance to my happiness." She expressed pity for the unfortunate princess he might choose, "convinced that she herself would not be made the victim of policy." When the news of her betrothal became generally known, she wrote a letter to a friend, in which she begs her to "pray for me," and adds – "I am ready to sacrifice my own happiness for the good of the State." Her consent was asked, but merely as a matter of form. Archduchesses have no opinions but those of their fathers. She was resigned; but none the less, Napoleon seemed to her like some ogre in a fairy tale. Nor was this surprising, when we reflect that she saw in him the embodiment of the revolutionary spirit, the man by whom her country had been four times overthrown and dismembered, who had twice made his triumphal entry into Vienna, who had compelled *His Sacred and Imperial Majesty*, her father, to come to his camp, a suppliant for peace. Every feeling of the aristocrat and the patriot, the princess and the daughter, all that is most sacred in human affection and most susceptible in patrician pride, rose in revolt at his name.

But once married to him, all these impressions seem to have faded. Her education had made her little more than an automaton; her narrow brain could cope with very few ideas at a time, and from the very first, the material side of her nature seems to have asserted itself, dominating the emotional and the reflective. It is not impossible that Napoleon was right in his belief that Marie-Louise's chief objection to her marriage with him had been her distaste for his supposed appearance. "She had been told," he said, "that Berthier exactly resembled me. But she soon confided to me that she noticed a very pleasing difference." Are we then to suppose that all past impressions had been effaced by the fact that she had become his wife, and that personally he was not repugnant to her? Incredible as it may seem, it was probably true of Marie-Louise.

Napoleon's first care, therefore, was to prove himself a devoted husband. He had ceased to share his apartments with Josephine soon after the establishment of the Consulate, excusing himself on the plea of increased work and absorbing occupations, his true motive being to secure his freedom of action. He would have submitted to the restraint, however, for Marie-Louise, had she wished it; but she, brought up in the vast and icy palaces of Vienna, could not endure heat, while he was always chilly, and had fires in his apartments nearly all the summer. Often, when he begged her to visit him in his rooms, she would plead, in her harsh German accent, that they were too hot for her. When, on the other hand, he went down into the Empress's apartments, and ordered a fire, she had it promptly extinguished. As her Majesty was on her own territory here, the "red women" obeyed her, and the shivering Emperor retired. Opportunities were not wanting for infidelities if any such had been in his mind. But if any such took place they were either quite unimportant, or concealed with such care as to leave no trace.

In 1811 he paid some attention to the Princess Aldobrandini Borghese, Mademoiselle de la Rochefoucauld, whom he had married to Pauline's brother-in-law, with a dowry of 800,000 francs, and appointed Lady-in-Waiting to the Empress. But he seems to have felt only a passing admiration for the youth, elegance, and vivacity of the young lady. At least we have no evidences of anything further. He was also thought to have a weakness for the Duchesse de Montebello, another of the Empress's ladies, and a good deal of scandal was circulated in private correspondence about their relations; but here again we have only rumour to go upon, and the Duchess herself seems to have been recalcitrant. The lapses of which he was really guilty at this period were obscure adventures, carefully hidden from the world, which, knowing nothing of them, was unable to gossip about them. During the visit to Normandy, he encountered – perhaps not for the first time – Madame Pellapra, wife of the Receiver-General of Calvados, the Pellapra of the Teste-Cubières lawsuit. They met again at Lyons in 1815, after his escape from Elba, and hostile pamphleteers published the most virulent attacks on "Madame Ventreplat." A passing caprice for a certain Lise B_ at St. Cloud recalls his earlier intrigues with Josephine's readers, though this was of a still less serious character, and went no further than two or three secret interviews. His fidelity was so far authentic that he now made no mystery of the little room at Compiègne, which opened by a secret door on to the corridor where the lady-visitors were bestowed, and communicated by a secret staircase with his apartments.

He went even further than this. Knowing, or supposing, that Marie-Louise might take umbrage at his visits to Malmaison and the Rue de la Victoire, he took care to make the latter so secretly that no gossip on the subject was possible; while the former, which became less and less frequent year by year, as Josephine gave him increasing causes of displeasure, were also planned with the utmost discretion. He desired his household officers never to mention them. "My wife," he said, "might feel hurt."

It may be that his temperament had cooled with advancing years, for he was now over forty. Besides which, his young wife's fresh beauty was very attractive to him. His fidelity is not inexplicable. But his whole course of life was changed. A youth of solitude, poverty, and sadness had left, as it were, an untouched reserve of animal spirits in him, which inclined him to all sorts of noisy pastimes and practical jokes in later life. This tendency effectually did away with the superficial disparity between himself at forty-one and Marie-Louise at eighteen. He was more of a child than she, and had a passion for school-boy pranks. Thus he would ride races with her among the flower-beds of St. Cloud. Sometimes the horse would stumble, throwing his rider, who was up again in a moment, laughing and shouting. She had stipulated for only one indulgence when agreeing to the almost conventual rule of life he had laid down for her, and this was permission to ride, a pastime very much affected by the princesses of Lorraine so soon as they were emancipated from the maternal control. Marie-Antoinette had indulged in the same fancy, to the great scandal of Marie-Thérèse. Napoleon had consented, but he would allow no

one but himself to be riding-master. He himself always placed the
Empress in the saddle; he gave her her first lessons, leading her
horse by the bridle, and running beside her. When his pupil began
to gain confidence, and to get her seat, he had a horse brought
round every morning after breakfast, and not waiting to pull on his
boots, would mount in his silk stockings and trot by his wife's side
up and down the avenue, where grooms were stationed at intervals
of a few yards to guard against accidents. Shouting at the horses to
excite them, he would laugh heartily at the screams she uttered
when they broke into a gallop, often falling himself from the
saddle. In the evenings they spent in private he would start
drawing-room games, which were then very fashionable, and they
played Blind-man's Buff with its innumerable variations, and
games of forfeits of every description. He joined in them all, but
with a certain impatience, declining to undertake the more
onerous parts in some of them that the ladies would fain have
assigned him.

Up to the time of her marriage Marie-Louise possessed but one
social talent, on which she prided herself not a little – the power of
moving her ears without stirring a muscle of her face. It proved a
somewhat insufficient means of amusement, and was neglected in
favor of billiards, of which she became inordinately fond. She often
challenged the Emperor to a match with her, but he was a very
indifferent player, and was obliged to take lessons from one of the
chamberlains before he could compete with her.

His patience and gentleness with her were unvarying, whatever the fancy of the moment might be. Sometimes she insisted on
sketching him in profile, and he was always ready to pose for her,
though it was with the greatest difficulty he could be induced to sit
to any artist. Sometimes she would go to her harpsichord, and play
him German sonatas very little to his taste; or display him her
needlework, the belt or baldric she – or rather Madame Rousseau,
her teacher – had embroidered for him. In all such trifles he
showed himself full of interest and attention, seeking in every
possible way to amuse and cheer his "good Louise Marie," as he
called her. His homely "thees" and "thous" astonished the Court,
where the most rigid etiquette now obtained, the husbands of the
Faubourg St. Germain carefully refraining from any such
unfashionable freedom towards their wives.

Marie-Louise, however, took such familiarities in excellent
part. She soon caught the trick herself, returning her husband's
"thees" and "thous," bestowing pet names on her sisters-in-law,

and calling her mother-in-law "mamma." She nevertheless contrived to make it tacitly understood that she exacted one condition. Her husband must be constantly with her, and always at her disposal; and to this he agreed, not unwillingly.

He whose habits had hitherto been strictly subordinated to his occupations, now found himself forced to reconcile, and often to sacrifice, his occupations to the tastes, wishes, occasionally to the caprices, of his wife. He had been for years in the habit of breakfasting hastily and alone, on a corner of his worktable, at such time as he could best snatch a few minutes from business. Now (for the first two years at least; he emancipated himself after 1811) he sat down with his wife at a fixed hour to a heavy meal, at which the menu comprised soup, three entrées, a roast, two *entremets*, four *hors-d'oeuvre*, and dessert in place of the four little dishes formerly served to him.

When they travelled (they took five State journeys between 1810 and 1812, to Normandy, Belgium, Holland, the Rhine, and Dresden), instead of waiting for the Emperor, as had been Josephine's practice, she invariably kept him waiting for her. She was never ready, either for a hunting-party, a reception, or the theatre, and he kept guard patiently, as he had learnt to do at Fontainebleau, humming a tune, and slashing the gravel with his whip.

She insisted on his remaining by her side, and he remained, though his presence with the army in Spain became a more imperative necessity each day. He made repeated efforts to start. His carriages were ready at the frontier, and there they remained.

His chief delight in hunting had been breathless runs across country at a hand-gallop, which refreshed both brain and body after long-continued mental toil. But now, as she liked to be present at every hunt, and yet would not allow the pastime to interfere with her regular hours, and above all, with her meals, he gave up this form of exercise, and rode at a pace which enabled the carriages to keep up with him, and ensured their return in good time for dinner.

He was not only a faithful but a loving and attentive husband, who missed no opportunity of giving pleasure to his wife. The Oriental magnificence of his offerings is a matter of history. But we lay little stress on such gifts as the set of Brazilian rubies, valued at 400,000 francs, given in place of one she had coveted at 46,000 francs, or the pearl necklace of eight rows, containing altogether 816 pearls, and valued at 500,000 francs, presented to her after the birth of the King of Rome, and afterwards stolen at Blois. Such gifts were to some extent official and Imperial – the homage of the Emperor to the Empress. But we recognize the lover and husband in such souvenirs as the bracelets with dates and names formed of precious stones, the lockets and caskets innumerable on which Napoleon's portrait figured. Marie-Louise herself bore eloquent witness to his tenderness in one of the offerings she made him in return – a miniature of herself, in a setting by Nitol, with the legend, "LOUISE, JE T'AIME," in pearls and gems.

If he had not loved her as he did, would he have been so keenly sensitive to every newspaper phrase or couplet which seemed to represent him in the light of an enamoured Corydon? Every allusion in the public prints which in any way violated his domestic privacy was fiercely resented, and evoked a furious letter to the Minister of Police, designed, not to deny the imputation, but to forbid its discussion.

He was careful to ingratiate himself with his wife by profuse attentions to her family. He was continually making presents of books and engravings to the Emperor Francis; of toilettes to the Empress Maria-Ludovica of Este; of books, furniture, dresses, arms, and playthings to the young archdukes and archduchesses; all this quite independently of Marie-Louise's gifts, waggon-loads of which were perpetually on the road from Paris to Vienna. On one occasion alone, after the meeting at Dresden, when the Empress of Austria literally stripped her step-daughter's wardrobes, the Emperor sent the various members of his wife's family a consignment which included eight dressing-cases, one valued at 28,000 francs, two gold watches, nine shawls, thirty-one dresses in the piece, twenty-six ready-made dresses, thirty hats, turbans, and caps – goods the value of which amounted altogether to 122,642 francs.

At Court, the most flattering marks of distinction were lavished on the Grand Duke of Wurtemburg, his wife's uncle, and on Metternich, Schwartzenburg, and every one of Austrian birth. He "gorged them with diamonds," as he himself said.

But perhaps the strongest proof of his love lay in the fact that, jealous as he was, he never ventured to find fault. His distrust had by no means abated, in spite of the lapse of time, his wife's evident affection for him, and the precautions, no less stringent than at first, by which he sought to assure himself of her fidelity. When the outbreak of the war with Russia forced him from her side, every post brought him a circumstantial report of her drives and walks, the visitors she had received during the day, and the manner in which she had spent the evening. These reports were drawn up by a subordinate official of the household, who used kitchen-paper to write upon, and spelt Ville d'Avray, *Vildavre*. Always punctilious in such matters, he himself carefully annotated these rambling communications by notes of interrogation and reminder on the flimsy margins. It was characteristic of the man, and we could have no better evidence, not so much of his jealousy, as of his continued interest. But if any action of his wife's displeased him, he had not courage to rebuke her; on such occasions he cast about for an intermediary. One day at St. Cloud she allowed the Duchesse de Montebello, who was walking with her in the park, to present one of her relatives. The next morning the Emperor told the Austrian ambassador of the incident. Metternich, apologizing for his own obtuseness, explained that he failed to see the point of this confidence. "I want you," said Napoleon, "to remonstrate with the Empress." Metternich demurred, but the Emperor insisted. "The Empress is young," he said; "she might think me inclined to play the tyrant. A hint will come better from you than from me."

Nor was this all. If Napoleon had been a faithful and fervent worshipper of any one divinity, that divinity was Power – the only mistress to whom he had given absolute allegiance. He had shown himself prompt to resent the slightest encroachment on his prerogative. Josephine had been punished for some imprudent speech on political matters by the most scathing disclaimer in the *Moniteur*; neither to his brothers, his oldest counsellors, nor his most intimate friends had he ever been induced to grant a semblance of delegated authority. But in 1813, the hour of his Empire's greatest peril, he consented to share his power with his wife, whom he formally appointed Regent in his absence – Empress, Queen, and Regent!

Her responsibility, it may be urged, was apparent rather than actual; no decision of moment was made without his sanction. It may be that he had had a presentiment of disaster in Russia, had faced the possibility of his own defeat, and on his return, when preparing for dangers even greater than those already encountered, had recognized the necessity of securing the future of his crown. But even so, Marie-Louise was the one human being he admitted to a share in his power. Henceforth, all State decrees were issued by the Empress, in the Emperor's name. Pardons were granted, appointments ratified, and proclamations signed by the

Empress. The bulletins, in which the master's voice had echoed throughout his dominions from 1800 onwards, announcing his victories, distributing praises, and giving an account of his conquests, ceased to appear. By the new formula, "Her Majesty, the Empress, Queen, and Regent, received such and such news from the army; "the conscripts of the year of doom were enrolled in her name, and went by the nickname of "the Marie-Louises."

Meanwhile the structure of government was shaken to its very foundations by multiplied weaknesses, defections, and treacheries. He was no longer there to steady it. His very name had disappeared. That of Marie-Louise inspired no awe, and conveyed nothing to the ear of the nation. But Napoleon's confidence remained unshaken. His wife had more knowledge of his policy than Cambacérès and all the Bonapartes combined. The more imminent the catastrophe, the more deadly the peril, the more persuaded was he that she, and she alone, would save the situation.

And by a last irony of fate, chance made her the instrument of the supreme disaster! She cannot be held responsible for her departure from Paris, the capitulation, and all that followed. But a letter from Napoleon to her, not in cypher, described the supreme movement he proposed to attempt against the allies. The letter fell into the hands of Blucher's scouts, and Blucher hastened to lay it, unsealed, "at the feet of the august daughter of his Imperial Majesty, the Emperor of Austria."

Chapter 18
Elba

WAS it love alone which moved Napoleon to such a display of confidence and affection towards his wife, or had policy any part in his conduct? Did he imagine that the Austrian Emperor would be turned aside from his purpose when he encountered his daughter and his grandson, and would hold his hand, powerless to strike the threatened blow? By appointing the Empress to the Regency, did he hope to prepare the ground for an act of personal abdication, whereby his dynasty at least might be saved in the event of irreparable disaster? And did he dream that the sovereigns of Europe, finding his throne in the possession of a distinguished member of their own caste, would hesitate to overthrow it, would accept and confirm the substitution he had himself effected, and instead of driving out his son, would make it their common interest to protect his rights?

If we accept such hypotheses, we shall be forced to conclude that Napoleon despaired of his own fortunes so early as April, 1813, before the battle of Lutzen, before that first campaign, in which he gave evidences so numerous and striking of his continued faith in his star. It may, however, be readily admitted that he had occasional misgivings in connection with the Austrian alliance, that he looked upon Marie-Louise as a pledge of national friendship, and that he relied on the good faith of Francis II – his good faith less as Emperor than as his father-in-law.

It would have required a kindred baseness, of which no Frenchman of the revolutionary era – Talleyrand and Fouché hardly excepted – was capable, to divine the plot hatched against Napoleon by the aristocrats of Europe, and to recognize in the young girl they had thrown into his arms the decoy of an oligarchic coalition. The conception and execution of such a scheme, which brought the concentrated venom of all the ancient courts of Europe into play about his nuptial bed, could have emanated only from those depths of corruption peculiar to the patrician society of the time – a caste unscrupulous by tradition and education, obedient to no law, human or divine, beyond that of self-interest, and careless by what means a coveted end was attained; above all, conscious of no dishonor when they perverted love, the most sacred of human emotions, into an ambush for their enemy, for this was one of the stratagems most approved among them. In this case a wife, and not a mistress, had been required. They had given her. What matter if, when the avenging car crushed the blasphemer who had laid a sacrilegious hand on the ark, the wheels should rend the quivering flesh and blonde tresses of an Austrian archduchess? Should she survive the ordeal, her future should be cared for; she would be consoled! Should she die, so much the worse for her! Such a game was not to be played without a stake and here the stake was only a woman!

Napoleon seems to have had no suspicion of treachery. He would never suffer the hypothesis that his wife had been in league with his enemies, and he was right, for she had been kept entirely in the dark; and so well fitted was she by nature for her part, that no prompting could have improved her rendering of it. Whether he shrank instinctively from discussion of the subject, or was reluctant to recognize the chief cause of his overthrow, it was not till a much later period that Napoleon showed any disposition to connect his second marriage with the events that followed. "It was the abyss," he said at St. Helena, "but they covered it with flowers." He seems, however, to have avoided dwelling on the matter, as if recoiling from the depths of baseness further investigation would reveal. He wished no stigma to attach to his wife or her memory, and sought to exculpate her in the eyes of history, relieving her of all responsibility in the great catastrophe to which his own blind confidence had so largely contributed – a catastrophe which, to the uninitiated, ignorant of its baser causes, has all the vast and fateful simplicity of an Aeschylean tragedy.

Far from visiting his downfall on the woman by whose means he had been overthrown, his love and confidence seemed to increase with his misfortunes, as if to console her for the aggressions of her nation, and the raising of her father's standard against her husband – events she could not but regard as an outrage to herself. Even in this extremity he still preserved some confidence in himself and his fortunes. It was his nature to hope even against hope, and this virtue of great souls has made many days in the fatal campaign of France worthy of record on the same page as the immortal day of Castiglione. Not till the very last would he admit the possibility of the entry of the Allies into Paris, and the capture of the Empress and the King of Rome. When forced to face such a possibility, he dismissed the occupation of the capital as a temporary triumph by which his plan of operations would be very slightly affected. But he could not suffer his wife and son to fall into the hands of the victors. Rather than subject them to such an indignity, he ordered Joseph to abandon Paris, taking away with him all elements of resistance, and all Government officials. By this measure he dealt the death-blow to his own authority, for Talleyrand readily found a pretext for remaining behind. His web had long been ready woven; its meshes enclosed accomplices in every department of the State, among the immediate followers of Joseph and the Empress, in the Prefecture of the Seine, among the police, over all of whom he exercised an influence so mysterious as to suggest some mediaeval compact with the powers of darkness. By their help he accomplished in 1814 the work of treason he had begun at Tilsit.

But the overthrow of Napoleon's Empire by the help of five hundred thousand foreign bayonets was only an item in Talleyrand's program. He had further determined to destroy the ties he himself had chiefly contributed to form between Napoleon and Marie-Louise. The Emperor imagined that the supreme consolation of his wife and son's companionship would still be his in exile. He gave the Empress no positive injunctions to join him at Fontainebleau, believing, no doubt, that her tears would touch the Emperor Francis, and that her personal intercession would best guarantee her own future. But he made up his mind that she would come to him as soon as his establishment was organized; that some independent sovereignty would be assigned her, adjoining the petty principality he had resigned himself – or thought he had resigned himself – to rule. Knowing, as he said, that she had loved "the man rather than the Emperor" in him, he hoped that life might still hold some happiness for them, and for the child they would see growing to manhood beside them.

Marie-Louise was perfectly ready to play the part assigned her in these dreams. She loved her husband, and would gladly have followed him. But for every faithful heart around her, there were a hundred utterly venal and corrupt! She, who from her earliest childhood had never been allowed to think for herself, who had all her life been subjected to the severest discipline, and in whom obedience to some superior will had become second nature, found herself suddenly thrown on her own resources. Her father's hand closed slowly upon her. She struggled at first, her love for her husband getting the better of her filial respect. But Talleyrand determined to crush that love. Among Marie-Louise's ladies was one whom he had secured for his own purposes, and who was notoriously one of the most astute and scheming spirits of her time. She knew neither scruples nor gratitude. In her youth she had been given to amorous adventures of the Italian type, and had retained her passion for intrigue in all its vigour. She was in her element in any diplomatic imbroglio. Unlike the greater number of the Empress's ladies-in-waiting, who had retired to their homes, she had remained at the palace, and finding herself practically alone with her mistress, she promptly opened her batteries. Acting throughout on Talleyrand's instructions, she first hinted, then boldly affirmed, that the Emperor had never loved his wife, and had persistently deceived her. Finding the Empress hard to convince, Madame de Brignole produced the two valets who had just abandoned their master and benefactor at Fontainebleau. These men had been previously schooled by Talleyrand and herself, and were prepared to swear to anything she wished.

At this crisis, Marie-Louise's soft and yielding temperament looked in vain for support and sympathy. There was no one to defend the absent, to breathe courage and resolution into that girlish heart. Marie-Louise's nature was an eminently material one; and her mortification at these disclosures was far greater than her despair at the downfall of her throne. Just as she had allowed herself to be given up, a passive victim, a modern Iphigenia, so now she suffered herself to be recaptured. Policy, as Schwarzenburg declared, should untie the knot which policy had tied. It was not the work of an hour. For nearly a whole year she struggled against the combined forces of Europe, and all the wiles of diplomacy were called into action to get the better of her school-girl heart. Pride, vanity, jealousy, and envy were played upon in turn. But the victory was only accomplished when she had been induced to replace love by love, and the respectable Emperor of Austria had driven his daughter into open concubinage. Then all monarchical Europe applauded, and adultery was rewarded by a kingdom.

Of this final degradation Napoleon knew nothing. At every stage of his melancholy journey he despatched a letter to his wife, just as in those happier days when she was advancing in triumph to the Imperial territory, with peal of bells and salvos of cannon, the army and the people drawn up in array to greet her, the Marshals of the Empire saluting her, sword in hand. He, escorted by the commissaries of the Allies, pursued by the shouts of death and vengeance of a mob subsidized by the Verdets, was now making his way to that island which Europe, still retaining some remnant of her awe, had given up to him, intending some day to snatch it from him. His friend and comrade, the former Elector of Salzburg and Duke of Wurzburg, his guest at Compiègne and the Tuileries, now once more Grand Duke of Tuscany as in 1797, when General Bonaparte sat at his table, was already preparing to dispute the possession of Elba with him.

It would be deeply interesting to compare those stiff and courtly letters, dictated by etiquette to an unknown bride, with this second series. Only two have been published. They are addressed to his "good Louise," his "good Louise Marie." Forgetting his own sufferings, he dwells only on her griefs. He expresses anxiety about her health, a pretext for delaying their reunion having been found in the supposed necessity for a sojourn at Aix, prescribed by Corvisart, who, consciously or not, played into the hands of the Emperor's enemies in this connection. Napoleon shows himself as unsuspicious of this manoeuvre as of all else. He applauds the devotion of Corvisart, to whom he wrote a letter from Fréjus, which, if merited, is the physician's best title to glory. Far from opposing the visit to Aix, he urges it himself, and desires its speedy accomplishment, as bringing the term of separation to an end. If she should be unable to come at once to Elba, he counts on her establishing herself in Parma, and will forthwith despatch a detachment of his Polish cavalry hither to form an escort, together with a hundred carriage-horses.

No sooner was he installed at Porto Ferrajo, than he set about the preparation of apartments for the Empress in each of the dreary palaces assigned to him as residences. At Porto Longone and at Porto Ferrajo six rooms were chosen for her use, and orders were given that they should be got ready with the utmost speed, as the Empress might arrive at any moment. Balls, excursions, displays of fireworks were organized for her reception. Every detail of his life was governed by some thought of her. Unusual as it was with him to publish his more intimate emotions, we find him instructing the painter who decorated the ceiling of the drawingroom to make a design of "two doves, fastened together by a cord, the knot of which tightens as they fly asunder."

Marie-Louise was undoubtedly in his mind when he took such elaborate precautions to conceal Madame Walewska's visit of September 1. She was on her way to Naples, to claim payment from Murat of the pension settled upon her by Napoleon, and derived from certain estates he had reserved to himself, which Murat had nevertheless confiscated. Her vessel touched at Porto Ferrajo, and she begged to be allowed an interview with the Emperor. Napoleon had been driven by the intense heat to take refuge at the Hermitage of Our Lady of Marciana, where he had arrived on August 20. It was a small, one-storeyed chalet of four rooms, attached to a fine chapel, situated in the heart of a forest of chestnuts. The hermits occupied the cellars, resigning the upper storey to their guest. The suite, which consisted only of Paoli, the captain of the guard, Bernotti, the orderly officer, two or three Mamelukes, and the two valets, Marchand and St. Denis, were lodged in a large tent under the chestnuts, by the side of a spring, the mossy banks of which were fragrant with heliotrope, lilies of the valley, violets, and other wild-flowers. There was no kitchen. The Emperor dined at Marciana, where Madame Bonaparte was installed, and returned in the evening to his hermitage.

On the receipt of Madame Walewska's letter,[1] orders were immediately given to ensure the utmost secrecy in connection with her visit. She landed after nightfall on September 1; a carriage with four horses, and three saddle-horses were in waiting at the port. She at once entered the carriage with her son. Her sister, who had accompanied her, and her brother, dressed in the uniform of a

---

[1] It is possible, and indeed probable, that Madame Walewska's brother, Colonel Laczinski, had come to Elba before her visit. A certain Colonel Laczinski was entrusted with some commission for the Emperor on August 4. It may be that he brought letters from Madame Walewska, and that the Emperor desired him to fetch her. It is, however, not absolutely certain that he was the same Laczinski who accompanied her to Marciana, for Madame Walewska had two brothers, one who seems to have been a general in Poland, and a colonel, at least, in France, another who was unquestionably a colonel in the grand ducal army. The glorious history of Napoleonic Poland has yet to be written, as far as France is concerned.

Polish colonel, mounted the horses, and the cavalcade set out by moonlight. At Procchio they encountered the Emperor, who had come to meet them, attended by Paoli and two Mamelukes. Madame Walewska then mounted the third horse, for the carriage could go no further. Bernotti took charge of the child, and after a toilsome ascent, they reached the top of the mountain. On entering the house, the Emperor bowed to his visitor, and said "Madam, this is my palace." Beds had been put up for the strangers, and the four little rooms were placed at their disposal. He himself took refuge with the valets in the tent. A storm of wind and rain came on towards the end of the night. At dawn the Emperor, who had not slept at all, called Marchand. The valet told him a rumour had got abroad in Porto Ferrajo that the visitor was Marie-Louise, and the child the King of Rome, on hearing which Doctor Foureau had hastened to the Hermitage to offer his services, and was awaiting the Emperor's orders.

Napoleon dressed hastily and emerged from the tent. The sunshine, streaming gaily through the chestnut-branches, had already dried the ground. The mysterious child was playing beside the stream, gathering the mountain flowers. The Emperor called him, and seating himself on a chair Marchand brought from the tent, took the boy on his knee. Then he sent for Foureau, who was walking in the forest. "Well, Foureau," he demanded, "what do you think of him?" "Sire," replied the doctor, "I think the King has grown very much." Napoleon laughed, for the little Walewski was a year older than the King of Rome, though his beautiful features and abundant golden curls made him strikingly like Marie-Louise's son, or, rather, like the popular portrait by Isabey, in which the painter, perhaps intentionally, aged his youthful sitter by a year or two.

Napoleon jested for a few minutes with the doctor, and then dismissed him, thanking him for his zealous offer of service. Presently Madame Walewska came out of the house. She had grown somewhat stouter than when she first met the Emperor, but her figure had not suffered, and her sweet, serene face was as attractive as ever. Her young sister of eighteen is described as having the "head of an angel." Her blonde, childish loveliness was that of some exquisite flower. The table was spread under the chestnuts. Breakfast had been sent up ready prepared from Marciana, and the little feast was gay and cheerful. The day was spent in conversation, and walks in the neighbouring woods. The child had not breakfasted with them, but the Emperor insisted on having him by his side at dinner. Madame Walewska demurred, saying that he would find her son too turbulent a neighbour. The Emperor assured her that he should not mind the child's pranks; he had been very wilful and mischievous himself as a boy. "I used to hit Joseph, and make him do my lessons for me. When I was given dry bread as a punishment, I used to go and change it with the shepherds for some of their chestnut cakes, or I would go to my nurse for dainties." The child, who behaved with great decorum at first, became somewhat boisterous as his shyness wore off. "Ah!" said the Emperor; "you are not afraid of the whip. Well, I advise you not to deserve it. I only had it once, and I never forgot it." He went on to tell how he and Pauline had once made fun of their grandmother, and how Madame Bonaparte, who was not to be trifled with in such matters, had whipped them both. "But I don't make fun of mamma," cried the child, with a little contrite air that delighted the Emperor. "That is a pretty answer," he said, kissing him tenderly.

Night was approaching, and at nine o'clock the visitors set out for the port. Napoleon accompanied them to the shore, and was heard to murmur, as he embraced his son – "Farewell, dear child of my heart!" Madame Walewska carried away with her a draft on the Emperor's treasurer of 61,000 francs, payable to bearer, by way of compensation for the property seized by Murat. She is said to have remained in Naples for some time, and was still there in March, 1815.

In spite of all the precautions taken, and the arrival and departure of the visitors at night, there were too many persons interested in the Emperor's movements to allow the episode to pass unnoticed. The Elbans were all persuaded that the visitor was Marie-Louise; the English residents, and the spies of the Bourbons, were better informed; they concluded that the unknown was a mistress of the Emperor's. But they suspected a love-story, where there had been no question of any feeling beyond gratitude and affection. The presence of Mademoiselle Laczinska sufficiently proves this.

If the Emperor indeed consoled himself for his wife's absence at Elba, it was certainly not with the so-called Comtesse de Rohan, a mere vulgar *intrigante*, who is said to have come to him with all sorts of protestations and offers of service. A more probable heroine for such an adventure is to be found in the more mysterious beauty who had visited him occasionally at the Orangery at St. Cloud and who came on her own initiative to Porto Ferrajo. Was she already the wife of Colonel B_ on her arrival, or did she marry him at Elba? In 1815 she arrived at Rambouillet, and implored Napoleon's permission to follow him into exile. Her distress at his refusal was overwhelming. She is said to have taken her passage to the United States with three thousand francs that were given her, hoping to rejoin him.

No one seems even to have suspected that Napoleon held any communication with this woman at Elba. On the other hand, there have been several reprints of a series of letters, forged by a miserable priest in the pay of the Duc de Blacas, in support of certain calumnies against the Emperor. They call for no further comment.

During the sojourn at Elba, Napoleon was in the midst of a moral and political crisis that demanded the utmost circumspection of conduct. He knew Marie-Louise well enough to be aware that the slightest infidelity, reaching her through the distorted medium of those who now surrounded her, would cut her to the heart. He had despatched Captain Hurault de Sorbée, the husband of one of the "red women," to Aix-les-Bains, with instructions to approach the Empress, and get speech of her, if possible. He had lately been given grounds to hope that a regular correspondence would be allowed. The moment would have been ill-chosen for a scandal.

Time went on. The month of September passed, bringing no letter nor communication of any kind from his wife. On October 10 he determined to write to the Grand Duke of Tuscany, on whose friendship he still placed some reliance, and whom he had already pointed out to Marie-Louise, on the preceding 19th of April, as the natural intermediary between them. His letter is hardly that of a suppliant; the tone in which he approaches his "Brother and very dear uncle," shows that he remembered, and expected his sometime parasite of Compiègne to remember: "Having received no news of my wife since the 10th of August, nor of my son for the last six months, I beg your Royal Highness's permission to send you a letter for the Empress once a week; and I would further ask you to send me in return letters from her, and from Madame la Comtesse de Montesquiou, my son's governess. I venture to hope that your Royal Highness has retained some friendship for me, in spite of the events which have changed so many others. It would be a great consolation to me to receive your personal assurance of this, in which case, I would crave your Royal Highness's consideration for this little province, which shares the attachment of all Tuscany to your person. I beg to assure your Royal Highness of my constant affection for you, as of my perfect esteem and high consideration. I desire to be remembered to your children."

It was a request rather than a petition. The consciousness of equality, of former superiority informs every line. But with what infinite skill and ingenuity does he appeal to the heart of this man, if indeed he had a heart! It was only a small family service to one who avows his misfortunes, recognizes his own fall, and with a proud and touching humility all but declares himself the subject of the prince who had been one of his most assiduous courtiers!

No answer was ever received. The drama was played out, and the Imperial family of Austria had brought about the dishonor of one of Austria's daughters, the Empress of the French. Napoleon may or may not have learnt the facts long after; he certainly knew nothing of them at this time. But he could write no more, after such a letter to such a man. They had taken his wife, they had taken his son. The Bourbons had failed to pay the annual sum agreed upon at Fontainebleau. He would soon be under the necessity of disbanding his guard. Then he would be unable to make even a semblance of resistance, or to die fighting among his veterans, when his enemies should order his deportation to some ocean island, the Azores, for instance, as suggested by Talleyrand on October 13; "because," as he said, "it is five hundred leagues from the mainland."

Which was preferable, assassination at the hands of Beulart's cut-throats, or the more lingering death decreed by the kings under Talleyrand's guidance? Was there not yet another alternative? He elected to strike one desperate blow for and with France, and made up his mind to flight.

Chapter 19
The Hundred Days

ON New Year's Day, 1815, Napoleon received a letter from Marie-Louise with an account of his son, who, she declared, would soon be able to write to his father himself. What prompted this letter is not very clear. Some lingering remorse, perhaps. However this may have been, Napoleon accepted it as an overture, an evidence that Marie-Louise had not renounced all idea of returning to him, and was silent only under coercion. He persuaded himself that if he were at liberty, she would hasten to join him; and further, that if he had once more a throne to offer her, her jailers would set her free. No sooner, therefore, was he fairly embarked on his enterprise than he hastened to communicate with the Empress from Lyons. She, however, laid the letter before her father, to whom she had handed all letters received from Elba. He in his turn submitted it to the plenipotentiaries of the Allies. No reply was made.

Immediately after his entry into Paris, the Emperor re-organized the Empress's household almost on the original scale, and gave orders that her apartments should be prepared for her reception. Ten days later, on April 17, he wrote an official letter to his "brother and very dear father-in-law," claiming "the objects of his dearest affections, his wife and son." "The long separation necessitated by recent events," he adds, "has caused me deeper suffering than I have ever experienced, and I cannot doubt that the reunion I so ardently desire is as eagerly longed for by the virtuous

201

princess confided to me by your Majesty." He concludes with these words – "I am so well acquainted with your Majesty's principles, and the great importance you attach to family ties, that I rely fully on your co-operation in this matter, whatever the disposition of your Cabinet and counsellors, and I rest assured that you will do all in your power to hasten the reunion of a wife with her husband, and a son with his father."

No answer was vouchsafed to this appeal. Finding that his official letters and those he had despatched by the Austrian diplomatists at the Bourbon Court on their withdrawal from Paris were alike ineffectual, Napoleon was confirmed in his belief that his wife's natural inclinations were paralyzed by her father's policy, and he attempted to gain her ear by secret means. He despatched Flahaut and Montrond to Vienna, judging them to be more likely than any agents at his disposal to reach Talleyrand and the Empress. Only Montrond succeeded in passing through the lines; but when he attempted to deliver the letter he had brought with him to Marie-Louise, Médneval, formerly private secretary to the Emperor, transferred to the Empress's household in 1813, interposed. He knew how matters stood with Neipperg, and it was in kindness to his former master that he burnt his letter. He did not venture to write explicitly in reply, dreading the effect of such a blow on the Emperor. He therefore had recourse to an anonymous letter, addressed to Lavallette, whose fidelity he knew to be unalterable, in which he hinted at the actual state of affairs. Lavallette, however, doubted its authenticity, persuading himself, and no doubt Napoleon as well, that the missive was a stroke of Austrian diplomacy.

This delusion, however, was presently to be dispelled. Ballouhey, keeper of the privy purse to both Empresses, an honest man, whose fidelity was above suspicion, had started from Vienna for Paris, taking Munich in his way, to receive certain instructions from Prince Eugène. The Emperor was so impatient to see him that he ordered his arrival to be announced by telegram from Belfort, and kept a sentry waiting at Ballouhey's lodgings, with orders to bring him at once to the Elysée. Ballouhey arrived on April 28, and was closeted with the Emperor for two hours. He brought a variety of useful suggestions from Prince Eugène, but failed to fully enlighten the Emperor on matters of more immediate moment. A man of scrupulous probity, but of a timorous disposition, deeply attached to Josephine, and almost equally so to Marie-Louise, he could not nerve himself to proclaim what at Vienna was an open secret to the Congress, the Court, and the whole town.

Méneval's arrival twelve days later, on his dismissal from Vienna, enlightened the Emperor to a certain extent. A letter written by Marie-Louise on March 12, in which she placed herself formally under the protection of the Powers, evoked the furious proclamation signed by the plenipotentiaries of the Allies on the following day. Her decision was recompensed by the appointment of Neipperg to be her chamberlain. On March 18 she agreed to give up the guardianship of her son, who was at once separated from Madame de Montesquieu, and all his French servants. When Méneval took leave of her, she herself charged him with this message to the Emperor – "I shall never consent to a divorce, but I flatter myself that he will agree to an amicable separation. This has become inevitable, but it will in no wise affect my feelings of gratitude and esteem towards him." She had made up her mind, and her decision was irrevocable. Even her father could not have forced her to return to France.

Méneval perhaps added some more intimate details, for it is barely possible that the whole truth can have been kept from the Emperor. The firstfruits of that adulterous connection which eventually peopled the avenue of the Burg with bastards, on whom the House of Austria, to its lasting shame, conferred the rank of princes, was already anticipated by Marie-Louise. When the *accoucheur*, Dubois, informed Napoleon, after the birth of the King of Rome, that another child would imperil the Empress's life, he accepted the verdict as final, greatly as he desired a numerous posterity, a second son to occupy the throne of Italy. No such scruples checked the multiplication of M. de Neipperg's progeny, who effectually proved the fallibility of Baron Dubois' opinion.

Though Napoleon could no longer have felt any doubt in his inmost heart, he still held it to be essential that the truth should be kept from the nation, and that the illusions he supposed the people to cherish with regard to the Empress should be maintained. Just as, a year ago, he had been persuaded that nothing could more effectually touch the hearts of Frenchmen than the thought of the woman and child he had confided to France; so now he judged that every generous emotion of men and patriots would be stirred by their captivity, by the separation which violated all laws human and divine, by the attack on conjugal faith and paternal love made by men who professed to have taken arms to restore the reign of order and morality in

France. He desired Méneval to draw up a report, to be held in readiness, in the event of "a resolution by the Chamber in the matter of the King of Rome." In this document Méneval was instructed to dwell on such details as the Empress's despair when she was torn away from her duties; the thirty sleepless nights she spent in 1814; her virtual captivity; the violation of the Treaty of Fontainebleau by the kings who had deprived the Emperor of his wife and son; the indignation of the old Queen, Marie-Caroline, and her suggestion to her grand-daughter, that if she were prevented from passing out through the door, she should let herself down from her window, and hasten to her husband; the removal of the King of Rome or, as Napoleon now styles his son, the Prince Imperial from his mother's guardianship; Madame de Montesquieu's dismissal, and her fears for her pupil.

During the Hundred Days, and throughout his six years of suffering and exile, no word reflecting in any way on his wife ever passed his lips. He never spoke of her but in terms of tenderness, pity, and affection. In all his recollections of her he dwelt on her youth, her freshness, her frank and loyal nature. "She was Innocence in all its loveliness." Every one of his comrades in captivity has recorded the same conversations, almost in the same words. When some trifling accident which had happened to her was mentioned in the newspapers, he had the notice read over to him three times. When a vessel from Europe weighed anchor at Jamestown, he persuaded himself that it brought him a letter from the Empress, and spent the day in a state of nervous expectation, unable to compose himself to work. When one of his followers was removed, Las Cases or O'Meara, for instance, he recommended them to the care of Marie-Louise, as in the following note – "*If he (his surgeon) should see my dear Louise, I beg her to allow him to kiss her hands.*" In his will, dated April 5, 1821, he wrote as follows – "*I have always had reason to be satisfied with my dearest wife, the Empress Marie-Louise. I retain the most tender affection for her to my last moment. I beseech her to watch over my son, and to guard him from the dangers that threaten his childhood.*" This was not all. Among the modest treasures of his wardrobe, now his sole fortune, he chose his lace as a legacy for her, and on April 28, seven days before his death, he supplemented this by a further bequest – his heart, which he desired Antonmarchi to remove after his death: "Put it in spirits of wine, and take it to my beloved Marie-Louise at Parma. Tell her that I loved her dearly, that I never ceased to love her. Tell her all you saw, everything connected with my last days and my death."

Hudson Lowe was well advised when he forced Antonmarchi to place the silver vase containing Napoleon's heart in his coffin. It would have been an embarrassing gift for M. de Neipperg's mistress.

In default of the wife, the Austrian, whose place was empty, other women, French, Irish, Polish, added the lustre of their faithful beauty to those last days of splendour, rejoicing the Emperor's heart throughout that brief reign of three months by their enthusiasm. Taught rather by instinct than by reason, even those among them who were least fitted by nature for political intrigue, divined the dangers that threatened him, kept a vigilant watch upon his enemies, and more than once gave him counsels he would have been wise to follow. We may quote Georges, in the case of Fouché; Madame Pellapra, who had hastened from Lyons, and surprised certain manoeuvres of the Duc d'Otrante; Madame Walewska, who had hurried from Naples to the Elysée with her son, bringing intelligence of Murat. Madame X was the first to welcome the Emperor. Resuming her rank and title as Lady-in-Waiting, she was one of the faithful who stood in the illuminated halls of the Tuileries on March 20, anxiously awaiting the arrival of the exile. Many others, among them Madame Dulauloy, Madame Lavallette, Madame Ney, Madame Regnault de St. Jean d'Angely, Madame de Beauvau, and Madame de Turenne, vied with each other in their homage. In those hours of exaltation, there breathed upon the graceful heads of these fair women, formed for love and laughter, something of that divine essence which creates martyrs and heroines, which fires the weak with courage and devotion, and nerves the shrinking soul to face danger unflinchingly.

Such a spirit shone conspicuous throughout that sinister period, still fitly described as the White Terror in spite of recent attempts to palliate its atrocities. The stars of the Imperial Court, those graceful and artificial beauties, the most luxurious and extravagant women of any age or country, displayed, in striking contrast to the universal cowardice of the men, a courage, an energy, a presence of mind that has immortalized their memories. At the Tuileries during the Hundred Days, as at Malmaison after Waterloo, they had already proved their devotion in adversity, and their courage in disaster.

The enthusiasm was not confined to the famous and distinguished. It animated the unknown and obscure. A woman approached the Emperor during the review of the federated troops, and under color of presenting a petition, thrust a rouleau containing twenty-five notes for a thousand francs each into his hand. Another, on June 23, the day before Napoleon left the Elysée for Malmaison, wrote to his valet, begging him to meet her at the Church of St. Philippe du Roule to receive an important communication. Marchand went, and found at the appointed place a kneeling woman, whose veil could not altogether conceal the exquisite beauty of her features. Approaching her, he asked what he could do for her. She was silent for a moment. Then, with evident embarrassment, she explained that she had been deeply touched by the Emperor's misfortunes, and that she longed to see him, express her admiration for him, and console him. On hearing of this request Napoleon smiled, and remarked that "admiration of this sort might end in an intrigue. It must go no further." But the naive offer of that heart, at such a crisis, touched him, and he afterwards referred on several occasions to the unknown of St. Philippe du Roule.

In his subsequent captivity, did he find that consolation which only woman can give to man? We know something of his playful intercourse with Miss Elizabeth Balcombe during his sojourn at Briars; and there were whispers of a connection with a woman whose conduct under the Empire might have been supposed to have made it impossible for her to approach him, who had been divorced, and whose third marriage had caused her husband's immediate disgrace. The bequest made to her in the Emperor's will seems to give some color to the statements of the foreign commissaries; and it is not improbable that her presence was the cause of the disagreements that arose among the Emperor's followers, and that her departure marked one of the final stages of suffering in his career. But this part of the drama of St. Helena is too little known to admit of positive assertion or denial. The woman certainly played some part in it; but this is all we can say.

In striking contrast to this worthless *intrigante*, whose calculating spirit brought her to Rochefort, and retained her at St. Helena, we note the dignified figure of the Comtesse de Bertrand. A devoted mother, a happy wife, she found her highest satisfaction in the discharge of a holy duty. Her birth, and connection with the Fitz-Jameses, would have entitled her to a place among the noblest at the Court of Paris. She chose instead a house, or rather a hovel, infested by rats, within easy reach of the Emperor, though she had not even the consolation of nursing him, or making herself in any way useful to him. She remained by his side to the end, lovely, grave, and tender, preserving her honor with all the loftiness of a Roman matron. She followed the sad procession to the Valley of Geraniums, and stood beside the grave of the dead captive like some statue of grief. And she, an Englishwoman by birth, was the only woman who wept over the hero England slew.

Chapter 20
Conclusion

AND now, what must be our opinion of Napoleon in his relations with women?

We must consider these in a double aspect. First, as purely material; secondly, as combined of the moral and the material, or rather, as the material expression of moral influences.

We have made no attempt to glose over those commonplace adventures in which the senses alone were concerned; not that they throw any particular light upon Napoleon's character; but had we concealed them, it might have been supposed that they were specially damaging to his reputation. Secrecy was out of the question for one in Napoleon's position. Careful as he was to veil all such passing intrigues in mystery, ladies of the Palace, waiting-women, aides-de-camp, and valets were always on the watch, taking note of the most insignificant events. In the same manner, all who lived within the zone of government around the Tuileries, all who were scheming for favors, or collecting gossip, duly registered any rumours that came to their ears. And as Napoleon's slightest actions have become history, as no details of his daily life, even to the casual variations of his health, have been found too insignificant for the public, whose interest and curiosity seem to have been stimulated rather than sated by a century of comment, all contemporary witnesses, no matter how dubious, have found credence. Pamphleteers have drawn largely upon them for the support of their various theses, and the most erroneous theories have been accepted. These it is only possible to refute by setting forth the actual facts, in a plain, unvarnished record of all such adventures as rest on the synthetic narratives of several contemporary witnesses. If we have neglected others, or noted them but in passing, in spite of their probable authenticity, it has been either because they are recorded only by one irresponsible chronicler, whose testimony lacks documentary corroboration; or because they were in themselves so trivial and commonplace that comment on them would have been but a repetition of facts already noted.

What conclusions are we to draw from adventures of this nature? Simply that Napoleon was a man; that he was thirty years old in 1799; that he was forty in 1809, and that he had made no vows of chastity. Women were ready to offer themselves at the slightest sign made by him, or by others for him. He took them, with more or less of satisfaction in the intrigue, but with little self-abandonment. His brain remained clear and active, his faculty for strenuous mental labour unimpaired. No woman was ever corrupted by him. Some among them may have been chaste hitherto; but these were for the most part astute virgins, whose virtue was a commodity they were willing to sell at a price.

Broadly speaking, these women, whether of the theatre or the Court, whether married or unmarried, were courtesans. Their love was a marketable commodity. He bought them on their own terms, and duly paid for his bargain. Sensuality can hardly be laid to his charge, for sensuality implies the refinement of pleasure. He, on the other hand, wasted little time in dalliance. His wooing was abrupt and peremptory. He has been called brutal, where perhaps he might be more justly described as hurried and pre-occupied. He took such distractions hastily, as he took his meals. In his case they were rather a concession to the weaknesses of the flesh, than an indulgence in voluptuous habits, or a realization of sensuous dreams.

Was such conduct an outrage upon the laws of morality? We may ask, what laws of morality? If these vary with latitudes, how much more with epochs!

It is obviously absurd to test the men of the Empire, and notably the Emperor himself, by the smug standards of contemporary middle class morality. In their wild career throughout Europe, under a perpetual hail of shot and shell, where every man rode with death on the crupper, a few may have carried mistresses in their train, whose presence was carefully concealed from the

Emperor. But the large majority of them lived hardily and chastely throughout a campaign. If it be true that at the close of a long war, or when they entered a conquered town, they sometimes broke out into fierce and riotous debauch, can it be denied that the most virtuous citizen of modern times is less continent than the most reckless of these men? Did not the very calling inclination had led them to adopt, and ambition had forced them to retain, mark them out as types of brutal and primitive humanity? Had not their career naturally tended to foster and exasperate the savage instinct of combativeness, and consequently of animalism? Because they were soldiers, were they therefore exempt from the tastes, the needs, the appetites of other men? And could it be expected that monogamous scruples would so far compel a man of this breed, as to keep him invariably faithful to an absent wife?

Some indeed attained even to this chaste ideal. Strange evidences are extant of such constancy; among these men of iron there were lovers whose hearts were capable of all the delicate fidelity attributed by romancers to the great Cyrus himself. Others, however, allowed themselves greater licence. They took no account of such camp courtships, and could not look upon them as infidelities; neither could they think with much compunction of the passing intrigues they occasionally indulged in in Paris – adventures of an hour, concealed with so much care that in many cases they were never heard of until after the death of the principal actors. Even these lax spirits combined with their grosser animality a vein of sentimental fancy and conjugal tenderness. Nothing was too rich, too beautiful, too rare for the woman nearly every one among them had married for love, without a thought of self-interest. They pillaged Europe to gratify the caprices of these women, and cast the spoils at their feet. They sought to win their smiles by a tact, a patience, an assiduity of devotion which might move to laughter, did it not rather incline to tears.

That Napoleon yielded to none among them in devotion to his wife, his letters, his presents, the enormous fortune he settled upon her sufficiently prove. But the strain of sentimentality in his character was wholly different.

They whom neither nature nor education had endowed with scruples, evolved a code of conduct for themselves, the basis of which was what they called honor – the honor of soldiers, differing in many respects from that which Montesquieu describes as the *appanage* of gentlemen, though they indeed held that their swords had made them the equals of the best in the land. They could not, however, find precedents on which to base their rules in their own times, and they had little reverence for the Lauzuns and Tillys of a past generation. They still hated those whose places they had taken, and disdained to ape their manners, claiming equality, not so much with them, as with the ancestors of the noblest among them. These ancestors were the Crusaders; and here we find the key to the extraordinary success of what was known as the *troubadour movement*, under the First Empire. Where must we look for the first impulse which set this stream of tendency in motion? Was it literature which created the romantic idea in the minds of men, or the romantic idea reflecting itself from those minds in the literature of their day? It matters little which. What it behooves us to see is, that never did art or literature respond more readily to national sentiment, nor exercise a deeper influence on national manners – an influence most potent and vivid, perhaps, in its action on minds that could boast little previous culture.

In 1806 the troubadour movement was at its height in France. Novels, history, the theatre, pictures, and costume alike proclaimed its sway. The troubadour himself, however, counted for far less in the matter than the knight whose exploits the troubadour had sung – the knight who professed the worship of his lady, and claimed as the sole reward of his exploits in the Holy Land, of infidels slaughtered, dragons overcome, cities won from the foe – a scarf of her colors to wear in battle, and a glance from her bright eyes. The warriors of the Empire all endeavoured to model themselves upon this ideal and imaginary knight. If they did not bind a scarf of their lady's colors across their breasts, hundreds of them carried on their swords a tassel embroidered by beloved hands, wore a portrait of her next their hearts, and decked themselves before a battle with some love-token.

Napoleon felt the influence of the movement less than many of his comrades. He was not carried away by it, like his stepson, Eugène, and some of his Marshals. But neither was he altogether unmoved by this manifestation of the age, as we may judge by many details of his relations with Marie-Louise. This, however, was not until the close of the Empire, when a feeling hitherto unknown to him had begun to dominate and efface all others. Up to this time his sentimentality owed nothing to the new literature, but much, indeed all, to that of the last generation. It was Rousseau, and Rousseau alone, who gave Napoleon his sentimental education. According to Josephine, he loved three women only – herself, Madame X, and Madame Walewska. His letters both to Josephine and Madame Walewska are pure

Rousseau. In his recorded conversations with them we also recognize the tone of young Lieutenant Bonaparte's writings, the phrases, the very words in which he lamented his solitude and poverty at Valence. Those reflections on the illusions and emptiness of life flow from the same source. The same sufferings inspired in him the same dreams, on three different occasions. As Rousseau's pupil, he seems to have so saturated himself with the spirit of the master that he made it his own; and he, who had attempted everything, and achieved the impossible in the world of realities, was oppressed by impotence, negation, and disgust in the realm of sentiment. It may be indeed, that though Rousseau's influence is apparent in the inception and expression of his youthful sentiment, his moral temperature developed independently on these lines, and received but a slight bias from literature. In his aspirations after the woman who would love him for himself alone, be absolutely his, thinking of none but him, and vying with him in the interchange of mutual tenderness, he was undoubtedly sincere; but we may ask how far he unconsciously adopted the tone of his literary memories, and how far he constrained himself to feel sensations which he supposed to be rare and novel.

That such a strain of exaltation was in some degree forced is shown, I think, by the fact that he soon wearied of it. It did not bring him the joys he had hoped for; the woman he loved, or imagined he loved, fell short of the ideal he had created.

Some incident roused his suspicions, and caused a revulsion of feeling. All was over. His acquired sentimentality vanished in the light of his keen and practical natural sense. But he turned at once to a fresh experience, in which he found a deep and enduring satisfaction.

In a man such as this we may well wonder at the fidelity, not indeed of his senses, but of his heart. He was unfaithful to Josephine; he had mistresses, some of whom he loved fondly and sincerely, with whom he sounded all the depths as well as all the puerilities of sentiment; yet throughout he retained such lasting tenderness, such real affection, such indestructible passion for the woman who had held the first place in his heart that he could forget all she had thought, done, and said against him. He did not forgive – he obliterated it.

He could dismiss, as though they had never been, all those details of treachery of which we can hardly suppose him to have been ignorant – her lovers, her venality, her debts. He remembered only that the woman he had raised to the proudest place in Europe, whom he had called to the throne, and consecrated by the hands of the Pope, whom he had associated with the most stupendous of destinies, was grace and charm personified. He invested her with good qualities, and even with virtues. He decked her with all the graces the most passionate lover could attribute to his mistress; if he found fault with her extravagance, his very reproaches spoke of love, for he had given her the means to gratify her prodigal tastes.

The true character of this woman, over whom he threw a mantle of immortality due to the glamour she exercised on him, and his unreal conception of all pertaining to her, was so entirely unknown to him, that if he deceived posterity about her it was because he was himself deceived. The illusion persisted till his death. At St. Helena she still appeared to his eyes, his heart, and his senses the Josephine whom "General Vendémiaire" saw for the first time in the little house of the Rue Chantereine, the Josephine of Milan and of Mombello, the first, the only woman, it might almost be said, who let loose the storms of passion in his breast, and taught him to know and rejoice in love.

Josephine was throughout rather a mistress than a wife; he loved, but he did not respect her. His passion, exacting, masterful, and intemperate, had in it a touch of half-contemptuous cynicism, which made it easy for him to pour out perilous confidences, to confess his own infidelities, to ask her help in breaking off a connection that had become irksome. Their intercourse towards the end partook of the free-and-easy familiarity of a quondam lover and his former mistress. At every turning-point in his career he recognized the expediency of putting an end to a connection which was not a marriage in his eyes. He felt that it could not go on for ever, that it was time for him to have done with it, and form more serious ties. His superstitious conscience was easily persuaded that a marriage without the blessing of the Church was no marriage; and that the tardy ceremony of eight years later was invalidated by the compulsion under which he consented to it. Yet had a child been born of their union, he would have held the contract, such as it was, to be binding; he would have recognized his obligations. But no child, no contract. In his parting with Josephine he maintained the same attitude. He offered her the consolations proper to a discarded mistress – plenty of money, a life of ease and opulence.

In spite of his unconquerable weakness for this woman, in spite of his lavish generosity to her, his adoption of her children, the exalted positions to which he raised her nieces and cousins, we may doubt whether Napoleon ever looked upon her as belonging to his *family*, when we see how different was his feeling for her to that he developed after his marriage with Marie-Louise, especially when Marie-Louise had given him a son. After his second marriage, the *conjugal spirit* took possession of him, and modified his whole character. His love for Marie-Louise had little of the passion with which Josephine had inspired him. Her attraction for him was that of the wife, and not that of the mistress. He felt that an infidelity to her would be an unpardonable offence, and his infrequent lapses were concealed with a care that bore witness to his respect for his marriage vows. He indulged in no intimacies, and took part in no amusements his wife did not share. It was commonly reported that his delay in undertaking the settlement of affairs in Spain was caused by his reluctance to leave her. He had rigidly excluded Josephine from any participation in the government of the Empire; but he called upon Marie-Louise to share his power, and made her Regent. He gave her credit for more intelligence, judgment, and reason than he discerned in his oldest counsellors, or any of his brothers. He treated her thus, not only because she was the mother of his son, though this, no doubt, had due weight with him, but because he felt for her that conjugal respect he had never felt for Josephine.

Whereas to Josephine he was always the *lover* – even after her death – to Marie-Louise he was always the *husband*. The sentimental education he had received from Rousseau influenced all his relations with the former. With the latter his Corsican atavism, the old tradition of his mountains, reasserted itself, heightened, no doubt, to some extent by assimilation of the monarchic idea. He worshipped the *wife*, sanctified and sublimated by the *mother*.

He would not admit that his wife had abandoned him; he refused to know that she was false to him; being his wife, he supposed her beyond the reach of ordinary temptations. So strong was this conjugal loyalty in him, that he maintained it to the end, as we know from his will. He, whose jealousy was so inordinate that he complained bitterly of Madame d'Ornano's marriage, had only words of praise and tenderness for Marie-Louise. Was this merely an extreme application of the monarchic principle of respect to crowned heads? Or was he anxious to keep up his own illusion to the last? Did he make special allowance for the weaknesses of the Archduchess, or did he suppose that the secret he guarded to the end would be respected by history? There may have been a mingling of all these influences in his mind. But above all, he was silent because she was his wife, and his wife was above suspicion.

Setting aside those purely physical distractions of which we have spoken, we recognize in Napoleon a faculty for love as great as was his faculty for thought or action; we see him to have been no less extraordinary as lover and husband than as warrior and statesman. As a husband, he suffered in silence to save his wife from the obloquy of posterity; and from 1815 to 1821, consistently played a part to preserve her honor. He showed that he could be faithful, tender, and respectful. He could lay aside his imperious mood, and woo her with all the timid flatteries of a youthful husband. Jealous as he was by temperament, he was able so far to control himself as to conceal his feelings entirely in his wife's presence, and to affect the most perfect confidence in her devotion when an ocean lay between them, and she had forsaken and betrayed him.

As a lover he was even more abnormal, if we consider the strength of his passions, and the amativity, if we may be allowed the word, which he developed. There was not a note in the gamut of human passion he did not sound, passing from the fury of sensual and physical desire, to the most suave and delicate phases of sentimental emotion. Nothing escaped him, nothing was unknown to him in the whole range of amorous sensation, and as far as he himself was concerned, from the personal and egotistic point of view, he was an ideal lover. Women, perhaps, judged him differently, and with the generality of them he seems to have been capable of arousing an antagonism so pronounced, that it may be questioned whether he was ever really loved. For women can rarely love the man in whom they recognize their master, the superior, who bends them to his will, and refuses to bow to theirs, who lays the impress of his mind upon them, and declines to conform to their opinions. Who can know that he is truly loved? Is it not enough to have loved, to have tasted all the delights of love to a degree undreamed-of by lesser men?

We have one last question to consider. Did any of the women loved by Napoleon, whether as husband or lover, exercise an appreciable influence on his policy? Did they so far sway his mind as to determine his public action? We can find no trace of direct intervention, either on the part of wife or mistress. But it is indisputable that the impressions he received of and from several among them, his conversations with them, the circumstances connected with certain *liaisons*, led to the conception of new ideas, the modification of old ones, and even to the determination of his course in certain crises of his career.

Passionately as he loved fier, Josephine is not foremost among the women to whom we may trace the genesis of certain political resolutions. It would be an error to conceive of her as stimulating his social ambition by attracting the old nobility to his cause, and inducing him occasionally to sacrifice the spirit of the revolution to the traditions of the ancient order. It was he himself who was bent on gaining the aristocrats, at the price, as it proved, of being sold and betrayed by them. Josephine recruited among them by his orders. Josephine distributed his bounty, but this was because he thought it would come better from her hands, and produce a more favorable impression. As a matter of policy, he allowed reversals of decrees against emigrants, restitution of estates, and all such favors as he thought likely to dispose nobles and great ladies to gratitude, or at least to neutrality, to pass through Josephine's hands. But to such measures he was himself inclined; and, except on those rare occasions when he was taken by surprise, he only allowed such favors to be solicited as he had already made up his mind to grant. His kingly instinct was not sufficiently pronounced to make him take pleasure in repulsing a weeping woman, begging for the life of her husband or brother. A few useful hints, together with many false impressions, and indications more or less exact, seem to be all he owed to Josephine socially.

But to others we may trace, directly or indirectly, some of the most decisive acts of his career. When Mademoiselle Dénuelle de la Plaigne became *enceinte* by him, he made up his mind to the divorce, and the approaching birth of Madame Walewska's child finally confirmed him in this determination. A new light is thrown upon his whole policy in connection with Poland, when we remember who was his mistress in 1807, 1808, and 1809. Again, his extraordinary forbearance to Bernadotte is clearly referable to his early affection for Désirée. As soon as he had become the husband of Marie-Louise, and through her a member of the Austrian royal family, he considered the ties thus formed as close and durable as those which bound him to his own family. Hence that confident reliance on the continued friendship and support of Austria which was his own undoing. If his sense of family obligations was so strong that he relied on them alone to cement political alliances – as he undoubtedly did in his negotiations with Bavaria, Baden, and Wurtemburg, to say nothing of Austria – it is hardly surprising that the conjugal spirit should have dominated him so absolutely; nor can we wonder that Marie-Louise, not by direct intervention, but by virtue of the place he accorded her in his combinations, and the prestige with which he surrounded her, should have exercised an unprecedented influence on his policy, both at home and abroad.

Would he have been a man had it been otherwise? Was it not because he was keenly susceptible to the highest feelings of humanity; because he retained a faithful and tender recollection of his first love; because he had the family instincts of his race, and the conjugal devotion enjoined by monogamic morality, that his downfall was so stupendous and so irreparable?

If woman had played no part in his life, Napoleon would not have been what he is, the most complete and extraordinary type of masculine genius on record. He would have been a something sexless and supernatural, a being in whom humanity could feel no interest, because he had neither shared its passions nor followed its traditions. Whereas he, whose intellectual powers were greater than those of any man before or after him, who, rising to the level of his extraordinary fortunes, found in his mighty mind resources equal to his splendid opportunities, and who accomplished the grandest task ever undertaken by mortal, was essentially a man to whom no human emotion was unknown.

It is human to feel the influence of woman, to love her, to believe in her, to experience every sentiment and sensation she can inspire. And here, as in all other phases of character, Napoleon was the superior of other men.

I HAVE to thank Monsieur Paul Le Blanc of Brioude, for calling my attention to two articles by Monsieur H. Mosnier, published in the *Haute-Loire* of August 23 and 24, 1892. In these articles Monsieur Mosnier gives an exhaustive account of *The Adventures of Monsieur de Ranchoup*, correcting my narrative in several points of some interest. The Ranchoups, he says, occupied a very humble position in the seventeenth century. They were, in fact, agricultural labourers in the villages of Bougernes, Solages, and Ranchoup, near Craponne. In 1651, one of the family attained the dignity of Consul of Craponne, and after this date they seem to have risen considerably in the social scale, intermarrying with various highly respectable families of the town. At the beginning of the eighteenth century, one Pierre Ranchoup settled at Puy, practising as a surgeon; he had five sons, one of whom became tutor to the Comte de Mailly; another, a canon of Chartres; a third emigrated to the West Indies, settled at San Domingo, where he held the post of lieutenant to the Provost, and married Mademoiselle Denain, daughter of a Bordeaux shipowner, by whom he became the father of Madame Fourès' second husband, Pierre-Henri Ranchoup.

The said Pierre-Henri, born at Cap-Francais, was sent to France at an early age, his uncles undertaking the care of his education, an office they found to be no sinecure by the time he had reached his sixteenth year. A commission was obtained for him in the Anjou Regiment, in which he rose to the rank of sub-lieutenant a year later. In 1781 he went to India, where he fought with some distinction, and was badly wounded. His mother died shortly aftenvards, leaving him a legacy of thirty thousand francs, which he returned to France to squander.

When he had spent every penny of his fortune, he took shelter for a time with his uncle at Chartres, and in 1787 started for Constantinople, where he became a major in the Turkish army, fighting in the Moldavian and Wallachian campaigns. In 1795 he was still in Turkey, directing a military school, and forming a Turkish army corps on Western principles.

When the Egyptian campaign began he was in Paris. He offered his services to the Directory, and seems to have been employed on a mission to Hungary. On his return from Hungary in 1800, he met Madame Fourès, who, dazzled by the "de," and the title of Chevalier assumed by Ranchoup, married him, and on Brumaire 11, year X (October 19, 1801), obtained the appointment of Sub-Commissary of Trade at Santander for him. Three years later he was made Consul, and in 1807 was transferred to Cartagena. Madame de Ranchoup complains of the transfer in a very curious letter to Talleyrand, enclosing a direct request to the Emperor for a Consul-Generalship, either at Dantzic or Hamburg. This, she tells Napoleon, *is the last request she will ever make to him*, a statement somewhat difficult to reconcile with her description of it to Talleyrand, as "the first favor she had ever asked of the Emperor in her life."

It was not, however, till June 27, 1810, that Ranchoup was appointed Consul at Gothenburg. His wife does not appear to have accompanied him to Sweden. In 1812 and 1813 she spent a considerable part of the year at Craponne. Was this an exile, as Monsieur Boutin supposed? Monsieur Mosnier thinks not, and indeed there seems to be little ground for a contrary opinion. About 1814 or 1815 the couple, who lived on somewhat indifferent terms with each other, formally separated. In 1816 Ranchoup obtained the management of the Theatre of Nantes, and soon became bankrupt. He then embarked on a long persecution of the Minister for Foreign Affairs, whom he bombarded with requests and solicitations. The following note is written on the margin of his last petition – "These incessant appeals seem to be the result of mania. In future, they need not be answered." He seems nevertheless to have been in receipt of a salary of some sort in 1826. Towards the close of the year, however, we find him in the

Hospital of St. Louis, from whence he sent out what was probably his final cry of distress. The story of the adventurer whom Madame Fourès married completes her history so far. That of Monsieur Auguste Bellard remains to be discovered. There is also a second point which calls for investigation, namely, the history of a young girl of twenty, who was with Madame de Ranchoup during her sojourn in Paris in 1825, on her return from Brazil. The young lady was known as Mademoiselle Longchamp, but was commonly supposed to be Madame de Ranchoup's daughter. We find from the police reports, that Madame de Ranchoup herself passed occasionally as Madame Longchamp. The clearing up of this little mystery might prove interesting. I venture to recommend a study of the facts to my learned and amiable correspondents of the *Haute-Loire*.

Appendix B
On the French Calendar

See you next Octidi? [1]

The third list presented even more difficulties, because indicating how many of those under construction on 13 Messidor could be completed by 14 Thermidor would depend on the number of workmen being employed...

Ah, those crafty French are at it again. Ramage has obviously intercepted a coded message. 13 Messidor? 14 Thermidor? How will he ever crack the code? Actually, he could crack it by simply buying a French calendar at any bookstore.

I can only imagine that the thinking went something like this. If you are going to reinvent yourself with a "revolution," and the revolution was based on "rational thought," why not apply that thought to other irrational things like... the Gregorian calendar. So, they did. On October 24, 1793 the Republic of France abandoned the calendar that was used by the rest of the world and adopted one of their own design.

In the Revolutionary French Calendar the year was divided into four seasons and each season had three 30-day months, as follows:

---

[1] From: Grundner, T.M. (2007) *The Ramage Companion.* Tucson: Fireship Press, pp. 87-88

SPRING (PRINTEMPS)	SUMMER (ETÉ)
Germinal - (Budding) Floréal - (Flowery) Prairial - (Meadow)	Messidor - (Corn Harvest) Thermidor - (Heat) Fructidor - (Fruit)
AUTUMN (AUTOMNE)	WINTER (HIVER)
Vendémiaire - (Grape Harvest) Brumaire - (Fog) Frimaire - (Hoarfrost)	Nivôse - (Snowy) Pluviôse - (Rainy) Ventôse - (Windy)

The Months of the French Revolutionary Calendar
(The British, ever eager to help the French out, immediately renamed these months: Showery, Flowery, Bowery, Wheaty, Heaty, Sweety, Slippy, Nippy, Drippy, Freezy, Wheezy and Sneezy.)

I know, 12 months with 30 days only equals 360 days. They solved that problem by making the inconvenient remaining five days disappear into holidays. These were added as supplementary days after Fructidor. For leap year, they threw in another holiday: "Jour de la Révolution."

Each month had three weeks of ten days each. They too were renamed: primidi (oneday), duodi (twoday), tridi (threeday), quartidi (fourday), quintidi (fiveday and so on), sextidi, septidi, octidi, nonidi and décadi.

Not content to stop there, each *day* of the year also had a name. These included the names of fruits, flowers and trees; but also included some classics such as Grub-hoe, Plaster of Paris, Horseradish and Manure. Can you imagine keeping a straight face as someone proudly arranges their revolutionary cap and announces that they were born on: Manure, the 8th of Snow.

Mercifully, Napoleon I abolished the calendar on September 9 1805 (excuse me: Hazelnut, 22 Fruit, Year 13) with a *Décret Impérial*. The Republican calendar had lasted only 13 years but, you guessed it, there are people even today who want to bring it back.

CPSIA information can be obtained at www.ICGtesting.com
Printed in the USA
LVOW120049050113

314425LV00019B/985/P